Sound Reporting

CONTRIBUTORS

Deborah Amos
Jonathan "Smokey" Baer
Ted Clark
John Dinges
Carl Kasell
Karen Kearns
William E. Kennard
Jacqueline R. Kinney
Christopher Koch
Robert Krulwich
Skip Pizzi
Marcus D. Rosenbaum
Robert Siegel
Scott Simon
Flawn Williams

Sound Reporting

The National Public Radio Guide
to
Radio Journalism and Production

Marcus D. Rosenbaum & John Dinges
Editors

Flawn Williams
Technical Editor

Karen Kearns
Consulting Editor

KENDALL/HUNT PUBLISHING COMPANY
2460 Kerper Boulevard   P.O. Box 539   Dubuque, Iowa 52004-0539

© 1992 by National Public Radio

Library of Congress Catalog Card Number: 92–72794

ISBN 0–8403–7202–7

Printed in the United States of America
10 9 8 7 6 5 4 3 2

CONTENTS

Preface

Today, it would be hard to imagine life in the United States without National Public Radio. It is not an exaggeration to say that America's understanding of itself and the world would be significantly diminished. Of course, commercial broadcasting, both television and radio, also provides information and entertainment every day. Some of it is highly laudable. But nowhere else in American broadcasting is there as much high-quality journalism provided for no other reason than the well-being and education of the intelligent listener. Instead of delivering a mass audience of consumers to advertisers, NPR's purpose is to speak to citizens of a democracy, providing information that a free society cannot live without. That is the "big idea" behind NPR. *Sound Reporting: The National Public Radio Guide to Radio Journalism and Production* is the map with the details we use to get there.

When Frank Mankiewicz, then president of NPR, wrote a preface for the first version of this book (called *Telling the Story*) in the early 1980s, he rejoiced in the fact that radio in America was surprisingly alive and flourishing. He gave credit to National Public Radio for this "second age" of radio and modestly predicted that quality radio journalism would continue to attract a new generation of listeners, as well as a hardy breed of radio journalists. He was right on both counts.

In 1981, National Public Radio was made up of 270 noncommercial stations and counted a weekly audience of about 7 million people. Today, there are almost 450 NPR stations around the country, and the weekly audience has grown to more than 13.7 million people. The audience tuning in just to hear NPR news programs has tripled during the past 10 years, from 3 million to more than 9 million people. And not coincidentally, the number of NPR news programs has also increased. A decade ago, there were only ALL THINGS CONSIDERED and MORNING EDITION. Today, with WEEKEND EDITION on Saturday and Sunday mornings, a national weekday call-in program called TALK OF THE NATION, and newscasts nearly 24 hours a day, there are live news programs seven days a week—mornings and evenings.

This growth has required more reporters, editors, and news bureaus. In 1981, NPR had just one foreign bureau—in London. Now there are a dozen reporters abroad, from Moscow to Hong Kong, Southern Africa to South America. Domestically, in addition to major NPR bureaus in New York, Chicago, and Los

Angeles, there are half a dozen other cities with NPR reporters. In many other locations NPR member stations have strong news operations. Altogether, a staff of more than 160 professional journalists write, edit, and produce NPR's distinctive brand of radio journalism.

Finances are always tight in public radio, but this evolution over time has meant that, in general, NPR is now likely to have its own reporters on the scene at important news events. They were present, for example, to witness the fall of the Berlin Wall, the war in the Persian Gulf, and the death of Communism in the Soviet Union. Instead of interviewing reporters from other news organizations—a staple of the early years of NPR—NPR programs now rely on our own reporters to provide stories and documentaries. Indeed, NPR reporters now regularly find themselves interviewed by other networks.

Despite such changes, what remains as true today as when the network first went on the air in May 1971, is the NPR emphasis on high-quality radio journalism. It was Bill Siemering, the first producer of ALL THINGS CONSIDERED, who spelled out four guiding principles more than 20 years ago. The NPR staff knows these by heart, and it is worthwhile to repeat them here. From the beginning, Siemering emphasized:

- *Excellent writing:* using crisp, clear, memorable language.

- *Imaginative production:* exploiting the advantages of sound to the fullest extent possible.

- *Authentic approach:* getting out of the studio as much as possible to hear real people speaking, while respectfully celebrating the human experience in all its diversity.

- *Conversational style:* making programs accessible through normal voices, comfortably earnest and honest.

Today's audience still hears news and features in which accuracy and in-depth analysis are constants, but also where natural sound ambience brings stories alive in carefully produced reports that combine fine writing with imaginative tape editing. Such sound portraits and fully mixed, or produced, pieces have always been NPR's hallmark, providing reports of a style and content heard nowhere else.

That NPR sets a high standard for quality journalism was confirmed in a survey by the Times Mirror Center for the People and the Press. In a nationwide poll of business leaders, educators, government officials, and journalists, the Times Mirror Center found that of all media, National Public Radio has had the single most positive influence on American journalism. That survey was published in November 1989, but there is every indication that NPR's stature has only grown since then. Increasingly, NPR is becoming the broadcast of record—the place where people turn for accurate, understandable information vital to a democratic society.

So, welcome to the world of radio journalism where the mission is to inform the audience at the highest level of understanding—and where not everyone wants to be on television. *Sound Reporting: The National Public Radio Guide to Radio Journalism and Production* contains practical tips, personal insights, and fundamental policies that underpin this unique brand of American broadcasting. Its authors are the best in our business; all are current or former NPR staff members, and their advice comes from their own hard-won experience. In my own case, working as a reporter for NPR was the single most difficult, demanding, and enjoyable job I ever had—and that has never changed. As Robert Krulwich said during my first week on the job in 1978, "The work doesn't get any easier over time, but it does get better."

This book is dedicated to that idea. Nothing worthwhile comes easily, but hard work and steady improvement go hand in hand. Few other news organizations do what NPR does. To do our job, we need more skilled and dedicated journalists willing to engage in the fine art of radio journalism. I hope *Sound Reporting* will guide you in that direction.

William E. Buzenberg
Vice President, News and Information
Washington, D.C.
April, 1992

Introduction

by Marcus D. Rosenbaum and John Dinges

How does an upstart radio network on a shoestring budget metamorphose into a respected, mainstream news organization? Simple. It produces programs like ALL THINGS CONSIDERED, MORNING EDITION, WEEKEND EDITION, and TALK OF THE NATION. Everyone who listens to National Public Radio knows it is unique. This book will tell you what makes it so—its sound on the air, its approach to the news, its rapport with its listeners. And it will teach you how NPR does it— how we define journalism, and how we practice it. In the process we hope to encourage you toward a career in radio journalism.

To be sure, radio journalism is a lot of work. It is more difficult than print to produce, and it offers a lot less glamour than television. But it also can make for the best, most compelling journalism there is.

If you decide that radio journalism is for you, there are certain skills you must have to succeed:

- *You must be an excellent journalist.* This is not a medium of pretty faces—or just of pretty voices. Nor is it only a medium of high-tech equipment and fancy production. Radio journalism is first and foremost *journalism*: explaining the world in a way that expands people's knowledge and helps them understand their surroundings. That means you need an inquisitive mind and the ability to ferret out the truth. You need to develop good news judgment—to decide what is important and what is not—and you need to understand what is fair and what is balanced.

- *You must be an excellent writer.* Once you've learned the facts, you need to be able to tell them to others. And radio requires the most precise, most mellifluous writing of any medium.

- *You must be an excellent producer.* Reporting the story and writing the story are only one part of the process. You also need to produce your story—recording it on broadcast-quality equipment, mixing the sound at the appropriate levels, and cutting the piece together with seamless edits. In many instances, in addition to being an excellent journalist, you also must be a skilled recording engineer.

- *You must be an excellent listener.* This is sometimes called having a "good ear." Radio is, after all, an aural medium in which you must be able to listen to something and understand it the first time through and to distinguish one sound from another.

This book is designed to help you learn about all of this. It is divided into four parts.

- **Part I, Defining the News,** is a basic introduction to journalism in general and reporting in particular. It opens with a chapter on ethics and then explains story selection, reporting skills, and interviewing techniques.

- **Part II, Telling the Story,** begins with a discussion of the role of the editor, who is involved in every stage of the process. It then offers a guide to writing news for radio and concludes with a chapter on how to use your voice to tell a story.

- **Part III, Features,** offers two approaches to reporting and writing features, as opposed to news stories, and also contains a chapter on how to produce a feature.

- **Part IV, Recording, Tape Editing, and Production,** is full of advice about the technical side of radio journalism. There are chapters on field recording, tape editing, and studio production.

After Part IV is the first edition of **The NPR Stylebook**, which will be published separately for internal NPR and member station use. The complete Stylebook consists of the three chapters presented here—on usage, grammar, and pronunciation; editorial and production guidelines; and the law—plus an additional chapter on standards and ethics.

We believe this book will be helpful to anyone interested in the field of radio journalism—students who are just entering the profession, experienced journalists who want to try out a new medium, and practicing radio journalists at NPR and at NPR member stations who want to improve their skills. Indeed, the NPR Training Department will use the book in its workshops and other programs. For more information about NPR Training, write the department at National Public Radio, 2025 M Street N.W., Washington, D.C. 20036.

A note on using this book: Certain words used in this book are presented in **boldface**. Definitions of these words are included in the glossary.

Acknowledgements: We want to thank the authors of all the chapters of this book, who took time from their busy schedules to share their knowledge. Special thanks goes to Flawn Williams, whose assistance ensured the technical accuracy of this book; Mary Morgan, whose careful copy editing omitted many needless words; Alice Taylor, whose additional copy editing omitted many more; Karen Kearns, who had the original idea to update *Telling the Story*; Bill Buzenberg, who found the financial resources to make this publication possible; and Doug Bennet for his overall support for this project.

Part I

DEFINING
THE
NEWS

The Rules of the Game

John Dinges

The news programs produced by National Public Radio have a short history—the first one went on the air in 1971. From the beginning, NPR reporting and production were intended to be carried out within the finest tradition of American journalism, both print and broadcast. That tradition prescribes a free press that aspires first and unconditionally to independence, nonpartisanship, and the pursuit of truth. NPR also embraces the idea that the news media have an explicit mission of public service and play a vital and constructive role in democratic society.

NPR's view of itself, and its aspirations, were described in a mission statement written in 1979:

> Through its programming services, NPR will respect differences among people and will celebrate the human experience as being infinitely varied by speaking with many voices and dialects; it will reflect the joy and satisfaction of life as well as its problems and frustrations; it will encourage individual growth and active, constructive participation in society. National Public Radio programs will explore, investigate, analyze, and interpret issues and ideas that help listeners better understand themselves, their government, their institutions, and their natural and social environments. As public trustee of resources and expertise for the production, stimulation, and distribution of noncommercial radio programming, NPR and its members will take advantage of the inherent values of the aural medium—immediacy, actuality, ubiquity, economy, and the ability to capture and stimulate the imagination.

In attempting to live up to these objectives, NPR strives to produce a mix of domestic and international coverage that uses intelligent writing, a variety of voices and opinions, and a relaxed, accessible style. And whatever else might be said about NPR journalism, NPR does it with an amazingly small budget.

Journalism at NPR

Coverage. The old joke in NPR's earlier, even leaner years was that NPR did the news a day late and called it analysis. No longer. With a staff of reporters in all parts of the United States and foreign correspondents stationed around the world, NPR can cover most major stories on location.

Nevertheless, NPR editors constantly try to avoid mistaking staged "events" for real news. The orchestrated White House "press opportunity" may be on all the daybooks, but it should get minimal mention from NPR if it doesn't advance the story. We try to resist the temptation to give such events more coverage than they deserve simply because they provide a fresh sound bite.

Analysis. In addition to providing up-to-the-minute coverage, NPR uses interviews and long-form features to examine the most important questions raised by the news. On the eve of the president's State of the Union message in an election year, for example, reporters in four regions of the country explored people's questions and expectations for the country's leadership. To track the momentous changes in Russia after the dissolution of the Soviet Union, ALL THINGS CONSIDERED sent a reporter to visit and revisit the same small city to get to know the people there and track how their lives were changing.

NPR analysis also includes reports that examine historical causes and background, personalities and ideologies. It is a conscious attempt to counteract the often-heard charge that Americans forget their own past and ignore that of others, and it is the kind of journalism that imputes a high degree of intelligence, interest, and social awareness to its listeners.

Voices. One of the most important characteristics of NPR journalism is that it lets people speak for themselves. Newsmakers, opinion-makers, experts, average citizens, the weak, and the powerful are the voices of NPR interviews. In conversation with an NPR host, each is given a full opportunity to explain, argue, cajole—even to bluster or whine. The style is direct but friendly. There is time for the interviewer to probe for contradictions, for a guest to outline an elegant philosophical insight, and for the listener to sense a moment of genuine emotion. Some interviews run more than 10 minutes on the air. Most are four or five minutes

long. But that is still many times the length of the typical television interview.*
And in newspapers the interview format is becoming a rarity.

The extensive air time devoted to interviews is both an opportunity and a
responsibility. It provides a forum for a vastly broader spectrum of voices than is
available in any other medium. There is time and interest for the traditional and
the avant garde, the mainstream and the marginal, the comforting center and the
disquieting voices on the edge. But in stepping beyond the ordinary, NPR must
make sure that the choice of interview subjects is carefully balanced and fair.

Style. There is clearly an NPR style, recognizable to listeners and highly
valued by most of them. It distinguishes NPR from commercial radio and from
television news. Adjectives sometimes used to describe this style include unpre-
tentious, self-effacing, irreverent, iconoclastic, compassionate, culturally diverse,
relaxed, outgoing. On the same program, NPR News can alternate between earnest discourse and April Fool's jokes.

Editing. Everything that goes on the air is subject to NPR's rigorous editorial process. In most cases, at least two editors must hear and approve a piece
before it is broadcast—the reporter's supervising desk editor and the show editor
or producer. The desk editor shares the reporter's responsibility for the accuracy,
integrity, and fairness of a report, and therefore must pay attention to all the
details of a script as well as its overall structure. The show editor or producer
provides a more detached ear—and a final check before broadcast. Show interviews are conducted in the presence of an editor or producer who shares with
the host the responsibility of avoiding omissions or misrepresentations. These
editing procedures apply as well to the highly produced, long-form features that are
a staple of NPR news programs. These features offer an opportunity for
experimentation in writing and production techniques. They follow looser structural
forms and often employ less formal language. They are vehicles with which
producers and editors may strive for originality, to push the limits of radio. No
matter how original, however, features are held to the same strict stan- dards of
journalism as other NPR stories—standards that guarantee what goes on the air is
fair, balanced, thoroughly researched, and includes all elements the listener needs to
form an independent judgment about the story. In other words, advocacy reporting,
point-of-view writing, and the use of production devices or "hot tape" to slant a
piece toward a position not warranted by the facts is no more permissible in feature
production than in news writing. (Other elements of the craft of editing for radio are
discussed in Chapter 5, "The Editor.")

---

*Even in interviews used as "actuality" within a reporter's piece, the NPR rule is to allow enough
time for the expression of a concise but fully coherent thought. That usually means that an actuality
on NPR runs longer than the eight or nine seconds typical of television or commercial radio.

Ethics and Standards

Journalism in the United States has evolved over the course of many generations. A press once unabashedly at the service of particular business and political interests has been replaced by media avowing strict standards of independence. Still, each organization's claim that it cannot be bought is a claim that must be defended constantly and openly in day-to-day practice. Guidelines vary from organization to organization; knowledge of what is appropriate may vary even more widely from one journalist to another, particularly when an individual has had little formal training in a newsroom environment.

There are many books that discuss general ethical principles and their application. The aspects included here are some of the questions that arise most often at NPR.

Conflict of Interest

For individual reporters, the rules are straightforward: They receive nothing of value from those about whom they report or who are sources of information for their reporting. Likewise, NPR does not pay for information or for access to sources of information. There are common-sense exceptions: Sharing a meal and picking up a check, or accepting a dinner invitation at a source's home, are often essential elements of the reporting environment; the amounts involved are not significant enough to allow even the impression of a bribe or influence peddling. Free transportation may be acceptable if it involves only a ride in an automobile, but inappropriate if the ride is in a Lear jet. Likewise, although a reporter should not accept free lodging from someone promoting the story being covered, few would question the ethics of a reporter who stayed overnight in a priest's home in a remote village where human rights violations had occurred, even though the priest was passionately interested in the story's getting out.

Free tickets to a movie or play, when such tickets generally are made available to the press, are acceptable if intended for use in on-air coverage and as long as the decision to cover or not to cover such an event is not made on the basis of the availability of free tickets. Likewise, NPR accepts promotional copies of books whose authors may be interviewed. Unsolicited books and tickets are the property of NPR—the news organization to which they were sent—not the staff members who happen to receive them, and it is up to news managers to determine their disposal.

Free-lance reporters and producers are required to tell their NPR assignment editor if they have received funding or payments of any kind in relation to their assignment; it is also the responsibility of assignment editors to ask about outside funding, especially when the story involves travel or other expenses not paid by NPR.

Institutional funding. It is a truism that all money comes with interests. In the commercial media, the acceptance of advertising, even when editorial decision-making is rigorously shielded from contact with those who sell ads, is enough to raise charges that news content is muted to avoid offending advertisers. And there are enough examples of commercial advertisers threatening to pull lucrative ads in protest over treatment of their product to make this more than a theoretical concern.

Although NPR does not accept advertising, conflict-of-interest questions arise because NPR solicits and accepts money earmarked or "restricted" for covering specific subjects. Because of NPR's noncommercial status, such grants are often a vital supplementary source of revenue without which NPR's news coverage would be significantly diminished. NPR President Douglas Bennet has issued the following guidelines governing the acceptance of such funds:

Policy for Accepting Project Grants

To avoid conflict of interest or the appearance thereof, when National Public Radio's News Division accepts project grants through the Development Office,* the policies below should be followed:

  I. Associations, corporations, foundations, and other interest groups, including governments both domestic and foreign, can contribute to the News Fund* for general support.

 II. Restricted grants must not be so narrow in concept as to coincide with the donor's area of economic or advocacy interest—e.g., an automobile corporation supporting coverage of the car industry.

III. When deciding whether to accept restricted grants from domestic or foreign government sources, NPR will take account not only of the considerations in II, but also of whether the structure of the donor agency provides adequate safeguards against interference or the appearance thereof.

 IV. In a case that seems unclear, a final determination will be made by the vice presidents of News and Development. No contacts with funders shall be made by anyone in the News Division other than news managers and then only in conjunction with a member of the Development Office.

Needless to say, these guidelines require interpretation using good common sense on a case-by-case basis. Their purpose is to ensure that NPR makes editorial

---

*NPR's Development Office raises funds from foundations and corporations to support NPR operations. Funds for general support of NPR News go into the News Fund.

decisions based solely on sound news judgment, and that it does not leave the perception that those decisions are affected by the wishes of its funders. This principle is key: The idea for coverage must originate from NPR, not from the funder. Funders may not be directly involved in story assignments or any other part of the editorial process.

Two examples illustrate the guidelines. The Ford Foundation has a distinguished record in funding projects that promote the study of foreign affairs. This broad interest, because it does not extend to lobbying or other forms of advocacy of specific policies, is not a barrier to NPR's receiving money from the foundation for the coverage of Eastern Europe. Applying the same standards, clearly a conflict would exist—and be perceived as such—if General Motors funded NPR's coverage of the auto industry or international trade issues. In that case, even if GM had nothing to do with the choice of stories, or their content, there would still be the inevitable impression that NPR was tailoring its stories on those subjects to please the automaker.

Between these two obvious cases are many others that are less clear and must be decided by applying the guidelines, good common sense, and the "Caesar's wife" maxim—that NPR as a journalistic institution must not only be virtuous, but appear to be virtuous.

Funding is a difficult subject in public radio, no less so at the station level than at the network level. These practical rules can help guide day-to-day decision-making:

- News staff should have as little contact with funders as possible. Under no circumstances should news staff contact funders directly to propose grants for projects in which they would personally benefit through assignments or travel. Reporters and editors working on grant-funded projects should not speculate about whether what they are doing will please or displease the funder, nor should they attempt to limit or expand coverage according to what they believe the grant requires.

- The separation of funding from editorial content should be evident on the air. News personnel should not read funding credits.

- A news organization should pay its own way when gathering news. NPR and many other news organizations acknowledge exceptions to this rule when the story is of paramount interest and access is difficult without special assistance. The most obvious example is accepting military transportation to a battle zone. In such cases, special care must be taken in writing and editing to ensure that the special treatment does not slant the stories in favor of the organization providing assistance.

Ethical Decision-Making

Ethics, by definition, involves the collective wisdom about what is right and wrong within the context of a group with shared values. Do not try to make decisions in a vacuum, or simply by reading a chapter on journalistic ethics. Make every effort to avoid confronting ethical decisions on deadline. Anticipate them at the assignment level and during the reporting process, and give yourself and your colleagues reasonable time to talk the problem over and air all opinions.

Usually, the process will have several stages: an initial gut reaction about what is right or wrong; a second stage exploring rules or guidelines that might apply; and a final period of reason and reflection in which a decision is made. The gut reaction often is right, particularly among veteran journalists, but it is risky to trust that first reaction until it has been measured against the conclusions of the second and, if necessary, the third stages.

This chapter contains few rules and no dogmas. It is not a substitute for good judgment and common sense; the best guidance comes not in statements of policy but in a strong sense of mission as journalist, citizen, and human being.

Politics and causes. People do not leave behind their opinions, experiences, specialized knowledge, and pet peeves when they become journalists. They are not and never have been automatons devoid of emotion and critical intellect. Many come into the profession and leave it with their sense of outrage intact, with a deep and probing concern for what is wrong with society, and with a living compassion for their fellow human beings. These qualities are considered assets for NPR reporters, editors, and producers. Callousness and cynicism are recognized liabilities.

Some of the thorniest decisions we face concern whether and to what degree a journalist may be personally involved in advocacy organizations and politics. Most news organizations restrict news staff from personal involvement in activity, especially political activity, that reasonably could be perceived as compromising their journalistic independence in reporting on such activity. Clearly this does not apply to the exercise of a reporter's right and duty as a citizen to vote. It may apply to electoral campaign activity, speech writing, lobbying, and public endorsement of candidates. Other public and leadership roles in advocacy activities also may be a conflict.

In general, however, there are only a few activities that would be out of bounds for all news staff, say, running for Congress. In almost all cases, our judgment depends on several factors: First of all, does the reporter, producer or editor make editorial decisions about stories affecting the interest of the cause he wants to promote. Does he have a major role in those decisions, i.e. is his role more than peripheral? If the answer is yes, there may be a conflict, and the journalist should discuss the situation with colleagues and editors. It is a good idea to ask oneself whether those on the other side in a controversy involving the cause would consider a reporter fair if his advocacy role were known.

As journalists, we are free to be active in our professional organizations, religions, communities, schools, philanthropic and service organizations. The presumption is on the side of freedom of action. We should be concerned only if a reasonable and substantive argument is likely to be made that the activity calls our impartiality into question.

These ethical considerations, of course, do not apply to relatives of news staff. But in cases in which a direct family member (spouse, companion, parent, sibling) is involved in activities about which the news staffer may make editorial decisions, common-sense ethics requires that the staffer disclose the relative's activities to an editorial supervisor.

Speeches. Journalists are often asked to make speeches in the area of their expertise, and few news organizations discourage this activity. A potential conflict of interest can arise, however, when substantial payments are involved. A reporter who covers an interest organization or trade association would have difficulty justifying the acceptance of payments from those groups, whatever the reason.

Fairness and Objectivity

NPR is committed to the strictest principles of fairness in reporting. Some people have a problem with the term "objectivity." I have always understood it in the very simple sense of **fact-based reporting.** Everything that goes on the air, from the most straightforward news voicer to the most elaborate news analysis, is anchored in the pursuit and description of facts—those verifiable bits of information that are the raw material of accurate communication.

The reporter's first duty is to get the facts—all the facts that are relevant—to be honest with the listener about the facts that could not be found or verified, and to put the information in intelligible context. Fairness is a natural byproduct of fact-based reporting.

Reporting the facts from all relevant points of view is the first tenet of fairness. "I just reported what I was told" is the dodge of a lazy reporter. It is the reporter's most basic obligation to seek out the other side, the third side and the fourth side, and not to rely on the one-dimensional, possibly biased version provided by those who may have promoted the story.

To report and write a story without attempting to contact those who are involved and are likely to disagree is unprofessional and unethical conduct. Likewise, honesty in reporting dictates that a reporter not mislead listeners by failing to disclose relevant information, such as the possible political motives and partisan interests of a person accusing another of wrongdoing.

In describing people and their points of view, be sure to use terms that the person you are describing would consider accurate. Avoid loaded terms that betray your personal bias—terms such as "claim" when "said" would do; "refused" to comment when "declined" is accurate; "admit" when "said" or "acknowledge" would suffice. Similarly, take care with descriptions. Describing a female political leader's hair, giving an Italian politician's nickname, and commenting on physical traits are not necessarily inappropriate, but may inadvertently feed into possible stereotypes. Was it fair, for example, for news reports to dwell on General Manuel Noriega's facial scars and to repeat the term "pineapple face"?

Fairness is particularly important in stories involving people who are not public figures. People asked to appear on the air or involved by no design of their own in a prominent story are entitled to protection of their privacy and dignity in every way possible. They should never be exposed to ridicule or derogatory description of any kind. Nor should anyone else with access to the air be allowed to make derogatory or belittling remarks about people not otherwise in the public eye.

Keeping an open mind is indispensible to fair reporting and must be practiced at every stage of the editorial process, from assignment to final edit. It is good mental discipline—and a hallmark of sound journalism—to assume during editorial discussions that you do not know the personal views of your colleagues. This is especially important when discussing coverage of controversial issues like abortion.

Sources, Credit, and Plagiarism

It is the reporter's responsibility to attribute all facts to a reliable **source** and to identify that source as accurately and completely as possible. The only exception is background information so widely known that it constitutes general knowledge. The more important and controversial the information, the stronger the sourcing must be. In general, a reporter must have at least two sources, both of whom have independent ways of knowing the information. For facts of great importance, such as the winner of an election, the beginning of the ground offensive against Iraq in the Gulf War, an indictment of a public figure, the two-source rule is absolute unless there has been an official, public announcement. The rule is not based on arithmetic and should not be applied mechanically. In some cases even two sources are not enough if the sources' access to the information is at all questionable. If the source of information is providing an eyewitness account, a single source, properly described, may be enough.

A source who declines to be identified greatly diminishes the value of the information. Reporters should make every effort to persuade sources to speak on the record. When you promise a source confidentiality, be sure the source understands that an editor may decide not to allow the anonymous information on the air. The source also should understand that confidentiality is the joint responsibility of the reporter and the editor; an editor may require the reporter to tell him the name of the source if it is necessary to judge the source's credibility.

It is not uncommon for journalists to be manipulated by unnamed sources, particularly government officials who use anonymity to avoid accountability for unsubstantiated political rhetoric. Whenever possible, a reporter should identify the political interest the source may have in revealing the information. When an opposing political camp leaks anonymous information, that information must be independently verified. If verification depends solely on anonymous sources, the political interest of those sources must be revealed in the report.

Plagiarism is the misappropriation of another writer's work, either writing or reporting, and passing it off as one's own work. The *Washington Post*'s former executive editor, Ben Bradlee, called it "one of journalism's unforgivable sins."

Clearly, you should not copy someone else's work. But even when you write something based on information contained in wire service reports, for instance, avoid lifting phrases and verbatim descriptions. This is not a legal issue; you simply should not convey a wire service's descriptions and analytical points as if they were your own, because they are not. Write it in your own words. And when information is based on the exclusive report of another news organization, always give full credit. Likewise, identify the source of tape obtained from another organization's broadcast.

Correcting Errors

Mistakes are an unavoidable part of daily journalism. When they happen, and are more than trivial, the errors should be acknowledged and corrected on the air (and in the transcript of the program). Often the letters segment of a program provides an appropriate format for corrections. But serious errors should not wait for the arrival of a complaining letter to be corrected.

Ego and Personal Style

The broadcast media, even more than the print media, have fomented an era of "ego journalism." Highly paid, often glamorous reporters and anchors are foisted on viewers in much the same way advertisers sell products. Although some are indeed top-notch professionals, they are marketed not for their journalistic skills but for their ability to drive up ratings.

At the other extreme, mostly in the past, were the virtually anonymous reporters who turned out stories like so many cookies, with little or no personal identification with the product. Virtue, said the wise man, usually stands in the middle. A reporter's earned reputation and public image are invaluable assets and should be cultivated. Not only does a good reputation help get your calls returned, it instills pride and responsibility.

In radio, a reporter's voice and identity are part of the story's presentation. That is as far as it should go. A reporter should not get directly involved in the story by frequently using the first person in writing or using tape that calls attention to the reporter rather than the story's subject. Personal experience, when editorially relevant to the story, should be described in as straightforward a manner as possible, using the first person.

A reporter is one of a news organization's most public representatives. His public demeanor should be in keeping with that role. Reporters do not resort to subterfuges, such as assuming false identities, in order to get a story. Nor do they tape record another person without that person's express permission.

Going after the Tough Stories

High standards and strict ethics are not self-censorship. They more often dictate what should be *added* to a story than what should be left out. Ethical violations frequently involve faintheartedness in confronting a source and the omission of hard-edged material out of fear of offending a valued news contact.

The best journalism is **green-light journalism**—a professional newsroom atmosphere imbued with solid traditions of fairness, sensitivity, and the confident exercise of news judgment. In such a newsroom, reporters and editors are not looking over their shoulders to avoid criticism that their stories have offended some special interest group or failed to measure up to someone's idea of political correctness. Rather, they are going for the jugular, seeking out the toughest, not the easiest, stories to cover.

It was that attitude that led NPR into some of its biggest stories—for example, its ground-breaking coverage of the AIDS epidemic, its controversial reports on the Anita Hill-Clarence Thomas sexual harassment charges, and its investigation of the *Challenger* disaster.

Some of us were brought up with the social rule that in polite company you don't bring up religion and politics. Being polite has never been the top priority for the best journalists. They find and write about human problems that have the fewest pat answers, stories without good guys and bad guys, rife with moral ambiguity and social polarization—stories about abortion, religious experience, race, guns—yes, even sex, drugs, and rock 'n' roll.

John Dinges is NPR's managing editor. Before coming to NPR in 1985, he was an editor and reporter on the foreign desk of the Washington Post *and reported extensively on Latin America. He is the author of* Our Man in Panama: The Shrewd Rise and Brutal Fall of Manuel Noriega (*Random House, Times Books, 1990, 1991) and (with Saul Landau)* Assassination on Embassy Row (*Pantheon, 1980). He has a B.A. in English, studied theology for three years in Austria at the University of Innsbruck, and received an M.A. in Latin American studies from Stanford University.*

2
Getting Started

Christopher Koch

Every journalist, whether broadcast or print, must answer one crucial question: What is news? There are probably as many definitions of news as there are journalists, but all definitions seem to have common threads. News generally involves an event that is observed either by the journalist or another individual, and this observation is then reported to an audience. It is helpful to remember that news isn't news until someone decides that it is: News is the report of an event, not the event itself.

You can waste time trying to do news stories on vague ideas. Broadcast journalists, in particular, get into trouble when they try to do pieces about poverty, poor education, crime in the streets, corruption, inflation, freedom of speech, and other abstractions. These may be good topics for columnists and professors, but abstractions alone are not news stories. If journalists are interested in these things and want to do stories about them, they will look for events.

A march by poor people or the formation of a welfare rights organization are legitimate stories about poverty. A patrol of a big city park by a local vigilante group or the police routine at precinct headquarters are ways of doing news stories about crime in the streets. Unemployment lines, pandemonium on Wall Street, or the release of the latest economic indicators may be legitimate ways to cover inflation. Look for events.

In general, the more powerful the event, the easier it will be to do a story, because strong stories tell themselves. If you are working on a story about prison conditions and a riot breaks out, your only problems are getting to the riot, recording the right sounds, asking the right questions of the right people, and getting out in one piece. But if the prison is quiet, you will have to look for the events that evoke prison life—perhaps the slow movement of a new prisoner through a tough entry procedure, or the sounds of the night lock-up, or the Sunday sermon at the chapel, or the conversations of guards and prisoners about past events.

There are different kinds of events and correspondingly different kinds of news stories about them. These stories are given different names, and, even though the names are by no means precise (popular jargon varies from place to place), it is helpful to keep some distinctions in mind before you go to work.

Hard news generally refers to the breaking, daily stories that make up the front page of the newspapers, the bulk of the TV news shows, and the leading articles in the newsweeklies. Hard news stories are about those political, military, economic, and social events that appear to have a shaping influence on our lives.

The basic hard news story will convey the sense of such events—the taking of American hostages, the concession speech of an incumbent president, the agony of people's uncertainty after a volcanic eruption.

On extended news programs—those that go beyond the capsule summary of the day's main events—these major stories will be accompanied by **sidebars,** reports that spin off from the main event and help explain it.

Types of Sidebars

If the major story is new or complicated, then it may be important to explain the events that led up to it. In these **backgrounders,** reporters are interested in events that took place in the past. In radio, they will need archival tape and interviews with people who can describe earlier events.

Interviews with newsmakers also provide a useful type of sidebar. So do **news analyses** drawn from several participants or knowledgeable observers of the events.

The **sound portrait** is another typical sidebar. Here a reporter gathers sound from a series of small events and weaves it with interviews, creating a sound impression of persons, places, or things.

"Vox pop"—from the Latin *vox populi* (voice of the people)—provides comments of ordinary people, collected at random, usually in public places. Sometimes the vox pop is strung together in a montage of different voices (one following the other) with no narration or linking comments by the reporter. Other times the reporter is heard asking questions.

Other types of sidebars may include stories on related topics and commentaries.

Know the Show

You can learn several different things by listening carefully to the news programs you hope to work for—and to other news programs as well. For one thing, you can begin to develop critical standards that you can apply to your own work.

Listen carefully and consistently with a notebook in hand, asking yourself questions like these: Which reporters appear most frequently? Does anything distinguish their work from the work of reporters who **file** less frequently? What pieces compel your attention and why?

Record the show and select several particularly interesting stories for closer study. How long are they? What is the ratio between the narration (the things that reporters say) and **actualities** (the voices and sounds that they record)? How many different interviews have been used? What other kinds of sounds have been incorporated into the report?

Transcribe the narration and analyze stories that seem particularly well-written. How long are the sentences? Are they full of vivid images, packed with information, or are they sparse links between actualities? No one way is necessarily any better than any other. Nor should you try to imitate anyone. You are only figuring out what works and why. Everyone has a different style, and you shouldn't be afraid to develop your own. Good journalism can happen even when rules are broken.

Each news program has its own style, and that is another thing to listen for. Some programs give straight interviews to reporters, and others insist that hosts do all one-on-one interviews. Some news shows are designed for a national audience, and others are regional or local. If it's a national show, your stories will have to be interesting to a national audience. This does not necessarily mean you should look for national personalities who are visiting your local area. Usually, the news staff of a national news organization will have access to these public figures and will prefer to do their own interviews.

Look, instead, for the local stories that address issues shared by people nationwide. And remember: If you listen carefully to the news programs, you'll get a much better idea about what might interest their editors and producers, the range of styles they will accept, the gaps in their coverage you could fill, and other things that will help you file effectively and frequently.

Selecting a Story

An infinite number of things happen every day, but not many of them are news. What makes something news? Primarily, enough interest in the event. In order to make people interested, the story needs to have an **angle**. This is not an opinion or a point of view, but the approach to a story that gets the audience to pay attention. It's part of your job as a reporter to find the angle and work it clearly into the story. Without it, you'll waste time pursuing ideas that never quite work out.

What follows are some truisms that should be chanted regularly or otherwise impressed on the mind of every beginning journalist.

- *Never do a story because people ought to know about it for their own good or the good of the republic.* Journalists are not professional moralists, and they have no special insight into what people ought to know. Leave moralizing to preachers and politicians.

- *People care about things that affect them.* A famine in North Africa is less interesting to most Americans than an earthquake in California, even though the famine may kill thousands more people.

- *Bad news, like gossip, travels more quickly and farther than good news.* Let's face it, you may hear about Uncle Harry's divorce faster than you hear about his marriage. Grandma calls when Junior breaks his leg, but you may never hear about Junior winning a school trophy. The completion of a new wing at a local prison may get brief mention on local programs, but a riot at the same prison could be national news.

- *Unusual events are more interesting to people than ordinary ones.* Thirty-five successful landings at a local airport are not newsworthy (unless the airport is under siege or the controllers are on strike), but the crash of the 36th plane is news.

These are general principles that will help you recognize good stories. They may also help you structure a questionable assignment by reminding you to look for an angle that will get people to listen to the story.

Where do the story ideas themselves come from?

- *Read the wires.* The international, national, and local services of the Associated Press (AP), United Press International (UPI), and Reuters carry the major stories on their **wire services**. If you have access to the wires, check them regularly. (If you don't, you should look into joining one of the many computer databases that will give you access.) When you get an assignment, pull the wire copy. It will give you a head start on your research. But don't trust the wire services (or anyone else, for that matter) to be accurate or thorough. Do your own checking.

- *Keep in touch with the local papers.* Read them carefully, and don't ignore the small stories on page 10. Many news stories work their way to the front page over a period of time. Pay particular attention to specialty newspapers and magazines. They will announce events and cover stories that could be interesting to a national audience before the major news organizations discover them.

- *Cultivate your sources.* The best ideas frequently come from sources. These are people who, for one reason or another, know about events before you do. Sources may work inside organizations and recognize good stories when they see them. They may be other reporters who can't use a particular good idea. They are frequently people on whom you have reported in the past, people who respect your journalism and trust you.

- *Keep your story ideas and your sources in a notebook.* Don't expect them all to be useful to you when you first hear about them. In many cases local stories can wait for a national **news peg**—a major news story to which you can tie a minor one. For example, if a national news program decided to do a piece on the worker-ownership of failing companies, it could give you a peg for a local story on a specific experiment in your community. If Congress were to withdraw funding from the food stamp program, you could do a story on the effect of that legislation in your area if you talked to the local grocers, government officials, welfare rights leaders, and poor people who might be affected.

- *Keep your eyes and ears open for events that nobody else has noticed.* Be curious about the world around you. When you see something unusual, find out about it. Often the best stories are the ones that have *not* been in the newspaper yet.

Understand the Assignment

Sometimes you will be assigned a story. Sometimes you will think up the idea yourself and get it accepted by the program for which you are filing. Occasionally, you will be working entirely on your own. In any case, someone is going to have to act as your **editor** and give you an outside, independent critique of your story idea. If this editing can be done by the people for whom you are filing, so much the better. They can help you tailor your story to their needs. If not, find a friend who can function as your editor.

Although editors are sometimes the final arbiters of what gets on the air, when they are working with reporters they should not act as judge, censor, or professor deciding on a grade. Editors do not usually know more about the story than reporters. In their editing capacity, they are essentially surrogates for the audience. They listen to the reporter's story idea with the ears of an intelligent listener, raising all the questions that any listener might raise. What do we need to know to understand this story? What story elements are redundant or obvious or too specialized? When does the story need more information to make sense?

If, in addition to being an intelligent, inquisitive listener, the editor knows something about the possibilities of broadcasting, he can be helpful in making the piece more "effective radio," but that isn't essential. It *is* essential to have some outsider listen to your work before it goes on the air.

Before you begin to work, you and your editor should have a common understanding of the idea, the reason the story is of interest, the length to file, the number of different components to include, the amount of research expected, and the conditions and amount of your payment, if any. Decide on a deadline for filing and make sure that the time available is realistic for your story.

These early decisions should not lock you into any final conclusions. The story may change as a result of your research and field interviews. But your original conception will serve as a road map, and your subsequent conversations with your editor will help you discuss the story from common premises.

The key here is outside input. You need to talk your pieces through with other people, getting as much advice and input as you can. Of course, the advice sometimes will be conflicting, and in the end you will have to rely on your own news instincts. The quality of your judgment in these instances will measure your skill as a journalist.

Getting Started

If the story is dramatic enough, getting started is easy. If a ghetto is burning, or a plane has crashed, or prisoners are rioting, grab your tape recorder and head for the action. But sooner or later you are probably going to have to do your homework and go back to the place most stories begin: in research.

You can start your research with a press release, a wire story, a newspaper clipping, or a tip from a source, but you will soon be on the phone. Because news is timely, there is rarely an extensive written record to look at. Because you are working under a deadline, there is seldom time to spend hours in the library or the county clerk's office.

Talk to the people involved in the story. What do they have to gain or lose? The losers are usually more valuable than the winners, by the way. Having already lost, they tend to be more reckless and more honest.

As people present their cases to you, they will buttress their arguments with information. Check the key points with the **primary source** of the fact if you can. Remember, people frequently disagree on the facts. If it's a quote, the primary source is the person who said it. If it's a statistic, the primary source is the person who compiled it.

When you are talking to people in sensitive positions or about sensitive issues, make sure that you distinguish between information given **on the record** and **off the record.** If it's on the record, you can attribute the information to your source, and you will probably want to record it on tape. If it's off the record, you must protect the confidentiality of your source—despite pressure from some prosecutors and courts to reveal the name—or your credibility as a journalist will be ruined.

The amount of research you do will depend on the story and the time available. You could prepare a story on a prison riot from notes gathered during an afternoon at the scene, or you could research the causes of the riot for six months.

When you have finished your research, you should know the key people, the major issues and conflicts, and the upcoming events. You should be in a position to rework your original idea, to structure your story, and to make some preliminary decisions about what to record and what to look for in the field.

Before you set out, have a second conversation with your editor. Decide how you want to tell the story. You can simply write and read a script, or you can produce a mini-documentary with all the sounds and devices of a full-scale documentary—interviews, recordings of events, and different kinds of **ambience** (the sound environment of the story). You need to know what kind of story you plan to do so you can collect the right kind of tape in the field.

Keep in mind that you are telling a story. It should have a beginning, a middle, and an end. At the *beginning* the audience must be involved: Something dramatic is going to happen; some goal important to us all is going to be contested; the situation of people we care about is going to change. In the *middle* we may meet other characters and listen to pros and cons about the issues. We may get additional information and be exposed to other situations that bear on the main event. The *end* should tie the various threads together and take the listener to a stopping place. The expectations set out in the beginning should be fulfilled.

Objectivity and Fairness

Objectivity is always hotly debated in journalism. Today there is a school of journalists who argue that objectivity is impossible to achieve, so reporters might as well abandon the attempt and put all their own values and biases directly into their reporting where the audience can see them clearly and take them into account.

Some compelling journalism has been done this way, such as Hunter Thompson's account of his time with the Hell's Angels and Michael Herr's extraordinary look at the Vietnam War, *Dispatches*. But a lot of drivel has been written in the name of "new journalism," too. Unless the reporter's perceptions are particularly revealing, unless his experiences are as powerful as the story that's being told, the reporter's biases just get in the way of the main event—and they are usually boring to boot.

Of course, objectivity and fairness *are* impossible goals in an absolute sense. Any story is infinitely complex and any telling of it is a massive simplification. The reporter talks to some people but not others, uses some remarks and not others, records certain sounds and ignores others.

At every point in the reporting process, the journalist is making decisions about what to look for, what to ask, where to go, and what words to use to describe the things he has heard and seen. All these decisions are made on the basis of each reporter's unique instincts, biases, and preconceptions. Different journalists tell the same story differently.

However, even though there may be no such thing as complete objectivity, you can strive for it by keeping your own opinions out of the story and making sure you are absolutely fair.

- *Be self-critical.* Bend over backward to hear all sides and make a particular point of trying to understand the arguments of all sides.

- *Be skeptical.* Pay the most attention to people closest to the event—their biases will be most obvious, their recollections more vivid, and their explanations less filtered through value systems. Distrust secondary sources.

- *Be specific.* Stay with things that are actually happening and avoid speculation about motives, causes, feelings, meanings, and all such imponderables. Trust what you observe. Distrust the theories that people use to explain things.

If the people who appear in your piece feel comfortable with the way you have portrayed them—including those on opposite sides of some controversial issue—then you probably have been objective and fair. Honest journalism inevitably will anger some people. Be prepared for that and make sure your facts support your portrayal.

Final Planning

Do one more thing before you go out to record. Sit down with your notebook and plan your field recordings and your production schedule. If you haven't already talked to the people you want to interview, do so before you arrive ready to record. Keep the conversation general. Find out what is on their minds. Be a good listener. You will find out more if you are sympathetic and genuinely want to get their story. Save your key questions for the taping. Most people say it best the first time. After that, they are more cautious and rehearsed. Make appointments and keep them.

If your story includes events, you will want to plan your interviews around them. For example, if you want to talk to people about why they are going to do something, it's best to interview them before they do it. If you want a vivid reaction to an event, talk to them as the event is going on or immediately afterward. Obviously, if you want to know what effect the event has had on them, you will have to wait until it's over.

Make some preliminary decisions about how you will record the event. What elements are important to your story? Where do you have to be, and when should you be there? What other sounds do you need to enrich your report? These may be background sounds that help place the story in a concrete location: the sounds of a receptionist answering a busy phone, the sounds of a car leaving a paved highway and turning onto a gravel road, the din of a factory in full production, or the hollow emptiness of a factory shut down during a strike.

Music can add realism and convey feeling, particularly if it's part of the location or the event, such as the Muzak of a hospital waiting room conveying the long and restless waiting in a public place, or a radio or television clip that relates to the story, or the songs of demonstrators. According to FCC regulations, you must get written permission to rebroadcast another (American) TV or radio station. (See Part III of the NPR Stylebook, "A Legal Guide for the Radio Journalist," for details.)

Make a list of the information you need to collect to complete the story and ask people in the field for it. The more you get down as you go along, the less likely you are to get stuck later trying to collect it over the phone.

Make some preliminary judgments about your **recording ratio**—the relationship between the raw tape you bring back and the length of the final story. New reporters tend to record too much. If you keep some ratio in mind—say 20 to one (that's one hour's tape for a three-minute piece) you will remind yourself to stay focused on the story and avoid an editing nightmare when you start putting the piece together later.

Finally, remember that when you are in the field, the best laid plans may become irrelevant. Problems can occur that you didn't foresee, or the story may go in a direction that you couldn't anticipate. Despite the pre-interview, the person to whom you are talking may have a whole new story to tell. Go with the story in the field even when it takes off in a different direction. Your advance planning may help you get back on course. At the very least, it will provide a yardstick against which you can measure your new story idea. But don't let yourself be locked into a weaker idea when a stronger one emerges.

Journalism is fascinating because the world is unpredictable and irreconcilable. Every situation has a craps-game quality that eludes the moralists and ideologues. People are far more complicated, and good and bad are distributed far more randomly, than the true believers and social planners want to accept. The moral and social ambiguity of real events is apparent to all good journalists. True believers frequently call that recognition cynicism, but it can just as easily be called compassion. If you infuse your reporting with a search for the truth and a respect for different points of view, you won't go far wrong.

Christopher Koch has spent 30 years in radio and television production, working for the ABC Documentary Unit program, "Close-Up," the Public Broadcasting Service, and NPR, where he was executive producer of ALL THINGS CONSIDERED. Koch currently has his own TV production company, Koch TV Productions Inc., in Cabin John, Maryland. His work has won many awards, including three national Emmys, the Overseas Press Club's Edward R. Murrow Award, an Alfred I. Dupont-Columbia University Award, a George Polk, several Gold Cindys, an Ohio Sate Award, and a National Headliners Award. He graduated from Reed College in 1958, and, in 1959, on a Woodrow Wilson National Fellowship, earned a masters degree with honors from Columbia University.

3
The Reporter

Ted Clark

There are two ways to approach journalism. You can simply report the story, or you can advance it. You can simply report the information at hand, or you can push beyond it. You can wait for developments to move the story forward, or you can move it forward yourself by reaching for new information and new insights.

The purpose of real journalism is to add to the body of information. That's why people listen. If your story adds nothing to what your listeners already know, it is simply a recounting of events—well written perhaps, professionally delivered, but just a recounting.

It's especially important for broadcast journalists to bear this in mind. It's tempting to think you have performed a service by taking a print story and rendering it for broadcast. Getting politicians to say the same thing on tape that they said in the morning paper may seem like a useful endeavor, but it's a recipe for mediocre journalism. Newspapers generally have more reporters than radio stations, and it's tempting to let newspapers do the real reporting while you simply transform it into radio. But don't yield to that temptation. *Advance the story.*

Try to find questions that haven't been answered. Eavesdrop on conversations in the bus, on the street. Find out what people are asking each other about the issue. Chances are they're asking some questions that haven't yet occurred to the reporters. Find answers.

Some reporters keep a "call list" of community leaders, interest groups, or just thoughtful people—people to be telephoned on a regular basis. Their insights help to advance stories, and often they can provide tips about stories that are not yet in the news.

Reporters always call "the other side" in a story, but not just because it helps assure a fair story. It also helps advance the story, because the other side will have researched the issue in a different way to find new information in its own defense.

Think the story "forward." Imagine it's a game of chess and you have to think three or four moves ahead. For example, Iraq's invasion of Kuwait in August 1990 raised vital questions about the future. Would Iraq continue its advance and take over Saudi Arabia's oil fields? What would that mean for U.S. energy supplies, and those of U.S. allies? Would the United States go to war to protect those energy supplies? Would the United States be able to act unilaterally? Would Arab states in the region ask for U.S. help? Did the United States have the military strength to repel the Iraqi invasion of Kuwait? How would the Iraqi invasion affect the Israeli-Palestinian conflict? These were questions asked within hours of the Iraqi invasion by reporters who tried to think the story forward.

You should think the story "outward." What were the secondary effects of the Iraqi invasion on the rest of the Arab world? On the Muslim world? On oil prices? On Israel—already worried about Iraqi military strength? On Jordan—economically intertwined with Iraq? On the United Nations? On U.S.-Soviet relations?

Think the story "backward." What were the origins of the Iraqi-Kuwaiti border dispute? How had Iraq behaved in earlier confrontations? Why had the Arab world become so mistrustful of Europe and the United States? Why did the world fail to see the Iraqi invasion coming?

Another way to advance the story is to profile the key players. What kind of men are Iraqi President Saddam Hussein, King Fahd of Saudi Arabia, the Emir of Kuwait? In profiling the newsmakers, you provide insights into the news. The point is to make the listener think new thoughts.

With that in mind, there are times you should try to abandon the popular assumptions about a story. For example, consider the Panama Canal story. The popular assumption in the United States was that this country had won friends in Latin America in the late 1970s by agreeing to return the waterway. But the story is very different if you begin with the assumption, common in Central and South America, that the United States had no right to the canal in the first place. Pursue that assumption, and you'll gather very different information. You'll advance the story. Then try out a very different assumption about the Panama Canal— that the United States should never have returned the canal because it is vital to our national security. If you had done that in 1978, you might have met many of the people who later were swept into power with the Reagan Administration.

By trying out different assumptions, you'll be exploring the meaning of the story. Almost any story can be made more interesting this way. So push beyond the obvious. Transcend boring assignments; advance the story.

Some of the Perils

As a journalist, you deal in an elusive commodity: truth. Truth changes with every new piece of information. *And perhaps the greatest peril of reporting is thinking that you know the truth about the story before you begin*—that you know the truth and all you have to do is to gather the evidence. Reporters with that attitude are often blind to facts before their very eyes. They talk when they should be listening. They miss opportunities to advance the story.

In 1948, with all the experts predicting that Thomas Dewey would easily defeat President Harry Truman, one newspaper boldly went to press announcing that Dewey had won before all the votes had been tallied. Harry Truman, of course, served another four years, much to the newspaper's chagrin.

While journalists shouldn't be too sure about the truth, they can, and should, be sure about their values. Journalists must never lose the capacity to be angered, when the facts justify their anger.

One thing that is sure to raise journalists' ire is when they face another peril: lies. Not just outright lies, but incorrect or misleading information from the best-intentioned people—inadvertent distortions, lies of omission, lies of dissimulation. There are many kinds.

There are artful denials. Political candidates sometimes allow their campaign workers to launch smear campaigns against opponents. The candidates say they did not approve the smear campaigns—and can even disavow them. Candidates who do this are being truthful only in the narrowest sense of the word.

There are diversionary techniques. After the 1989 massacre of pro-democracy students in Tiananmen Square, an American reporter asked a Chinese official about the incident. The official's response: "I understand you Americans also shot your students at Kent State University."

There are attempts to belittle the truth. Watergate was a "third-rate burglary," according to White House Press Secretary Ron Ziegler in 1972. There is disinformation, stories planted in the press by governments eager to discredit their enemies. There are flat-out lies when the stakes are high enough. And there are innocent untruths, told not out of malice, but out of simple ignorance. If reporters pass along any of these lies unchallenged in their stories, they become accomplices to some degree. Their reports circulate the lies more widely.

There are other hazards. You will be flattered by people you are covering. Press secretaries will tell you they admire your work. Watch out. It will be a little harder to be critical the next time. Richard Dudman, who wrote for the *St. Louis Post-Dispatch*, once told this story: "[Former Secretary of State Henry] Kissinger asked my opinion on what he should say, in some great matter, and for a second I felt the headiness of being an important guy. But the truth is, Kissinger couldn't have cared less what I thought—it was a form of flattery. Reporters have to remember they are not sought out in Washington for their charm."

You will hear things out of context. A White House reporter had just heard President Ronald Reagan talk about the decline of Communism. Later, the reporter overheard a couple of the president's advisers chatting. One said, "The president told me, 'It's the end of one era, but the beginning of another.' " The reporter thought Mr. Reagan had been elaborating on his earlier remarks about Communism and said so in the report he filed. But it later turned out the president had been talking to his aides about the sale of a major league baseball team in Chicago.

You will encounter the trappings of power, and you will be awed. Huge front offices, receptionists with frosty voices, countless reminders that you are about to talk to a very busy person. You might want to rush through your questions, and you will not think to follow up on them. Or perhaps you will find that the official is charming, witty—like the "good cop" after the "bad cop." And your skepticism might fail. Just remember that powerful people are well schooled in these techniques.

And finally, you will occasionally cover people or causes you deeply admire. The perils here are obvious. It helps to bear in mind that honest and even harsh criticism is constructive and should be welcomed by people or causes that are honest.

General Assignment Reporting

The appeal of general assignment reporting is its variety. There are a million stories to choose from. While the diet of a general assignment reporter is varied, there are a few staples.

One of these is the press conference. It's not the place to go for scoops, but a press conference is often where news is announced. Press conferences are most useful to reporters who prepare before they go, who read the clip file, who "call the other side," who have questions ready.

At a press conference, you'll be sharing the newsmaker with many other reporters, and it can be difficult to get your question in. You should learn to seize the pauses. The first pause comes after the initial introduction and presentation: a brief instant of awkwardness when no one knows who should talk first. Ask your question then, before the others do. Not only have you managed to get your first question in, you've made an impression on the person holding the news conference. You have become more visible, and it's easier to ask the next question.

Once the question and answer session (the "Q and A") is underway, if you're in a particularly competitive crowd of reporters, you may have to get the jump on them by asking your question before there's a pause, just as the speaker is concluding a sentence or a thought. This technique borders on the obnoxious, and if you don't want to risk seeming obnoxious you can often go up at the end of a press conference and pose a few questions quietly.

But while it's important to get your questions in, it's also very important to let the collective intelligence of the press conference work. Each reporter brings a different perspective and different information to the press conference, and the overall questioning can be much more provocative as a result. If a successful line of questioning is going on, join in if you like, but try not to interrupt it.

The press conference is an occasional event, but press offices are forever. Every general assignment reporter encounters them in corporations, in government, and in sports. Often they arrange daily briefings. The people who work in these offices are called "public information officers" or "press officers." Remember: *Press offices are there to make their bosses look as good as possible.*

Providing useful information is not always the primary goal of press offices. But if you want on-the-record reactions, if you want someone to describe the mayor's position on rodenticides, if you want to get an interview with just the right official on a non-controversial subject, if you want information on schedules and itineraries—press offices can help.

Be prepared to go around them at times. A press officer may not want reporters to talk to controversial figures, and they may warn the officials not to talk if it's known you're trying to contact them. Similarly, if you're onto a story that's damaging to the institution in question, the press office will probably steer you away from the people who know what you need to know.

The Defense Department press office did not help Seymour Hersh break the Mylai Massacre story. He walked quietly into Lt. Calley's barracks one day, before anyone understood the enormity of what had happened at Mylai, and had a long talk with Calley about that day in March when U.S. troops opened fire on Vietnamese civilians.

The White House press office did not help Woodward and Bernstein with the Watergate story.

You may not always be able to talk to officials about controversial stories in their offices. Call them at home if necessary.

If you want to tape telephone interviews, remember that the people on the other end of the line have no way of knowing that they're being recorded unless you tell them. Make it clear that you want to tape and then make it clear when you've started the tape. In some cases the law requires it; in all cases fairness does. A young reporter once lost his job because the congressman he interviewed on the phone didn't know his comments were being recorded. The reporter claimed he had abided by the letter, if not the spirit, of the rules. He began the interview by saying: "Hello, this is Jack taping." The congressman thought the "taping" was the reporter's last name.

As with press conferences, it's good to have a list of questions ready when you interview someone. The list can be liberating, allowing you to explore tangents without worrying that you'll forget to ask an important question.

Before the interview, many reporters think about when to ask the controversial questions. If they're likely to anger the interviewee, reporters will hold these questions until after they have the non-controversial answers they need. If reporters already have those answers and are looking for an unrehearsed reaction, they will often ask the provocative questions right away.

When you talk to people in their official capacity—as representatives of the local steel mill, for example, or the school board—you should operate on the assumption that you have every right to ask them questions. Their actions affect the public, and the public has the right to know about them.

For private individuals, or the private lives of public individuals, the ethical considerations are different, and so is the law. (See Part III of the NPR Stylebook, "A Legal Guide for Radio Journalists.") You don't automatically have the right to know what they are thinking or doing. If you want their stories, you may have to use gentle persuasion.

On a Beat

The time may come when general assignment reporting loses its allure. The excitement of covering a different story every day may give way to frustration. You can rarely do that follow-up story. You can't develop any real expertise.

That's the time to try a beat. It could be city hall, it could be crime, it could be Japan, it could be the arts. But whatever your beat, the first thing to do is read all about it; read everything you can get your hands on, even articles that are marginally related. Become voracious for information about your beat.

Next, you must develop sources. Official spokespersons are not usually considered sources. Sources are people who do policy work within the organization you're covering. Many beat reporters try to meet mid-level sources to begin with: not the mayor, but the mayor's assistants; not the company president, but the vice-president in charge of operations. The big names make pronouncements, but the mid-level sources often develop policy and can help a reporter to understand it. In addition, they can describe their bosses' motives, fears, regrets, and follow-up moves.

Some reporters meet sources by simply inviting them to lunch. They say, "I'm covering city hall and believe that you can help me understand what goes on here. Your insights would make my reporting more fair. Let's have lunch."

Some reporters simply walk into the office of a potential source and introduce themselves. And some reporters make a point of going up to the dais after a press conference and introducing themselves to the newsmaker there. In every case, the idea is to get acquainted, get familiar with each other, so the reporter doesn't have to call out of the blue on the day of the really big story.

Sources usually have pet products or projects, and reporters will sometimes admit to having filed stories on these primarily to cultivate the sources. Another way to get acquainted is to do a series of portraits of people behind the scenes. Try not to pass up opportunities to meet sources.

Sources won't always want to be named. The confidentiality of sources must be protected when they ask for it and the reporter agrees to accept the information on that condition.

What motivates sources? Often it's a sincere desire to inform the public. Sometimes sources want to get air time for their point of view when a policy decision is pending. Sometimes they want to sabotage an opponent. And sometimes the object is to lull a reporter into complacency, to lure a reporter into the family, or worse—to sandbag a reporter by giving false information at a critical moment. As you cultivate your sources, be aware of their motives and motivations.

Pack Journalism

If you are covering a beat, you're likely to be with the same group of reporters for long periods of time, and it's easy to start writing for them rather than for your real audience. The "pack" can end up deciding what is or isn't the news. *The New Republic* once compared the Washington press corps to the pigeons in Lafayette Park, which tend to take off all at once, race madly around in a flock, and then settle together in another corner of the park, all without apparent reason.

But there are also benefits of being part of the group. Reporters on a beat often "pool" resources. ("You stake out the back door, I'll stake out the front, and we'll share whatever we get.") They can share insights and even sources on rare occasions.

To be or not to be part of that group is a dilemma with no easy answer. The late I.F. Stone, for many years one of the best-informed reporters in Washington, opted out of the "family." He once said, "You pay something for everything you got. The establishment reporters, without a doubt, know a lot of things I don't know. But a lot of what they know isn't true. And a lot of what they know that is true, they can't print."

Putting the Story Together

Some reporters have daily deadlines; some have weekly deadlines; many have monthly deadlines. You can't avoid them. Sooner or later you have to take all that information and extract the news. You have to write it down clearly and engagingly.

Paradoxically, the more you know about a story, the easier it is to write, once you have a basic outline in mind. If you know more than you need, you'll write with greater confidence. You'll know which word is exactly right. You won't have to be equivocal. Your syntax will not be tortured by your doubt.

Reporters who learn more than they file find the information valuable later. When you're gathering information, put out lots of calls. Really work the phone. Reporters can't afford to be idle while they're waiting for people to return their calls. There's almost always someone in another agency, in another office, or in a nearby town who has some useful information. Nearby colleges are often overlooked as sources of valuable information. Political science, history, and fine arts departments are full of experts and activists.

If there is just one person who knows what you need to know, be persistent. Don't be shy about calling back before that person has returned your call. Explain that you're on a tight deadline.

Wire services can provide useful information, but they should be used judiciously. They are especially useful close to deadline when they can bring news of late-breaking developments across town. But the wires should be a supplement, not a substitute for your own reporting. The more you use wire service information, the more your report will sound like dozens of others. And, of course, it's important to confirm information taken from the wires before you put it into your story.

Contact your editor. (You should already have talked to the editor at the beginning of the assignment. See Chapter 5, "The Editor.") Most reporters find that once they've managed to explain the story to the editor, it's easier to explain it on the radio.

As you talk to your editor, decide on your **lead.** A lead is the opening shot in a news story. In newspapers, the lead is one or two sentences long, contains the most important information, and conveys a sense of where the story is going. In radio, there's another factor. You must think about ways to divide the lead with the person anchoring your newscast. If you don't give the anchor something provocative or newsworthy to say about your story, the anchor will seem vacuous. Your report will not be an integral part of the news program, but only attached by the most tenuous of phrases: "And now for the latest on the economy we turn to . . . ." And no one will listen.

Many reporters find it useful to write the intros to their own stories, in consultation with the program editor. That way, there's the smoothest possible flow from anchor to reporter.

If it's a hard news story, you might give the anchor the latest development to report, or perhaps the most important development. Your report should then begin in the most vivid way possible. It's a kind of partnership: the anchor gets listeners interested, and then you take them to the scene of the action.

So while a newspaper story could begin this way: "Today the Senate Ethics Committee recommended unanimously to expel Senator X, amid growing evidence that the full Senate will concur," a radio program would have the anchor saying something like: "The vote was unanimous. The Senate Ethics Committee has recommended expelling Senator X. If the full Senate goes along, and that seems more and more likely, it will be the first time since the Civil War that Senators have thrown out one of their own. More from . . . ."

And your radio report could then begin: "It was painful for Senator X and his colleagues. The committee chairman announced the decision in a subdued voice, as the committee members looked on silently."

When you've settled on a lead, you have the heart of the story, and you should take a moment to sketch a rough outline. It will set your mind free. You can concentrate on writing, and not worry about forgetting an important element of the story.

As you write, remember that editors are there to be careful, reporters are there to be clear. Write as simply and forcefully as possible. Your editor should keep you from painting with too broad a brush.

Write conversationally. Many broadcast reporters read their stories out loud as they write them. They say each sentence, each paragraph. It's the best way to guarantee a comfortable, conversational style.

In radio, the active voice almost always sounds better than the passive voice. People usually talk in the active voice. They don't say, *"It was announced by the mayor* today . . . ."* They say, *"Today the mayor said . . . ."* But sometimes the passive voice is unavoidable. Sometimes you won't know who did something, and you'll have to write, *"A young man was killed in his apartment last night . . . ."* And sometimes reporters use the passive voice to help the pacing of their stories. (See Chapter 6, "Writing News for Radio," for more detailed information on writing.)

When the story is completely written, go back to your editor for the final edit.

Delivery

Before they go on the air, most reporters read their scripts as many times as possible. Then, when they're on the air, or when they're recording, the words sound spontaneous and the script is almost secondary. Delivery is a very personal matter, but there are some general guidelines, which add up to: Be natural. Pause when you need to, breathe normally, swallow if you have to. Let your voice respond to what you're reading just as it would in normal conversation.

A frequent problem for beginning reporters is speaking too quickly. Reading tends to make people talk faster, and you may have to make a deliberate effort to read more slowly than you think you should. Also, there's the danger of sounding "singsong." When you read out loud, your voice often rises and falls arbitrarily, and you may find your voice placing the same emphasis at the end of every sentence. You may find your pitch rising in the middle of every sentence, then falling at the end. In both cases, it's not natural—it's your voice doing arbitrary things. If you are really familiar with what you're reading, you can concentrate on the substance of it, and you'll find that your voice falls into more natural patterns. Sometimes, reporters will underline words that should be emphasized until reading comes to them naturally. Sometimes, they write cues to themselves (or use symbols) in the margins of their scripts to denote "pause here," or "read deliberately here."

Use the voice you were born with, not the one you think a broadcaster should have. The latter rarely fits.

To enliven your delivery, if that's a problem, you might try smiling while you read. It's something you can get away with in radio because no one can see you.

The point is to feel what you are reading. If you do that, your voice will assume the proper tone. It's almost like acting. In fact, hosting a newsmagazine or delivering a news report is a kind of performance. But in radio journalism, acting skills are used for the effective presentation of fact, not fantasy. (See Chapter 7, "Delivery: Using Your Voice," for more details.)

Being an Editor

The division of responsibility between reporters and editors can be seen this way: A reporter should know everything about something, and an editor should know something about everything.

A good editor has the same sensibilities as a good reporter, and the ethics are pretty much the same. But an editor's concerns are "macro." An editor provides the context into which reporters place their pieces. So, as you move from the role of reporter to that of editor and back to reporter again, you'll have to adjust your world view.

As editors make assignments, they try to create a good "mix" of stories: not just hard news; not just features. This mix helps to assure a lively and well-paced news program. And, of course, the assignment process is a consultative one.

Reporters and editors will have arguments, but their conflicts should be constructive. A better story often will emerge from that inevitable tension. Good editors respect reporters who are prepared to fight to keep an important point of information or style in their reports but will listen and make changes where necessary, too. It's a sign of intellectual rigor. And good reporters welcome tough editors who pay close attention. For when editors care about stories, they really care about reporters who write those stories, and about the listeners—most important of all.

Ted Clark is diplomatic correspondent for National Public Radio. His reports on U.S. foreign policy are heard on MORNING EDITION, WEEKEND EDITION, and ALL THINGS CONSIDERED. From 1983 to 1987, he was executive producer of ALL THINGS CONSIDERED. From 1981 to 1983, he was NPR's White House correspondent, and from 1979 to 1981, he was editor of ATC. Before working at NPR, Clark was Washington bureau chief for Pacifica Radio. In 1987, he was a Jefferson Fellow at the East-West Center in Hawaii. He was awarded a 1990 George Foster Peabody Award for his coverage of Mozambique. Clark received his B.A. from Harvard University in 1968.

4

Interviewing

Robert Siegel

An interview for radio easily can be mistaken for a spontaneous conversation. After some editing, it often resembles one. Good interviews, though, are studied, calculated events that—when they succeed—convey the impression of conversation. On ALL THINGS CONSIDERED, I have found that my favorite interview situations are barely conversations by any common definition.

In fact, I prefer pre-taped interviews with a guest in a remote studio, connected by satellite or fiber optic line, to those where the guest is in the studio with me. The sound quality is about the same, and, during the guest's answers, I can write and consult notes, talk with my editor by intercom, and address the microphone without struggling to maintain eye-contact.

Some of my favorite face-to-face interviews are with foreign-language speakers and interpreters providing consecutive translation. They permit me to do the interview and think about it at the same time: While my question is being translated, and during the untranslated answers, I have time to plan my strategy for the next question.

In both these situations, the illusion of conversation is absent in the taping but may, as a result, be more evident in the finished product.

For example, during 1990 and 1991 I conducted several telephone interviews with Vytautas Landsbergis, the president of Lithuania. The audience heard it this way: I would ask a question in English. Then Landsbergis would begin to answer in Lithuanian. His voice would then fade under an interpreter, speaking in English. At the end of the answer, I would return with a second question in English.

At times these interviews, during the days when Moscow was trying to prevent Lithuanian independence, were dramatic exchanges that led ALL THINGS

CONSIDERED. They usually ran about four minutes on the air. In the taping, however, they were typically 15 minutes of consecutive translation. Landsbergis was in Vilnius, the interpreter was on a conference call from Arlington, Va., I was in the studio, and my editor was in the control room. We could virtually edit the interview in progress.

Situations like this happened often:

Interpreter (completing Landsbergis' previous answer): We are the rightful government of a rightful independent nation.

Siegel: Mr. Landsbergis, the United States does not recognize your republic's independence. The State Department says you don't control the territory of Lithuania. Moscow has ordered Soviet troops into the streets of Vilnius. What hope do you have of achieving real independence at this rate?

Landsbergis might speak for, say, 20 seconds. The interpretation would tell us it was rhetoric repeating what he had said earlier. The question was misfiring. The previous answer was definitely good, but not this one. The editor might suggest in my earphone, "Ask if the U.S. has indicated it might change its standard for recognition." I would then strategize. With my previous question destined for the trash, we would lose the facts of U.S. non-recognition and Moscow's dispatch of troops to Vilnius. So I would pose the next question this way:

Siegel (recalling end of earlier question): President Landsbergis, you speak of a rightfully independent nation, but Moscow has ordered Soviet troops into the streets of your capital, the U.S. says you don't control the territory of your nation, and, without that control, it won't recognize you. Do have any indication the United States might change its standard for recognition?

In this hypothetical (but entirely plausible) exchange, we made a mental "cut" while the interview was under way and adjusted the questioning accordingly. Don't try this in a social conversation.

Obviously, my guidance for interviews reflects my own experiences, preferences, and the job I perform at NPR. Interviews vary in purpose, place and quality. But there is one thing they all have in common. They all require preparation: editorial, technical and psychological.

Before You Start, Know What You're After

Bone up on the story. Before the interview, check recent newspaper and wire service reports; if your radio station did a story on the same subject, get the tape and listen to it. If there are aspects to the story you don't understand (what is a debenture? a carotid endarterectomy? a Yazidi?), consult a reference book or call an authority on the subject. (Local college faculties are full of people in possession of esoteric knowledge that has not aroused the genuine curiosity of a student in years. They would be flattered by a call from the press.)

Find out all that you can about the person you're about to interview. What is his organization? Or her most important achievement? What do his detractors think of him? What facts might he know that aren't widely known to the public? What would her harshest critics want to ask her?

Above all, decide what it is you want to get out of the interview. What is *the* question you want to make sure gets answered on tape? Then, make a list of the things you want to ask about in a reporter's notebook, think of some questions you intend to ask, and rehearse a couple of them to yourself—out loud, if possible.

I find scripted questions or an entire menu of questions can get in the way of hearing the answers and following up on them. I like to write down subjects in my notebook, rather than the questions themselves, because the questions can become too narrowly crafted.

That once led to the most stunning, nearly catastrophic event of my reporting career. I was in London, based at NPR's office at the BBC on the day Pope John Paul II was shot. I had heard that a suspect, not Italian, had been apprehended. I had taken a year of college Italian to satisfy the requirements of a French literature major and so devised the following plan: I told a BBC secretary that the instant the suspect was identified she should telephone the Rome embassy of the suspect's country of origin. I recalled barely enough Italian to rehearse the line: "Is there someone there who speaks English? If not, French?" The plan worked. It turned out that the suspect, Mehmet Ali Agca, was a Turk, and I was almost instantly questioning a Turkish diplomat in French.

Siegel (in nearly grammatical French): Do you know any details about this man, Mehmet Ali Agca—where he lived in Italy, what he did there, what kind of visa the Italians gave him?

Diplomat: I don't have any details.

Siegel (nearly grammatical and disheartened that this wasn't going to yield any news): Do you know when he entered the country? How long his visa was for?

Diplomat: No. I don't know any of that.

Siegel (dejected): No details.

Diplomat: None.

With no other questions on my list, I resolved to end the interview, until the diplomat piped up . . .

Diplomat: . . . except that he is the most famous convicted murderer in Turkey, who escaped from prison after assassinating the editor of one of our major newspapers.

Within half an hour, after confirming Agca's identity with the BBC's Turkish service (which wasn't broadcasting at the time) and digging up an *Economist* clipping from the BBC library, I filed for NPR on Agca's past. We were ahead of all the wires—and just about all non-Turkish news organizations. I almost lost a good story by asking narrow, secondary questions, instead of the big one. My first question should have been this: "Tell me about this Mehmet Ali Agca." I should have written on a reporter's notebook these words: "WHO AGCA."

Taking Charge

Most interviews in the field are recorded with one microphone. You will have to hold the microphone in such a way that you can comfortably reach the interview subject and yourself. If she is sitting behind a desk, reclining on a chair, or standing behind the deli counter of a supermarket, you may not be able to reach. So, before the interview starts, move the interview subject, yourself, or both of you to positions where you can comfortably record the interview.

Remember: You're the boss. You have to be prepared to take charge of the situation even though the person you're questioning may be older, more experienced, a government official, better dressed, and on home turf. Tell her where you would like her to sit. Tell him that he can't move out of your reach. Be polite, but firm. When they tell you that *ABC Nightline* somehow managed to record an interview without forcing them out of their favorite chairs, tell them we have higher technical standards (or worse equipment) than *Nightline*.

Some tried and true placements for an out-of-studio interview include:

- *Across the corner of a desk.* This gives you a surface for your reporter's notebook, not to mention your elbow. The problem here will be reclining desk chairs; when the governor leans back to take a puff off his cigar, he'll go way off-mike.

- *Across the corner of a coffee table.* Same virtues as above, with less risk of reclining.

- *Standing face to face.* This beats reaching across the deli counter. Hold the mike in one hand and the reporter's notebook in the other.

Social Distance

When you interview people standing up, certain phrases that we use figuratively resume concrete, literal meanings: arm's length, tête-à-tête, stand-offish.

Social distance is no mere figure of speech in this business, no allusion to class distinction. It describes the distance from another person at which one feels comfortable conversing. Come closer than that distance, and the person you're trying to question may recoil from you, as if by magnetic repulsion.

Many a beginning radio reporter assigned to gather "vox pop" at a local shopping mall has discovered that a microphone can work like a stave, pushing away the very people it is supposed to record. A conversation between two people with dramatically different comfort levels can become a kind of sidewalk rumba, one person backing away in search of more comfortable distance, the other persistently coming closer.

What complicates the problem of social distance is that it varies among individuals and among cultures. It's commonly reported that a northern European will recoil from a speaker at a distance of a foot or two—a distance a Latino speaker may find perfectly comfortable.

There are, however, some tricks for getting around the social distance problem—and preserving the technical quality you'll need for broadcast at the same time:

- Learn to probe for and work at the distance the other person favors. If at all possible, figure out ways to get around the technical problems when that distance is too far for satisfactory miking. Put the other person's mike on a clamp or a stand, for instance, and use two mikes if your voice needs to be on the tape. Try putting the corner of a desk or coffee table between you; the physical barrier may add to the psychological distance.

- In a sit-down interview recorded at, say, the mayor's office, explain to the mayor that she will have to remain closer to you than normal conversational distance. Anything extraordinary that you ask of people in an interview is worth an explanation. Tell her that your microphone can only pick her voice up well at a certain distance. Explain to her that if she wanders on- and off-mike, the effect can be irritating to the listeners (a.k.a. the voters). In short, be truthful, but blame any inconvenience or discomfort you cause her on the technology.

- On the sidewalk, don't buttonhole people straightaway. Try to engage them from a few feet away with a question, like: "Excuse me, sir. May I ask you a couple of questions about the mayor, for radio?" As you get consent, begin your approach and keep coming until you're close enough to mike him. Keep the mike below eye level. If you hold it out ahead of you, you may reduce the distance at which he feels comfortable talking to you.

Your relations with "vox pop" interview subjects are, of course, conditioned by social realities. In most American cities, nowadays, a person who stops strangers on the street is presumed to be a beggar. Women may find the entreaties of a male reporter to be more threatening than men do. It helps to look presentable and unthreatening.

Eye Contact

If you are face to face with your interview subject, you have to maintain eye contact. It's at the very least a sign of courtesy. In a radio interview, it is often a struggle. Between your eyes and the other person's is the microphone. Keep the mike below the line of eye contact, out of sight, and you stand a good chance, by Question 3 or 4, of putting it out of mind, too.

This is often easier to do in the field than in the studio despite (or, perhaps, because of) the best efforts of studio designers. NPR's current studios present a forest of mike stands, cables, and reading lamps between an interviewer and an interview subject, making unobstructed eye contact extremely difficult.

Establishing Rapport

This is a complicated business. Manuals for radio reporters have always assumed that the people we interview may be intimidated by the process, or suffer "mike fright" and go mute on us when the "On Air" light goes on. I think this was true in past decades but is now less and less a problem. Our society is a sophisticated communications environment in which millions of people have become familiar with microphones in one way or another: playing in garage bands, being in TV interviews, using home camcorders.

When I am in the field on a story, I am rarely concerned that the people I interview will lose composure before a microphone. But I am often concerned they will assume a formal, inauthentic composure, imitating "someone being interviewed." Often, the people I interview in the field (for radio) scan the area around me as they answer my questions, looking for the camera.

I try to establish sufficient rapport to get an interview with a real person, instead of an assumed persona. That is easiest in telephone interviews; people are accustomed to speaking effectively and authentically on the telephone (it's how they exchange news of births and deaths, for example; you don't get much more authentic than that). I begin phone interviews by asking for a voice level, partly for technical reasons and partly to establish rapport. As evidence in support of my theory that we are a people too accustomed to being interviewed, I would point out that very few people are even mildly surprised by this request. All Americans seem to know what voice levels are.

The most discouraging words I hear in response to the mention of "voice level" are "One-two-three-one-two-three-one-two-three." They signal potential disaster: a totally stylized exchange of questions and answers. To avoid it, I ask everyone the same question: "For voice level, can you tell me what you had for lunch today (or, if the time is inappropriate, your most recent meal)?" This question can be disarming. It takes the guest's mind off the subject of the interview, which she may have been concentrating on in anticipation of the interview, and puts it onto a subject that defies pomposity. Sometimes it's even revealing. A Jesuit priest involved in Central American peace work told me, for his voice level, that he had eaten a spoonful of peanut butter for lunch every day for years. At the other extreme, a French foreign policy analyst whom we call in Paris from time to time commonly relates lunches to us that are fit for the food columns of magazines.

In the field, there is often little time for prolonged voice levels. Even so, you can ask people to identify themselves by name, job, age and so on. I always say I'm asking for all that information on tape so as not to misidentify them on the air. This is, in fact, one reason for the question; I'll know how they pronounce their own names. But the deeper purpose is to make some contact with a real person. For example, say I am asking people on a street corner whether they give money to beggars, and why. If they reveal some of their identity to me, describe the background or outlook that informs their behavior, they will be less likely (I hope) to give me insincere, pat answers.

In these little conversations before the interview, try to establish a rhythm. You are not going to want one-word answers to your interview questions, so try to get the other person out of the rhythm of one-word answers to your voice level questions. If he says he's a teacher, ask where he teaches, what subject, whether he enjoys teaching. If she says she had a sandwich for lunch, ask about the condiments. Any side dishes? Salad? Was it tasty?

How Will the Interview Be Used on the Air?

There are two ways that interviews are used in radio:

- *As "actuality."* Extracts of the interview are inserted in a story or a newscast.

- *As an interview*, either live or taped.

When you prepare for an interview, know in advance how it is to be used on the air. An interview intended to produce actuality requires different tactics from one intended to air as an interview.

Going after a Quotation

When searching for actuality, you are trying to elicit statements that run 15–25 seconds. Your questions are probably going to end up on the floor, although one may survive as linkage between two brief answers. In general, don't worry about illogic or repetition in your questions if they're not going on the air anyway. They are the stimuli; you want responses only.

Ask the same question over and over. If you are interviewing people who escaped a burning building, the only important questions may be: "What did you do then?" "What did you see then?" "What happened next?" Don't worry about asking these same questions repeatedly. Even if you utter the words: "What happened then?" 50 times in four different interviews, they may only appear on the air once, if ever. The audience will not suffer from your lack of originality in questioning.

Also: Don't be afraid to ask for cooperation in getting a short, pointed answer. People nowadays know that interviews are edited for brevity. After someone gives you a two-minute answer describing what being inside a burning house felt like, you might ask: "If you had to explain to someone in just one sentence what it was like in there, what would you say?" Your question might not work, but it's always worth a try.

The Interview To Air as an Interview

Here your questions count for as much as the answers. They provide the thread of logic that runs through the interview. I assume that the first question I ask will be replaced by an introduction that I, or a tape editor, will write after the taping. But the other questions may go on the air. One of the most frustrating problems in an interview is making a factual error in a question. That may require editing out the question and, consequently, the answer it provoked.

Make sure the assertions in your questions are accurate. Master the vocabulary of the story so that when you are called upon to utter a strange word (debenture, carotid endarterectomy, Yazidi), you pronounce it with confidence. Speak grammatically and at a pace resembling the one you use when reading a story. If the interview is being prerecorded (as are nearly all interviews on ALL THINGS CONSIDERED), take advantage of the tape editing that will follow. For example, if the guest is slow to answer, don't feel obliged to stretch out your questions to fill dead air until he leaps in with a response. Let him pause. You can always cut the pause out later.

Some Questions for All Occasions

'The High Hard One'

Never forget to ask *the* one question that you want to hear the person answer on tape. Scott Simon, of NPR's WEEKEND EDITION, says this is the kind of question he *starts* his interviews with. Let's say the real purpose of your interview is to find out how Mayor Jones defends herself against the perception that she is no less corrupt than any of her predecessors. Ask her bluntly: "Are you any less corrupt than your predecessors?"

You can then follow with more detailed questions ("Your water commissioner is awaiting trial. The building commissioner is in jail. How do you explain that?")

By asking *the* underlying question of the interview, you avoid a common pitfall: spending 20 minutes with someone and never getting him on tape responding to what may be the lead of your story.

But you should be aware of the potential downsides to asking "the high, hard one." Many people you interview may be willing to open up to you and respond to your toughest questions. But others may respond differently: If you completely antagonize them, the interview may effectively end right at the beginning. At worst you might be asked to leave. And if the interview proceeds frostily, you may get no useful answers in response to softer, but nevertheless important and useful, questions. To guard against that possibility, many interviewers try to get the soft questions out of the way first and save the potential door-slammers for later.

You may also find that the rapport you establish in the less confrontational questions will pay dividends when you pose the tough ones. You are not out to make a friend in an interview, but you are a potentially sympathetic, or unsympathetic ear to that person. If you are perceived as sympathetic, "the high, hard one" may receive a more candid response.

Be careful, though. If the interview is for actuality in a story you're reporting, your posturing will end up on the floor, lost to posterity. If the interview is to be broadcast intact as an interview, it will be heard. While I believe in reporters asking bad questions so long as they get good answers, the questions hosts ask are partially posed on behalf of the audience. Fawning on others' behalf, without their consent, is presumptuous.

Getting Someone Else To Ask the Tough Ones

If it sticks in the craw to ask Mayor Jones "the high, hard one," you can always invent straw men.

For example, there is the *highly placed straw man*: "I've heard some of your critics say you're no less corrupt than your predecessors. What do you say to them?"

There is the *common man as straw man*: "A couple of days ago, I told a cab driver I would be interviewing you. And here's what he said: 'I used to think Lolita Jones was different from all those other guys, but now I can't see the difference. She's as crooked as the rest.' What do you have to say that man?" I suppose the best cut of tape you could get in response to that would be this response from the mayor: "I want to say to him, 'When is your hack license up for renewal?' " This might not be equally good news for any cab drivers you have recently patronized, but, then, whoever said the comments of cab drivers are off the record?

There is even the *most odious straw man of all*: "My news director told me I had to ask you this one . . . "

But best of all, you can try the *straw man as another person you have interviewed for this story*: "Here's what Sam Green wrote in his column in Tuesday's *Bugle*: 'Lolita Jones used to be . . . but now . . . ' etc."

The invocation of straw men or real players in the dispute you're covering can add a lot of heat to an interview, but it may keep the heat away from you. You are converting the conversation between yourself and the mayor into a conversation between the mayor and her nastiest critics on the City Council, or on the local op-ed pages. You remain a neutral in the dispute, but you present questions in the personae of other people who are not.

Definitions

Many of the best stories I have heard on NPR are simply definitions. "What does overheating the economy mean?" "What is a pardon?" "A smart bomb?" "What is AIDS?" This is a useful way to think of questioning, too. One of the main purposes of good journalism is to translate from narrow jargons of professionals, experts, and those bent on obfuscation into a common spoken English. Very often the people you interview will use words in a self-serving fashion. It's often fruitful to ask them to define their terms. "Mayor Jones, how do you define corruption?"

The Dozing Psychiatrist's Question

This is a question of last resort to pose when you haven't the slightest idea what to say, you've asked everything about every subject you listed in your reporter's notebook, yet the interview just doesn't feel complete. Repeat the last phrase of the person you're interviewing.

Reporter (asking your last question): Will you fire Commissioner Smith if he pleads guilty to a misdemeanor?

Mayor: I will do what I will do, in keeping with my responsibilities.
Reporter (caught without a clue): In keeping with your responsibilities?

This may or may not yield a more elaborate answer. At least it will give you some time to figure out what to do next. It is a close cousin to:

The Blank Silent Stare

At the end of an answer, no question at all is a statement on your part. It says: "Surely you don't think I think that's the end of your answer to my question." This tactic may get you more of an answer. It also may get a blank silent stare in return.

Parting Words

One last word of advice: You are not a collaborator with the people you interview, but you are not their enemy, either. You may ask a tough question right after a frivolous voice-level exchange. And you may let a person who has become tongue-tied restart his answer to a crucial question. Being polite is not the equivalent of being a patsy.

Robert Siegel is a host of NPR's ALL THINGS CONSIDERED. *He has served as NPR's director of news and information programming, and, prior to that, opened NPR's London Bureau as senior editor.*

PART II

TELLING THE STORY

5

The Editor

Marcus D. Rosenbaum

Everyone needs an editor. Good reporters *want* good editors; they know good editors are reporters' allies, not their enemies. Good editors will help them focus their stories, protect them against making stupid mistakes, save them from bad grammar, and help them tell their stories most effectively.

This chapter will explain what editors do and will give you some tips on how to be a good editor. Of course, this will be most useful to those of you who are or want to be an editor full time. But if you are a reporter, this chapter also will help you understand what your editors do and how they can best help you.

The Role of the Editor

Editors have the ultimate responsibility for the *content* of everything that goes on the air. Their job is to ensure that the right stories are covered, that those stories are covered properly, and that they are broadcast in a way that is responsible and accurate. In other words, they make the assignments, supervise the coverage, and guide the stories through production.

Some organizations split editors' assignment functions from their production functions. They have **assignment editors**, who dispatch reporters to cover the day's news and make sure that all the reporters don't show up in the same place at the same time. And they have **copy editors** or **production editors**, who shepherd the reporters' stories onto the air. Other organizations lump these functions together.*

Whatever their specific job, editors always play two very different roles simultaneously: As a surrogate for the listeners, they ask the "dumb questions" and ensure that stories are understandable on first hearing; as the reporters' supervisor, they ask the "smart questions," ensuring that stories are complete and accurate and fair.

Editors and reporters are in the same profession, but they have different instincts. Reporters thrive on the actual pursuit of the story—the developing of sources, the phone calls, the difficult interviews, the long stakeouts. Editors, on the other hand, are more interested in the big-picture questions about the story *idea* and in the details of how the finished story will sound on the air. This does not mean that editors and reporters never talk with each other during the course of an assignment; indeed, editors and reporters often work closely all the way through a story. But for the most part, editors focus on the beginning and the end—the assignment and the production.

The Assignment

In their assignment role, editors are likely to receive dozens of press releases each day. They also are likely to know of many other important events taking place. And they are not going to have enough staff available to cover everything—or enough air time to broadcast it even if they did. So an editor's first responsibility is to utilize scarce resources effectively.

News Judgment

Editors do this by exercising what is called **news judgment**—deciding which stories need to be covered and which ones can be skipped; which ones must get on the air now and which ones can be delayed; whether to cover an event or to devote the resources to an in-depth investigation.

Good news judgment is difficult to teach. Much of it comes from experience—learning what works and what doesn't from the good and bad decisions

---

*At NPR the assignment and production functions are combined, but there are still two different kinds of editors—**desk editors** and **show editors.** Desk editors function much like desk editors on newspapers; they deal most closely with reporters, supervising them directly, making the assignments, and usually editing the reports. There are four main desks at NPR—Foreign, National, Washington, and Science. Show editors have overall responsibility for the content of their programs. They coordinate with the desk editors to make sure that reporters are assigned in accordance with their shows' needs; and they work closely with the program hosts, prepping them for interviews, suggesting questions before and during the interviews, and editing host-produced reports.

you make yourself, and listening to other, more experienced editors justify their decisions. Good news judgment requires you to answer key questions like these: What is new about the story? What makes it interesting? Will I learn something? How can the news be advanced? What are the unanswered questions? Is there a way to cover the story that will go beyond the obvious?

To be able to answer those kinds of questions, you need to be knowledge-able about the world around you, abreast of the news, and ahead of upcoming events. There is no single way to do all of that. But there are some tricks of the trade:

- *Read as much as you can.* Good story ideas usually do not arrive over the transom, and when they do, you need to be able to recognize them for what they are. Daybooks, news releases, and public-relations hacks may let you know about events, but it is up to you to turn those events into news stories or features. To do that, you need to develop enough background and knowledge to get beyond the event itself to its meaning—so that you will know the "dumb" and "smart" questions you should ask. You develop that knowledge, in great part, by reading. Read all of your local paper every day, of course. But also read the suburban weeklies, the neighborhood shoppers, the city maga-zines. And then read at least one national or regional newspaper every day, too—the *New York Times*, the *Wall Street Journal*, the *Chicago Tribune*—and as many magazines as you have time for. These national journals will give you a broad perspective on the news that will bring depth to local stories and help you recognize when a local story has national implications.

- *Listen to your reporters.* Because they spend more time in direct contact with the public, reporters are likely to come up with many good story ideas on their own. They also are likely to be good sources to help you focus your own ideas. Run even partially formed story ideas past them. Listen to what the reporters say, and use the information wisely.

- *Watch the wires and the daybooks.* Follow the wires closely. Not only will they give you quick reads on events that can help you develop broader stories, but they also are an excellent short- and long-range planning tool. The short-range information often comes in the form of **advisories** or **daybooks**. The wires will send an advisory when they get word of an important news confer-ence, for instance. Their daybooks will list events for the upcoming day (or week or month). You also should get as many other calendar services as you can. Often local organizations publish their own events calendars and will be happy to put you on their mailing lists. Other calendars you may have to buy.

- *Set up a futures file.* Long-range information from the wires and from news-papers and magazines usually comes buried somewhere in a story. A piece about a local banker's arrest, for instance, may include a line that says his trial has been scheduled for March 23. Clip the story and put it in your **futures file**. There are many different ways to keep a futures file. You can do it electronically on your computer, or you can have a set of file folders, one for each day or each week, which you rotate so the most recent ones are in the front. Devise your own system, but be sure it's easy to use.

- *Trust your instincts.* You are, after all, a citizen as well as a journalist. If *you* are really puzzled about why the mayor said what she did, there's a good chance a lot of other people are puzzled, too. Maybe an explanation is in order. If *you* see inconsistencies in U.S. relations with Country A and its relations with Country B, maybe you should have a reporter ask the State Department for an explanation.

Whom To Assign

After you decide that a story should be covered, the next step is to decide *what is the best way to cover it*: Should it be a reporter piece, a host interview, host copy, or even a commentary? There are logistical issues to consider; they have to do with juggling scarce resources and time. But there are editorial issues to consider as well: Some stories are too complex to be done as a host interview; others will be more telling as an interview than as a report. As the editor, you have to decide.

The reporter piece. A reporter is usually your most flexible choice. Reporters can cover events *on the scene*, thus giving the listeners the best sense of being there. Reporters can handle complex and contentious ideas, giving all sides the opportunity to be heard and explaining what they say "between the lines." And reporters can analyze stories from a detached perspective that your listeners have come to trust. But be careful in your assignments. Reporters' time is scarce, and when they are covering one story, they are not covering another. You may miss important events if you make the wrong assignments. Some stories can be handled just as well—if not better—in another way.

If you decide the story should be covered by a reporter, you then have to decide which reporter. In many news organizations, some of the reporters have **beats**—that is, specialized areas of interest like education, the White House, city hall, Congress, police, etc. If the story falls within a beat, you probably will assign it to the beat reporter. But there are always other considerations, regardless of whether a beat reporter is involved: How complex is the story? How quickly does it need to be done? Does one reporter have a particular interest in the subject? Does it tie in with another story? Reporters have different strengths and weaknesses. Obviously, in making assignments you want to play to their strengths and not to their weaknesses.

The host report. At NPR, program hosts often do reporter pieces. The same considerations go into assigning a host report as go into assigning reporter pieces. But to do major stories the hosts must be away from their programs, which may cause scheduling problems.

The host interview. The host interview (or "two-way," as it has come to be known at NPR, to suggest that the host and the interviewee both have something to contribute) comes in many different flavors.

There is, first, the **newsmaker** or **participant interview**. An interview with Lech Walesa by a well-briefed host may be a much better way to cover the Polish president's visit to your city than assigning a reporter to cover his speech. Newsmaker interviews also work very well as sidebars to reporters' news stories. A program may lead with a report from Moscow on Boris Yeltsin's latest actions on the economy. Following that with a host interview with Yeltsin, or his spokesman, would be an excellent way to get some of the toughest questions asked—if not answered. However, remember that you're only getting one side of a story.

Participant interviews can be dangerous when the story is contentious or has more than one perspective. In some cases the interviews will work anyway, if the host is completely up-to-speed and asks tough questions.* Just be sure you are clear about what you are doing, because many participant interviews are inherently unbalanced. It would be fine to interview someone on a political campaign staff to get reaction to a just-revealed scandal about the candidate, for instance. But it wouldn't make sense to interview one of the candidate's committed supporters—or opponents—to find out how voters in general were reacting.

One of the best kinds of participant interviews is the **eyewitness interview**. If there's been a bank robbery, for instance, a fascinating and perceptive description might come from someone who actually saw it happen.

Closely related is the **light phoner**. Someone has invented a way to clean her entire house automatically. Talk to her and let her describe it herself. Doesn't everything get wet?

On a more serious note, the **expert interview** is often the best way to get background and an overview of a subject, particularly when it is used as a sidebar to a news story. Be careful; sometimes experts have axes to grind, and if they do, you need to make your listeners aware of them. Many local universities have faculty members who are qualified to talk about their areas of expertise—and usually will be happy to do so.

Another possibility is to do a **three-way**—that is, the host plus *two* participants, one from each side. Three-ways can become unwieldy, however, so be careful. And think closely about how it will *sound:* If both participants are men, will the listener be able to tell them apart without the host's having to identify them every time they speak? Should one of them be on a phone line so his voice will be easily distinguishable from the other's?

Finally, there is the **reporter two-way**. Sometimes, this format comes from necessity: The president makes a major announcement at 4:45, and there is not enough time for your White House reporter to write a story before going on the air at 5. At other times, however, the reporter two-way is the best choice. For one thing, the story may be one for which there is no tape—a federal trial, for instance, when the participants won't speak outside the courtroom—and the material cannot be crammed into the maximum-length voicer (usually three minutes or so). Breaking up the reporter's voice with the host's allows the story to run longer. In addition, two-ways are less formal than reporter pieces, and it is often easier to analyze events in a discussion than in a formal report.

Host copy. There are times when 30 seconds of host copy can be just what is needed. Add a choice cut of tape and you can cover important aspects of a story in just a minute or so. Maybe it is enough to tell the whole story. Maybe it's just added information to fill out another story. Either way, hosts can be excellent ways to plug up holes.

Commentary. Sometimes, you can even tell a story best with a commentary. Say it's Valentine's Day. You surely don't want to assign a reporter to do a story on it. Last year you did the Valentine's-ads-in-the-newspaper interview. What do you do this year? Suddenly, one of your commentators hands you a Valentine's love-letter to her husband. It's the perfect way to commemorate the day.

Making the Assignment

The first and most important rule in making an assignment is to *be as explicit as possible.* An event or an idea may be the basis for a story, but it is not the story itself.

Assigning reporters. "Bill, cover the school board meeting tonight" is not a good assignment. Instead, you should say: "Bill, I need you to cover the school board meeting tonight. They're going to be discussing how to cut the budget. We've already reported on why they need the cuts. But we haven't done enough on the competing interests—the janitors vs. the teachers vs. the administrators, and so on. There are going to be a lot of teachers demonstrating tonight, and I hear that the janitors' union will be out in force, too, so you ought to be able to get some good sound. Ask them why they think their budgets shouldn't be cut, of course. But ask them whose budget *should* be cut. And then bounce their responses off the people who would be affected. Try to talk to some people in central administration to find out why *their* jobs aren't on the line. If you can't get anyone there to talk, let's question the school board members themselves about this. Does this sound like a good way to go to you? What do you think? Let's shoot for four or so minutes on this. OK?"

Note in this example that the editor (a) gave details about what was going to happen, (b) explained in some detail the approach the reporter should take to the story, (c) gave some initial ideas about how the reporter should go about it, and (d) opened up the door to dialogue with the reporter to further refine and focus the story idea.

Now this example is the kind of discussion you might have with a beginning reporter. With more experienced reporters, of course, the dialogue would be much less one-sided. In fact, you probably would be coming to them for advice and ideas about how to cover an event—or even whether the event should be covered at all. Or they would come to you with many ideas of their own. Listen to them. Don't be afraid to take their advice. Many times I have called reporters in the field about stories that cross the wire—or with questions that cross my mind—to find out whether they should do a story. Sometimes the reporters say yes, sometimes no, and sometimes my initial idea sparks their interest in an angle that neither of us had considered before.

Whatever the reporter's level of experience, however, at the end of the discussion you both must be clear about what the assignment is—what the reporter is going to look for, what questions will be asked, and what questions will be answered.

Assigning hosts. For a host interview, a good approach to the assignment is to think through what specific questions you want answered, discuss with the host what questions the host wants answered, and then come up with a general outline of the flow of the interview. It also can be helpful to conduct a pre-interview to get the interviewee's ideas about what should be included. This isn't always possible with newsmakers, but it often can be very useful with experts. Once, when I was editing WEEKEND EDITION, we had set up an expert on negotiations to talk about how well the Mideast peace talks in Madrid were going. Because he was going to have to react to the news as it was breaking, we scheduled the interview for right before air. There would be little time to cut the tape, so we wanted to keep the interview as close to its scheduled length as possible. By calling him ahead, I learned that he wanted to talk about how he thought the negotiators should approach the issues that faced them. Initially, we had thought we would talk only about the negotiating process itself—deciding on the shape of the table, the rotation of the meetings, and so on. But by constructing the interview so that he could discuss his ideas about the real issues, he was able to broaden a simple process story into one of complexity and substance. It made for an excellent and interesting interview—and it was right to time.

Unlike the example in the preceding paragraph, most interviews are not recorded to time. Often, there will be four or five times as much tape as will end up on the air. In those cases, editors who are not cutting the tape themselves will need to explain to the **tape editor** what should remain and what should be cut out. (See Chapter 13, "Tape Editing.") Again, *be explicit*. While the interview is under way, listen carefully. Take notes if you want. You should be thinking about how it will hold together on the air. Make sure the host asks all of your questions: At times you will want to feed the host questions during the interview; at other times you will want to wait until the end. After the interview, discuss your ideas for how to structure it with the tape editor. Don't walk out of the studio and hand the tape to someone with the words, "Here, get this down to four minutes." At the very least say what the point of the interview is and what parts of the interview explain that point the best.

Before the Edit

There are some reporters who thrive on regular, sustained contact with their editors. One reporter comes immediately to mind. He was an investigative reporter, and during his investigations he would develop his questions and his analysis by talking the story over with me—daily and in as much depth as we had time to spare. In fact, we talked so often and so thoroughly as the story developed that the actual edit was virtually *pro forma*. All the issues had been ironed out ahead of time, an outline had been thoroughly vetted, and the analysis had been closely examined for flaws.

In most cases, however, time does not permit such an approach—and many reporters don't need or want it. They appreciate the focus at the assignment stage, but they pretty much want to be left alone. There will be times, of course, when the story changes, or when the reporter learns something that makes the initial approach unworkable. Then an editor-reporter discussion can keep the assignment on track.

As long as you trust the reporter's judgment (and if you don't, one of you is probably in the wrong job), there is nothing wrong with a hands-off approach. However, a certain minimal amount of contact is necessary after reporters have returned from the field and before they start to write or produce their stories. This is the time you *refine the assignment*. The reporters will tell you whether the original assignment panned out, and if the story changed, how it changed. Ask them to give you a **line**—a one- or two-sentence synopsis. It will help both of you to focus the story idea into something that is manageable. Watch out for reporters who can't distill their story into one or two sentences; they're probably so mired in the details that they have lost sight of the big picture and will have difficulty writing.

Use this opportunity to make sure reporters are on the right track and to ask any lingering questions you have after hearing their description of their stories. (You don't want to wait until the edit to resolve those issues.) You also can tell them about related stories that will run with theirs, so they can structure their pieces accordingly. As you talk through their stories, you will gather enough information to give to the shows so they can plan properly.

These discussions have a practical, logistical purpose, too. *They are when you schedule the edits.* They are also when you find out whether the reporters are in trouble: Will they meet their deadlines? If not, you can alert the show. Do they need any help? If so, you can work on the intros; someone else can cut tape; etc. If you're going to have to shift into crisis-management mode, be sure you know about it as early as possible.

If you're on a tight deadline, you will want the reporter to give you the host introduction to the piece as early as possible. Especially in news stories, it is essential that reporters write their intros first. This will allow you to ensure that they really say something and that they fit in with the preceding pieces. It also will help the reporters focus their stories.

The Edit

After reporters finish writing and before they record their voice tracks, you will give them an **edit**. If this were print journalism, the reporters would turn their stories in, and you would edit their copy—either by hand or, more likely, on your computer screen. But because this is radio, the edit works differently: Here, the reporters will read their scripts and play their tape while you run a stopwatch. (If possible, they will do this in person; if they are at a remote site, they will do it by telephone.) What matters, of course, is not what the scripts look like in print, but what they sound like; not how many pages they are, but how many minutes they are.

It is here that the editor's skills are put to the biggest test. As the last person to hear the report before it goes on the air, the editor must make sure that it makes sense, is complete, is to time, and contains no mistakes. But a good editor will do more: A good editor also will collaborate with the reporter so that the story is told in the best way possible.

Different editors take different approaches, but good editors need to operate on several different levels simultaneously during the edit. They need to pay attention to the big matters like content and accuracy, but at the same time they have to deal with prickly little things like grammar and production. As the listeners' surrogates, they need to be sure that ordinary people will understand the piece the first time they hear it and that there aren't any questions left unanswered. As the representative of their radio station or network, they need to be sure the piece meets the highest journalistic standards. It's a tricky balancing act: Editors need to know enough about the subject of the reports they edit to be able to catch errors, but not so much that they fail to notice when an ordinary listener would not understand its complexities. The trick is to know which questions to ask—and not to be afraid to ask them for fear of sounding "dumb."

- *Listen for content.* Does the story make sense? Is anything important left out? Is it interesting? Do any facts need to be checked? Do you understand the point? Was the lead right, or was it overstated? Was the analytical ending backed up by the facts in the story? Did the ending fall flat? Was the reporter too hesitant in the conclusion? Did the facts seem to substantiate more than the reporter actually said?

- *Listen for balance and objectivity.* Was the story weighted one way or the other? Did all sides get their say? Were loaded words ("claimed" or "maintained," for example, instead of "said") used without justification? Here is where you need to ask the "smartest" question of all: *How do you know that?* Make sure that the reporter's knowledge is based on reliable information—from reliable sources (note the plural), reliable texts, and so on. When reporters say they know something because someone told them, don't hesitate to ask how the other person knew it.

- *Listen for structure.* Did the story flow logically? Did you understand it the first time through, or did it bounce around? Is there a better way to tell the story? Did the intro work? Are there parts of the piece that duplicate what's in the intro? If so, you may be able to make them "second reference," so they don't sound like duplication.

- *Listen for pacing.* Did the piece keep moving, or did it bog down? Where did it bog down, and what can be done to perk it up? Was it all interesting, or did your mind drift during parts of it? Maybe those parts need trimming. Was the tape used well? Did it help move the piece along, or did it duplicate the script? On complex long-form pieces, pay particular attention to the scenes. How did they flow from one to another? Could you follow the shifts, or did you end up places without knowing how you got there or why you were there?

- *Listen for grammar and usage.* Make sure that bad grammar or usage does not get on the air. Little mistakes can ruin a story, because listeners who hear these little mistakes are likely to distrust the reporter on the big issues. If you don't know something for sure, look it up.

- *Listen for time.* Too long? Where do you trim? Too short? Should something be added? How?

It is not easy to do all of this at the same time. But it is necessary. It requires that you train your ear to listen very, very carefully. In fact, the first three rules of editing are *concentrate, concentrate,* and *concentrate.* It is absolutely essential that you do this. You will not be able to improve the story—or even catch the mistakes—if you're thinking about tonight's dinner or last night's date. Give the reporter your undivided attention. Shield yourself from telephone calls and other interruptions. And *concentrate*.

Before you start the edit, make sure you are prepared. Do you know what is on the wires? Do you know what was in the morning paper (so you can be sure the report *advances* the story and doesn't just repeat it)? Some editors like to review all of this just prior to the edit. Personally, I prefer a little more distance unless it's a breaking story; I feel it helps me in my role as the listener's surrogate. Either way, it's important that you *have a clear idea of what the story is about* before you begin to edit the report.

Different editors have different techniques for conducting an edit, but here is mine:

1. *Get out your stopwatch.* Tell the reporter when you're ready to begin. Should you read along with a script? Some editors do this, but I advise against it. The listener at home, after all, is not going to have a script. If *I* can't understand it the first time through, how can I expect the listener to? And there may be times when there is no script to look at, because the reporter is in a faraway place and on a tight deadline. So I recommend that you not read along, but just listen carefully. (A script *is* helpful to have after you've been through the piece the first time; it's an easy way to isolate your questions and your problems.)

2. *Take notes.* Don't interrupt the reporter, but when you have questions, jot down something so you can return to the problem areas after the reporter has finished. Some editors take a lot of notes; others take only a few. Develop your own style. But don't think about your questions too much or you will miss part of the report.

3. *Give initial feedback.* When the reporter has finished, it's your turn to talk. I find that it's helpful to begin this phase of each edit with a comment about my overall impression: "It was really good and I have just a few minor problems." Or, "I think there's something that doesn't work about the structure in the bottom third of the piece, but let's go through it top to bottom." Or, "It's really good, but we need to cut 30 seconds." Or sometimes, unfortunately, "It doesn't work. I think we need to rework it."

4. *Give detailed feedback.* I try to be honest without being harsh, but whatever the initial comment, good or bad, I always stress that it's a collaborative venture, a partnership, and that we both have something at stake. If I have problems with the report, it's not because I want to lord over the reporter. It's *our* report that *we* need to fix. Keep in mind, however, that it is the *reporter's* story. Try to keep as much of the reporter's style and wording as possible. Don't change something just because you would have done it differently. But *do* change it if it's confusing, and *do* offer suggestions for making it better.

Unless the report is a total disaster, I find it's easiest to go back through it from the top—in what I call chronological order—after my initial comments. Asking my questions from top to bottom (rather than, say, most important to least important) has two advantages: (1) It maintains the report's linear nature and thus makes it easier to think through the whole idea. And (2) it mixes up the important and the less important and thus discourages the reporter from second-guessing what your problem is. In effect, it helps the reporter to listen to what you are saying.

When you criticize, *be specific*. And always offer a suggestion for how to do it better. The worse the piece, the more important this becomes. Never say to a reporter, "Take it back and rewrite it." Always give direction. Even if the report needs a complete rewrite, give the reporter some ideas about how to do it; explain why the first version did not work, and collaborate with the reporter to devise a better way. In extreme instances—such as a fast-approaching deadline—you may need to do the rewrite yourself, with the reporter helping you. But even here it's a collaboration and must be treated as such.

5. *Listen as you revise.* Some problems, such as incorrect grammar or usage, can be fixed without further discussion. On the other extreme, there may be problems that will take additional reporting. And in the middle, some problems will require you to listen carefully to the reporter's explanations. The reporter may have had a specific reason for saying something in a certain way. This does not mean that the copy should not be changed. Trust your initial reaction. You are the listener's surrogate, and if you had a problem with that part of the story, it *is* a problem. If *you* didn't understand the sentence without the additional explanation from the reporter, the listener won't understand it, either. So explain to the reporter why you didn't understand the sentence, and then collaborate to revise it in such a way that the additional explanation is included or becomes unnecessary.

6a. *If you have time, go over the entire story again*, top to bottom, running a stopwatch and listening carefully as if from scratch. If you have made a lot of changes, you may find that when you hear the whole piece again, it doesn't hold together and needs further changes.

6b. *If time is short, prioritize what you're going to fix.* You may not be able to fix everything, but some things you cannot let on the air: factual errors, bad grammar, confusing syntax, unattributed information. You'll have to compromise in

---

*It's important when you're pushing through a piece on a tight deadline to keep an accurate account of the piece's length, so if it's long you can trim or beg for more time from the show. If you don't have time to hear the entire piece again, you'll need to time only those sections you've changed, and then add or subtract the time from the sections' original lengths.

other areas:* the sentence that could have been a little stronger, the cut that was a little long, etc. Set your priorities *as you edit*, so you won't have to think about it later. But no matter how little time you have, remember that *nothing can go on the air without first being checked by an editor.* Two brains have twice the chance of catching errors as one.

Who's the Boss?

An editor must approve the content of everything that goes on the air, so in a very real sense, when disputes arise, the editor's word is final. But as an editor, you should do your best to avoid situations in which you need to impose your will. Usually by explaining your objections carefully and listening closely to what the reporter says, you can work collaboratively toward a solution acceptable to both of you.

There are occasions—usually brought on by tight deadlines—when there simply isn't time for a long discussion, or even a short one. In those cases, of course, you don't discuss; you act. But if your general approach to editing is a collaborative, thoughtful, discussion-oriented one, you will develop the respect of the reporters you edit. They will understand the circumstances, and they will trust you without question.

Should You Be an Editor?

Here are some of the qualities of a successful editor. How many of them fit you?

- *Do you have broad knowledge and interests?* Do all those little factoids tend to stick with you? Can you shift easily from one subject to another? Are you naturally curious about many different things?

- *Do you instinctively ask the "big picture" questions?* Can you explore beyond the obvious and focus on what's behind the event rather than just the event itself? Are you willing to ask "dumb questions" because you don't think they've been answered adequately? Of *who, what, when, where,* and *why,* do you find yourself pondering over the *why* more than the other questions?

- *Are you a stickler for details?* Do you flinch at bad grammar? Do bad tape edits make you cringe? Do you want everything to be perfect?

- *Do you have an analytical mind?* When events occur, do you always try to find out why? When you read the morning paper, do you usually have unanswered questions about what you've read? When you are faced with a problem, do you easily come up with ways to solve it? When you hear a mistake, can you quickly figure out how to correct it?

• *Do you understand the principles of journalism?* Do you have an unwavering sense of fairness? Do you know when a premise has been proved and when it is speculation? Do you know the difference between fact and opinion, between analysis and bias? Do you know what it takes to get a story? Have you ever been a reporter? (You will be a better editor if you have experienced the difficulties reporters have in pursuing stories.)

• *Do you have an excellent knowledge of the English language?* Do you know how to use words correctly? Do you use good grammar?

• *Are you a good writer?* It's the editor's job to push writers beyond serviceable prose. News writing can be lackluster. It doesn't need to be.

• *Are you a teacher?* Although being an editor is a good way to learn about the world around you, editors often need to be teachers, too. When you correct reporters' errors, if you see your role as a teacher, you can help them avoid making the same mistakes again.

• *Are you articulate?* Can you explain why you like or don't like something in a clear and concise way? Can you quickly summarize the most important elements of a story?

• *Do you have a good attention span?* Can you concentrate and listen closely during an edit?

• *Can you work under pressure?* The producers, not the reporters, will be screaming at you as deadlines approach. Can you handle it?

• *Do you have confidence in your abilities?* An editor is in a leadership position. People will not follow you if you aren't self-confident.

• *Are you willing to let someone else take the credit?* You're unlikely to become famous being an editor. It's the reporter who goes on the air, not you. Does this bother you?

An editor's job is not an easy one. Editors must be able to use many different skills simultaneously. And they do not always get an adequate evaluation of their work. Although editors usually know when they have committed a major error—they're always the first ones to hear when there's a fact wrong or bad grammar or some other flaw in a story—they rarely get substantial feedback on how good they really are. Reporters don't criticize directly; after all, you're their boss. And your boss, particularly in radio, seldom hears the original version of a story and therefore has no way of knowing how much of the finished product comes from you.

Yet there can be great satisfaction in being an editor. The reporters know how good you are; even if they don't tell you directly, you'll find them maneuvering to avoid going to another editor, or you'll notice them queuing up outside your door while you're editing someone else.

And being an editor is a marvelous way to satisfy your intellectual curiosity without having to do all the legwork. You get to ask all those dumb questions you've always wanted to ask—and have someone else find out the answers.

Marcus D. Rosenbaum has served in many editing capacities at NPR. He was NPR's first foreign editor, the senior national editor, and editor of ALL THINGS CONSIDERED, *weekend* ALL THINGS CONSIDERED *and newscasts. Rosenbaum came to NPR in 1978 after a decade in print journalism. In 1988 he went to Congressional Quarterly Inc. as editor of* Editorial Research Reports. *In 1991 he returned to NPR to fill various editing positions. He is now senior producer of* TALK OF THE NATION.

6

Writing News for Radio

Carl Kasell & Marcus D. Rosenbaum

"The writer of news for radio must write the purest, most readily understood prose of any medium," veteran broadcaster and journalism professor Edward Bliss Jr. once wrote. "The reason is no secret. The writer for radio, unlike the writer for magazines or newspapers, must write so as to be understood the first time. The words are spoken and, once spoken, are irretrievable. There is no calling them back for review."

Mr. Bliss's words may be even more important today than they were when he wrote them a decade ago, because today's listeners get such a large part of their news from broadcast media. But the principle of writing for broadcast remains unchanged: Write for the ear. A radio report is written to be *heard*, not seen. Thus, it must be *linear* in structure—stories need a beginning, a middle, and an end. And it must be *conversational* in presentation—sentences must be short, direct, and simple; words must be readily understood or explained.

Now "short" does not mean that all sentences need to be just four or five words long. Too many short sentences will make your writing sound choppy. That's not the way you talk, so that's not the way you should write. A good story will have sentences of varying lengths.

But a good sentence for radio generally will contain only one idea. It will not be cluttered with useless words. It will be simple, the language uncomplicated.

Pity the listener who has to endure this:

> Stocks closed sharply higher in active trading yesterday, after a blue-chip rally helped the broad market shake off an initial weakness, which

was triggered by a sell-off in overseas markets and news of more economic woes at home.

Whew! How about this instead?

Stocks closed sharply higher in active trading yesterday. The market started off on the down side . . . reacting to weak markets abroad and more bad economic news at home. But blue-chip stocks rallied later in the day, and that helped push prices higher across the board.

Still perhaps not the most scintillating story, but at least the listener is likely to understand what you are saying—and, just as important, you can read it without gasping for air.

How do you know when you've written simply enough and when you're too complicated? First, write with your lips. That is, read your copy aloud. In fact, try saying your sentences out loud *before* you commit them to paper. Forget about how they *look* on the page. How do they *sound*? Do the sentences flow one to the next, or do they jump around? Are there pauses in appropriate places to allow you to breathe? Never forget: Radio is a medium to be heard, not read.

As for content and organization, think about someone like Aunt Martha— reasonably intelligent and informed, but no expert in any one field. Could you tell Aunt Martha a story about a complicated economics issue? Of course. Just start at the beginning, tell the story through to the end, and use simple, declarative sentences without a lot of jargon and subordinate clauses. No *idea* is too complicated to tell on the radio. Indeed, complicated ideas are best told in simple ways.

This chapter will give you some tips about how to do that. It will discuss structuring and writing stories as a reporter, and structuring and writing **newscasts**. It also will give you some practical do's and don'ts that should help improve your writing style.

The Reporter's Story

As a reporter, you will need to write stories of various lengths, from full-segment documentaries to 45-second **news spots**. Whatever the length, there are basic procedures you must follow. Some of them are common to all forms of journalism; others are specific to broadcast; still others are specific to radio.

Know Your Story

Whether you're writing a news spot or a documentary—or, indeed, a newspaper story or a book—it's essential that you know what you're talking about.

This may sound elementary. But you would be surprised how often inexperienced reporters and news writers read something on the wires and, without thinking about it, write it into their scripts. Terms, concepts, even events creep into copy in ways that demonstrate the writer did not understand them.

Make a rule of learning more about the story than you ever will use. Even if the on-air time is only a few minutes, those minutes must reflect a full understanding of the story. So research your story well. Read newspaper and magazine clippings, wire reports, books—anything you can get your hands on and can find the time to study and digest. Call sources for background information. Call the principals for details. Talk the story over with your editor to get more ideas and more questions to pursue.

You can never know too much about a story, although you never will have the time to know everything. Often, the constraints of deadlines will limit how much you can do. You must leave yourself enough time to write and produce your report. Experienced reporters learn to recognize when they have done enough reporting, even if they are not pressed by a deadline. Editors can help you decide if you are not sure when to stop.

Because this is a chapter on *writing*, not reporting, we will not dwell on this subject. Suffice it to say: When you have questions about your story, the listener is *bound* to have questions about it, too. So if you don't know something important, *find out* before you start writing.

Choose Your Tape as You Outline Your Ideas

After you have done your reporting and conducted your interviews, it's time to put your story together. Have a brief chat with your editor, who probably will ask you for a **line**—a one- or two-sentence synopsis of your story. This will help you focus what you want to say. Be sure to have a clear idea of the point of your story *before you start writing*, because if you do not, your story is likely to drift and sound disorganized. So think through your line carefully, and make sure it is straightforward and complete, but not complicated.

Be thinking about the details of your report, but don't try to get the logical flow of the story perfectly in order. First, choose your tape. If your report is a **stand-up,** or **voicer,** which uses no tape, you obviously will skip this step. But most reports you file will contain tape, and in radio, tape is the engine that drives the report.

Tape, called **actualities** or **cuts** in broadcast terminology, is roughly equivalent to the use of quotations in print. But there is a difference. In print journalism, quotations back up the main points of a story. In broadcast, however, tape *carries the story forward*. Not only does this affect the way you write in and out of actualities, but it also affects the way you structure your story. Many times as you are writing your story, it will seem that you are merely writing connecting matter for the tape. Indeed, an old broadcast term for the spoken part of a script is *continuity*.

However, those connecting words are very important. If tape is the engine that drives your report, the script is the transmission, which links power and movement, and makes sense of it all. A good radio news report will combine tape and script (actualities and voice tracks, or, in the lingo, "acts and tracks") to tell a complete story from beginning to end in a compelling manner.

But, to stick with the analogy, start with the engine: *Choose your tape first.* Let it guide the organization of your story. It is much easier to make your script fit your tape than to make your tape fit your script. Do not write your script and then try to plug in the tape afterward.

Choosing tape cuts is an art in itself. Some reporters make a log of every minute of tape to use as a guide. Others remember the most essential parts of the most essential interviews, and re-listen only to them. Others combine the two techniques, depending on the size of the report, the number of interviews, and how close their deadline looms. Develop a system that works for you in selecting the most important actualities for your report.

As you choose your tape, you should think through the details of what you want to say. What are the important facts to get across? What are the important events that took place? What are the main ideas? One easy way to do this is to make a list of those details, putting them in no particular order at first. Then you can look at your list and think about your tape simultaneously, putting the two together in logical sequence.

When you do so, you will be dealing with a puzzle of sorts, and you will find that you will discard some tape cuts and some ideas from your list. There's nothing wrong with this. Often those great actualities just don't work, and often you will realize that some of those "important" ideas aren't so important after all. But make sure that the finished product is a thorough one. *Never sacrifice content for form.* There is always a way to make a truly important point fit.

Start at the Beginning

Newspaper writing is often said to be structured in an "inverted pyramid"—that is, the most important information goes in the lead (or "lede," as it often is spelled), the next most important details come next, and the least important material comes last. This structure is probably the primary reason that a newspaper story read on the air often is hard to follow.

Broadcast writing is *linear*. It has a beginning, a middle, and an end. The broadcaster takes the listener through a story logically from Point A to Point B to Point C, until, finally, there is a conclusion. Often the most important part of the story comes at the end, not the beginning. But the beginning is crucial, because it sets up the story and prepares the listener for what will follow.

In broadcast writing, the beginning of a story is *not* the reporter's first words. It is the first words from the host or newscaster. This starting point is called the **lead-in** or **host introduction**. You should never consider it to be an unimportant afterthought or a throw-away element or something that an editor will fix later. It is an integral part of your story, and you should write it *first*. If you do not, you run the very real risk of structuring a piece in such a way that the host has nothing to say. It will make both of you sound bad.

The host intro should give the basic facts of the story and tell the listener why it is important. It should be written in such a way that it leads right into your part of the report, whether you start by taking a step back to provide background information, or continue moving forward. Here is an example of a host intro that allows the reporter to start with background:

Host: In a dramatic announcement at her weekly news conference, Mayor Smith said today that she will ask the City Council for a 14 percent property tax rate increase. If the council goes along, it will be the biggest tax hike in decades. Robert Reporter has the story:

Reporter: When Mayor Smith first ran for office six years ago, she made "no new taxes" the linchpin of her campaign. It worked. She was easily elected. And she used the same approach for her re-election four years later. . . .

Here is an example of a host intro that allows the reporter to pick up the story and carry it along, without delving into background information.

Host: Mayor Smith reversed years of campaign pledges today and said she will ask the City Council for a 14 percent increase in property tax rates. If the council goes along, it will be the biggest tax hike in decades. Robert Reporter has the story:

Reporter: The surprise announcement came at the mayor's regular weekly news conference. She told reporters that as difficult as the decision was for her, she saw no alternative, because the city is broke. . . .

Both of these constructions work. They give the host part of the story and let the reporter go on from there. But what if the reporter had started his part of the report like this?

Reporter: Mayor Smith announced today that she would ask the City Council for a 14 percent increase in property tax rates, and if the council goes along, it will be the biggest tax hike in decades. The announcement reversed years of "no-new-taxes" campaign pledges.

There would be nothing left for the host to say, except something like, "Mayor Smith surprised reporters at her news conference today." And that's not likely to grab the listener's attention.

So to reiterate: *Write your lead-in first.*

The Middle: Using Tape

Now you have thought through the point of your story, isolated your tape, figured out the report's structure, and written the host introduction. The rest is easy. You just need to link it all together in your script. Tell the story in a logical way that progresses from beginning to end. Each element—each sentence of your script, each actuality—should carry the story forward. The end of Point A should lead logically to the beginning of Point B, the end of Point B should lead logically to the beginning of Point C, and so on.

Listen to this example from MORNING EDITION in early March 1992—a report by Mike Shuster from Moscow. Note how the elements hold together, how the script flows into the tape, which flows into the script. Note how the intro sets the piece up. And note the linear nature of the piece, how it has a beginning, a middle, and an end.

Host: In Russia, Boris Yeltsin's government has now made public the elements of the next stage of its economic reform plan. Yeltsin's advisers believe the first shock of price rises, which began in early January, is over, and that the country must move on to face additional price hikes and austerity measures designed to hasten the transition to a market economy.

   The new reforms are also meant to conform to the wishes of the International Monetary Fund, which stands ready to provide additional loans to Russia if the reforms are implemented. NPR's Mike Shuster reports from Moscow.

Shuster: There is little doubt that economic conditions in Russia are changing. Prices on most goods are sharply higher than they were at the end of last year, but more goods are available in many stores—especially grocery stores. And what was most unexpected, the attitude of the majority of Russians to the price reform has been grudging acceptance, not rebellion. This led Finance Minister Yegor Gaidar to declare cautiously on national television two days ago that the first phase of the reform has been a success.

Gaidar: [*Voice in Russian established, then under for voiceover*] Now to the surprise of many, you can see that the reforms are working. Maybe slowly, maybe badly. We better than others know how weak these first signs of stabilization are, how easy it is by some clumsy actions to throw our economy back into sharp decline, into the catastrophe of hyperinflation.

Shuster: Nevertheless, the government has now made public its plans for further economic reforms, which are bound to shock the Russian public . . . perhaps even more deeply than the price rises. Not all prices were freed in January. Some basic food items, such as bread and milk, although now more expensive, are still regulated. That, according to Konstantin Kagalovsky, a member of Yeltsin's economic team, will end in March.

Kagalovsky: [*Voice in Russian established, then under for voiceover*] Firstly, what we all expect in the nearest future is the further freeing of prices. We are going to free all prices for consumer goods, with the exception of baby foods and medicine.

Shuster: Although Russian consumers might be alarmed to see the price of milk and bread climb higher, the Russian government is ready to take a step, according to Kagalovsky, that will certainly spark another round of sharp inflation throughout the economy.

Kagalovsky: [*Voice in Russian established, then under for voiceover*] After the end of the heating season in our cold country, about the middle of April, we are going to free prices on fuels, including oil and oil products.

Shuster: The price of electricity and natural gas will remain under state control. Fuel rises will hit the Russians most at the gas pump. A liter of gasoline now costs just over 1 ruble—three times its price in December. Crude oil could rise an additional seven times when its price is decontrolled in April, bringing sharp hikes at the fuel pump. Russian government officials estimate that such price increases will lead to a 10 to 15 percent drop in domestic fuel consumption. Finance Minister Gaidar says this will certainly worsen the overall performance of the Russian economy.

Gaidar: [*Voice in Russian established, then under for voiceover*] The increase of fuel prices will inevitably cause a decline in production. There has been no example of a post-Communist country in the world that has made the transition to the market with an industrial decline of less than 20 percent.

Shuster: Such a slump would come on top of production declines of some 30 percent over the past two years—in effect, a continuing depression of the Russian economy of at least three years' duration. Among other reforms the Russian government is planning is a tax on oil and oil products of 50 percent. It is with this tax that the Russian government plans to cover the better part of its budget deficit. The goal of the Russian government is to eliminate its enormous deficit by the end of the year, and in the process stabilize the shaky Russian currency. Other elements of the reform package include the rapid privatization of land and state business, which should begin immediately.

These reforms are meant to lead to Russian membership in the International Monetary Fund . . . probably in late April . . . and the establishment after that of a multi-billion dollar fund to stabilize the ruble. It is a plan of economic austerity that is bound to throw millions of Russians in heavily subsidized state enterprises out of work. Many here worry that the reality of unemployment in the coming months will be much harder for the Russian public to take than price rises to which they have already become accustomed.

This is Mike Shuster in Moscow.

Remember that you are writing for the ear. Your script is *not* the finished product; the finished product is your delivery on the air. So write the way you talk. Think of your script not as words to be read, but as a guide to help you tell a story. This does not mean that your script should not be carefully honed and polished.

As mentioned above, a lot of your script will consist of writing in and out of actualities, so that the actualities carry the story along. One good way to do that is to start out with actualities that are too long and cut them down as you write—putting one thought in your script and leaving the other for the actuality. For instance, you may have a rough-cut of tape that goes something like this:

> There are three reasons people should vote yes on the bond issue. First, the schools are overcrowded. They were built for, uh, 4,000 students, and there are now more than 6,000. And next year we're expecting to have even . . . uh . . . One survey shows, uh, 700 new students next year alone. Second, uh, the, uh, teachers are underpaid. I mean, they're starting as low as $19,000 a year. Who can afford to live on that in this day and age? And then, you know, the biggest thing is that this community can afford it. We have one of the highest income levels in the state, but our schools are ranked near the bottom. This is a rich county. Our children are our future. We should do better by them.

With that much tape, you can script the top and let the actuality run at the bottom:

Reporter: Jones said the schools are overcrowded. They were built for 4,000 students but now have more than 6,000 . . . with more expected next year. And he said the teachers are underpaid . . . starting at only 19-thousand dollars a year. But in Jones' opinion, the most important reason the bond issue should be passed is that the community can afford it.

Jones: We have one of the highest income levels in the state, but our schools are ranked near the bottom. This is a rich county. Our children are our future. We should do better by them.

This is not to say that you should pare your tape down to a distorted minimum. To the contrary, it is very important that you not cut speakers off in midthought. Your actualities should express complete ideas, not truncated fragments of ideas. For that reason, actualities at NPR often run much longer than they would in commercial broadcasting. But length is not so important as content. Some will be long, some short. Just be sure that the actualities fit with your script, so that together they tell a compelling and thorough story.

Print vs. broadcast. As noted earlier, using actualities in radio journalism is not the same as using quotations in print. Here's an example from a *Boston Globe* story about literacy:

> While many of the adults on literacy waiting lists do indeed hold jobs, business leaders say productivity is lost both because of errors made on the job and the exorbitant cost of training workers who cannot read.
>
> "Billions of dollars are being spent each year retraining workers with poor skills," noted Paul O'Brien, chief executive officer of New England Telephone Co. and co-founder of the Boston Adult Literacy Fund.
>
> "The quality and capability of the work force upon which we draw is a direct reflection of how productive we will be in the future. If we do not invest in public and private education and our people are ill prepared, we will have to provide remedial training at costs that will increase services or products or force us to import talent. Either way, that puts us at a disadvantage."

For print, that section works fine. Note how the reporter made a statement and then backed it up with a quotation. In radio, the quotation is a much more integral part of the story; it carries it forward. The same information in a radio script would be something like this:

Reporter: Paul O'Brien . . . the chief executive officer of New England Telephone Company . . . says the future of American productivity is at stake. Many adults on the literacy waiting lists do have jobs . . . but they can be very expensive employees. He says businesses are caught in a dilemma.

O'Brien: If we do not invest in public and private education and our people are ill prepared, we will have to provide remedial training at costs that will increase services or products or force us to import talent. Either way, that puts us at a disadvantage.

Reporter: O'Brien, a co-founder of the Boston Adult Literacy Fund, says it's costing American businesses *billions* of dollars each year to retrain workers with poor skills.

Bad places for tape. One other point about tape: Don't start or end your report with an actuality. Starting your report with an actuality is usually just a cheap shortcut. There's almost always a better way. Besides, if you start with tape, it's extremely difficult to write a host introduction. So start your report with your own voice and move that great cut of tape a little lower in the piece—or, if it really needs to go first, put it *in* the host intro.

Ending a report with tape is also a weak approach. In print writing, particularly for magazines, a quotation at the end is often the perfect conclusion. It can sum up the whole idea of the story in a very succinct way. But it doesn't work so well in radio. The reason is that in print the quotations carry more credibility than the reporter; the reporter is virtually invisible. In radio, however, it's the other way around; the reporter has the most credible voice in the story. So even if the actuality is the perfect summation for your report, you should say something after it. Or, in some rare cases, you can use the perfect quotation—but in your own voice. "As Jones put it, this city has one of the highest income levels in the state, but its schools are ranked near the bottom" may be a stronger end to a story than an actuality of Jones saying the same thing.

And So . . . the Conclusion

Take special care with your conclusion, also known as the **and so**. In broadcast writing, it often is the most important part of your report. It is when you sum up your report and prepare the listener for the next possible development in the story.

There's an old saying that if a story doesn't have an "and so," it isn't worth doing. That's not always true, of course, but listeners best remember the last words you say, so stories that say something important in their conclusions are most likely to stick with listeners.

Avoid being trite:

And so, this much is clear: Only time will tell whether it's just the tip of the iceberg.

If you have thought through the point of your story and organized it correctly, everything should lead up to the end, and you should not have trouble writing your conclusion.

Listen to this news spot by Anne Garrels from March 1992. It's instructive not only for the "and so," but for the way she explained a very complicated subject in a very short amount of time.

Newscaster: The Bush administration and Congress have been trying to find a way around their disagreement over 10 billion dollars in loan guarantees to Israel. But NPR's Anne Garrels reports they are still at an impasse.

Garrels: The administration has linked the loan guarantees to a freeze on settlements in the West Bank and Gaza. Israel's supporters on Capitol Hill oppose linkage. So Senator Patrick Leahy, a Democrat from Vermont, suggested a compromise—appropriate the money now, so it's at least available, and leave it to the administration to negotiate the terms later. But pro-Israel senators continue to balk at the tough terms . . . insisting Israel be granted at least two billion dollars in loan guarantees with no conditions to help resettle émigrés. But the administration is likely to veto this formula . . . so there's a good chance there will be no loans and no bill this year. I'm Anne Garrels in Washington.

Newscasts

A reporter generally covers a single story at a time. A newscaster's job is to cover many stories. On any one subject, newscasters may not have the same expertise as a reporter, but they need to have a good working knowledge of most stories that cross the desk. This is why good newscasters do a lot of homework. They read as much as possible to learn about as many different subjects as they can.

Using the Wires

Wire copy is the source of newscast stories at all levels of broadcasting—local and national. The wires are good sources and should be regarded as just that: sources. Remember, they can be wrong, so you shouldn't hesitate to question anything that appears mistaken. One way to question a fact is to check another wire. (This is just one reason to have more than one wire service; another is that one wire is likely to have details about a story that another wire does not.) If the wires are inconsistent, or if a fact on a single wire doesn't seem right, call the wire service or try to check the facts with a phone call to the source of the report.

As you use the wires, be aware of the fact that stories written on the news services' "A" wires are written in newspaper style. They have to be translated into language for the ear. Stories on the "broadcast" wire are written for radio, but they tend to be superficial. Good newscasters always rewrite the wires.

In fact, the best newscasters don't even look at the wires while they're writing, except to check an occasional fact. They'll read the wires, digest what is in them, and then write their story. It's the best way to make sense of an event; it ensures that you understand it before you say it on the air.

Fully understanding a story also makes it much easier to update, and if you're on the air at regular intervals during the day, you'll constantly be updating and rewriting to make the story fresh. Sometimes there's a development in the story that makes the updating easy. But face it: There are only so many ways to say, "A gunman is holding 10 hostages in the State Capitol. The siege has been underway for 48 hours." That's when you look at the bottom of the wire copy or question reporters covering the scene to find some element you may have missed in your earlier newscasts. Your listeners are tuning in to hear something new. You should try to give it to them.

Putting the Newscast Together

As a newscaster, you (and your editor) will decide which stories to use, how much time to spend on each one of them, and in what order to present them. The key criteria are how newsworthy and how new each item is. The less newsworthy and the older the story, the less likely it is to be used, and, if it is used, the less time it will receive and the later in the newscast it will appear.

Generally, you will start with the most important story of the hour. Most of the time, one story will stand out and clearly be the lead item. At other times, however, two or three items may qualify, so you may decide to rotate them from one newscast to the next.

Group stories according to subject. To bounce from Congress to China to New York to Paris to the White House to London to Cape Canaveral makes no sense if the stories are not somehow tied together. So you probably would want to have a section on Washington stories (Congress and the White House), a section on foreign stories (China, London, Paris), and a section on national stories (New York, Cape Canaveral). But if the New York story is about the economy, and the Congress and White House stories are about the same thing, you obviously would have something to link them together.

When you go from one story to another, let your audience know you are changing subjects. You can interrupt the flow with a change in pitch or inflection or reading speed. Listen to how good newscasters do this and emulate them.

The heart of any newscast is sound. Reporter news spots and actualities put the listener at the scene of the story. They break up your copy and allow you to catch your breath, and they lend credibility to your newscast. But they must be used properly. Don't bunch all the sound at the top of the newscast. Don't put it all at the end, either. Spread it out. Don't be afraid to use two bits of actuality in the lead story, but save some other sound to use later in the newscast.

The key to a good newscast is that it should hold together. It should be thorough without sounding choppy. So vary the lengths of your stories. Spread out the sound. And organize your newscast in a way that the listener will easily understand.

Hints

Most of this chapter has been devoted to conceptualizing your report or your newscast and organizing your ideas. Now here are some hints that will help you when you put fingers to keyboard. You can find additional tips in the "NPR Stylebook," which is reprinted later in this book.

Use the present tense. Newspapers and the wire services write almost everything in the past tense. Broadcasters should make more use of the present tense—even if, at times, it violates that difficult grammatical rule called sequence of tenses. The reason is, that's the way we talk. It sounds stiff to say out loud, "John Doe said he thought Christmas was a good idea." More natural (although, technically speaking, grammatically incorrect) is, "John Doe said he thinks Christmas is a good idea." Or better yet (and grammatically correct), "John Doe says he thinks Christmas is a good idea."

Use the active voice. It brings life to your copy. The passive voice usually is deadly.

No: Combat troops were sent by the president to . . .
Yes: The president sent combat troops to . . .

Advance the story. Listeners assume you are reporting what is happening now or something that happened in the immediate past. So even if the main part of the story occurred yesterday, use the element that carries it forward to today. Such as,

> The White House says President Bush will veto the jobs bill that Congress passed yesterday.

Use contractions. Contractions are part of our everyday speech, so to keep your copy conversational, use them. Be careful, however, that you are not misunderstood. "Joe Newsmaker says he can't take it" sounds a lot like "Joe Newsmaker says he can take it."

Put attributions high in the sentence. When writing for print, it is customary to put attributions at the end of sentences. Not so when writing for broadcast.

> *No:* The nation's economy will show great improvement in the third quarter, according to a report from the Federal Reserve Board.
> *Yes:* The Federal Reserve Board says the nation's economy will improve greatly in the third quarter.

Also, be specific in your attributions. Attributing information to unnamed "experts," "analysts," or "sources" really adds nothing to a story—except to demonstrate that you are unsure about your information.

Titles. Don't put too many titles and names close together in a sentence. Consider this:

> Secretary of Commerce Joe Scrivnek announced that James Scribner, chairman of General Motors Corporation, has succeeded Ralph Blumer, chairman of General Electric, as chairman of the Business Advisory Committee.

Not only is such a sentence awkward to read, but it's confusing to hear, too.

Many titles can and should be reduced to their bare essentials. Thus, "chairman of the Senate Select Committee on Intelligence" becomes "Senate Intelligence Committee chairman" and, on second reference, "chairman."

Avoid clichés. In fact, as the Stylebook says, "Avoid them like the plague." The familiar ones are easy to identify and eliminate. But try as you might, when you least expect it, a less common one sneaks into your copy. Often it's one of those new words or phrases. "At this point in time" became a cliché during the Watergate era—and it still grates on the ear today.

Labels can become hackneyed. "Conservative" Senator Jesse Helms, "controversial" football player Duane Thomas. These labels were used so often with these people they became almost a part of their names. Don't follow the pack.

Use proper grammar and good English. Good grammar and usage are the way we understand each other, and they are your road map to good journalism. They give you credibility. Don't believe it? Try using bad grammar deliberately on the air sometime. Then count the phone calls and letters. The "NPR Stylebook" (see page 229) will help point you in the right direction in this regard.

Nouns and verbs. Don't turn nouns into verbs. *Impact* is a noun. Use a word like *affect* for the verb.

Verbal booby traps. To repeat some advice from the beginning of this chapter: Read your copy aloud. It is an excellent way of self-editing, and it helps you avoid words and phrases you have trouble reading and should not use. Some people can't say "statistics." Others have problems with combinations of words, like "three tree twigs" or "the Joint Chiefs' chairman" or "the Earth's first space" or "in an uninhabited," and so on. Be aware of phrases that cause you trouble, and write around them. If you read your copy aloud before you go on the air, you'll never be caught before a microphone trying to say "six sick Sikhs."

Watch for homophones—words that sound alike but have different meanings—or near-homophones. They are understandable for the eye but can cause problems for the ear. Some examples:

aides	AIDS
brake	break
cache	cash
deceased	diseased
formally	formerly
miner	minor

Take care with the order of your words, especially modifiers. Take, for example, "the handsome airline pilot." Is it the airline that's handsome or the pilot? Or "the black doctor's bag."

Don't waste words. We hesitate to end this chapter with a quotation from a print essayist, but, in this case, the words fit—for content and for style. They are from E.B. White's *The Elements of Style.* (If you haven't read it lately, by the way, do so; it's a wonderful little book and easy and fun to read.) The book is White's version of a book of the same title written by his English professor, William Strunk Jr., in 1919.

This passage, from the introduction, not only carries a worthwhile message, but it does so with a quality of imagery and style that is rarely heard these days.

"Omit needless words!" cries the author . . . , and into that imperative Will Strunk really put his heart and soul. In the days when I was sitting in his class, he omitted so many needless words, and omitted them so forcibly and with such eagerness and obvious relish, that he often seemed in the position of having shortchanged himself—a man left with nothing more to say yet with time to fill, a radio prophet who had outdistanced the clock. Will Strunk got out of this predicament by a simple trick: he uttered every sentence three times. When he delivered his oration on brevity to the class, he leaned forward over the desk, grasped his coat lapels in his hands, and, in a husky, conspiratorial voice, said, "Rule Seventeen. Omit needless words! Omit needless words! Omit needless words!"

Now this passage may seem to violate one of the first rules of radio writing: The sentences are long. But how easy they are to read! There are places for breaths, and the pacing is comfortable. We should only hope that we all write as well as E.B. White—and follow Will Strunk's advice while we're at it.

George Orwell's Rules

In 1946, in an essay titled "Politics and the English Language," George Orwell listed six rules of English usage. "These rules sound elementary, and so they are," he wrote, "but they demand a deep change of attitude in anyone who has grown used to writing in the style now fashionable." What was fashionable in 1946 is no longer fashionable today, but today's "fashionable" writing is every bit as much in need of Orwell's rules as writing was when he wrote them. And they're as useful for radio writers as they are for essayists.

(i) Never use a metaphor, simile, or other figure of speech which you are used to seeing in print.

(ii) Never use a long word where a short one will do.

(iii) If it is possible to cut a word out, always cut it out.

(iv) Never use the passive where you can use the active.

(v) Never use a foreign phrase, a scientific word, or a jargon word if you can think of an everyday English equivalent.

(vi) Break any of these rules sooner than say anything outright barbarous.

Carl Kasell has been a morning newscaster for National Public Radio since 1977. He got his start in radio at WGBR in Goldsboro, N.C., in 1950. Marcus D. Rosenbaum, a long-time NPR editor, wrote Chapter 5 of this book.

7

Delivery: Using Your Voice

Karen Kearns

The last step in preparing a radio report is *telling* the story to the listener. Human beings have been sharing information through spoken words much longer than through written language, so telling your story may seem like the easy part of reporting. But reading aloud while sounding as if you are speaking spontaneously is one of the hardest radio skills to master. Radio journalism is really electronic story telling.

Radio is an intimate, person-to-person medium. It is a conversation between you and one other person even though there may be thousands in the listening audience. You are not announcing to someone, you are talking with that person. MORNING EDITION newscaster Carl Kasell says he imagines he's talking to "Aunt Martha." When the president gives a speech, he imagines calling Aunt Martha and saying, "Did you hear the president tonight?" Aunt Martha says, "No, what did he say?" Then he sums up the main points of the speech for her. The summary is the copy in Carl's newscast, and the delivery is his conversation with Aunt Martha.

The Voice

The voice is an instrument that requires training. Just as you wouldn't give a musical recital with an instrument on which you had never practiced, so you shouldn't go on the air without practicing your delivery. Remember that the radio audience hears the story *through* your delivery, and if your delivery doesn't clarify the meaning of the story, it can become a distraction.

In most public speaking, there is immediate feedback from the audience—eye contact, facial expressions, and vocalizations. If the feedback is negative—raised eyebrows or frowns, for instance—the speaker can adjust content or delivery to help the audience understand the message more clearly.

In broadcasting, it's different. There is no immediate feedback, so you don't know how the message is being received. It's just you, the microphone, and the copy. Read alone in the studio, the most polished script can become a monotonous collection of words. Having your imaginary listener give you feedback about your story can help you avoid this problem. Teddy Handfield, an associate professor of drama at Catholic University in Washington, D.C., says an effective radio communicator has three goals when voicing a story.

- *Clarity.* Your phrasing and emphasis should give listeners a clear understanding of the story. They immediately should *get it*. You should emphasize the words that illustrate the point of the story. You should pause to give the listener a chance to understand the message.

- *Change.* Your pitch, rhythm, and pauses should change with the thought pattern of the story. The delivery should be alive and melodious, but it should illustrate the meaning of the sentence. It should not be predictable.

- *Humanity.* Your voice should reflect the life of your mind. It should not be mechanical, but driven by the way you think and feel about the story. It should be spontaneous, natural, and dynamic—not computer-generated monotone.

Training the voice and practicing delivery are not intended to make everyone sound alike. Each voice is unique. Everyone has some regional accent or combination of accents. An accent is part of the uniqueness of the voice and only presents a problem if it distracts from the meaning of the story. Training your voice should allow you to find your style of delivery. Training should not force you to change your dialect or to become an "announcer." Rather, it should enable you to develop good speaking habits and techniques that will enhance your delivery.

In this, NPR differs from much commercial broadcasting. Commercial style can have a sense of artificial urgency. Some of that comes from the time constraints put on commercial news. When you have only one or two minutes to tell everything, it's hard to sound conversational. NPR allows more time for stories and details, so this allows slower, more expressive delivery. But there's more to it than that. As Carl Kasell says, "We think we don't need to shout at or preach to NPR listeners. We are *talking* to them rather than announcing the news." This is the personal contact that NPR develops with its listeners.

This does not mean that any delivery is good delivery. Far from it. Good delivery depends on **voice quality**, **pitch**, **tempo and rate**, and **volume**. All of these elements can be improved through practice and listening. "When you work for NPR there's a delivery style, and the way to learn it is through keen listening," says Lynn Neary, host of weekend ALL THINGS CONSIDERED. "I just think a good ear is the bottom line of everything in radio, and that includes delivery."

You can improve your delivery by recording your voice on a tape recorder and varying these elements for a more natural sound. There are many books available that offer exercises to improve diction and voice quality. However, you may have trouble doing this alone. Most people do not recognize their own voice the first time they hear it recorded. It takes time to adjust to hearing your voice emanating from outside of your body. Working with a speech or voice teacher, who will target specific areas for practice, can help you improve more quickly.

Voice Quality

Physically, the voice is produced by pushing air through the vocal folds of the larynx. The sound resonates in the hollow spaces of the head and neck. The size of the vocal folds and the hollow spaces give each voice its own quality. It is similar to the difference between musical instruments. You can play middle C on a piano and a violin, and while the pitch is the same, the quality of the tone varies because of the difference in the size of the instruments' wooden bodies and strings.

The breath is the motor that powers the voice. You breathe more deeply for speech. The air is taken in quickly and released gradually. Sitting or standing erect with relaxed shoulders allows the diaphragm to expand and contract for proper breath control. The movement of your mouth, tongue, and neck controls the resonance of the voice. The physics of sound production directly affects the quality of the voice.

But voice quality is more than physics. It also has to do with emotions. "An expressive face," says voice coach Marilyn Pittman, "creates an expressive voice." We are drawn to people who sound "warm" and "friendly," and we avoid people who sound "strident" or "unhappy." It's the difference between an open, resonant sound or a pinched, sharp, high-pitched sound. You can alter the quality of your voice by relaxing, releasing tension in the throat, shoulders, and neck, and opening your mouth more widely when you speak. A nasal sound can result from the back of the throat being closed by tension or poor posture.

The way you interpret a sentence can reveal your emotions. To make your copy work, synchronize the emotional state of your voice with the meaning of your copy. You must first understand what you are saying to make the connection between your *mind* and your *voice*. If you are reading copy about a fatal plane crash, it is inappropriate to have a "smile" in your voice.

Blending the physical nature of sound production with the appropriate emotional state for the content will make your delivery sound more natural and pleasant.

Pitch

The highness or lowness of your voice is determined by the **pitch.** We have many vocal stereotypes about pitch. For example, we expect people with high-pitched voices to be small and those with low-pitched voices to be large. Women are expected to have higher pitched voices than men. We believe lower pitched voices belong to stronger, more decisive people, and for the most part we find them more pleasant than high-pitched voices. In the early days of radio, women were not allowed to speak as announcers because their voices were considered too high-pitched to be pleasant. Ironically, women's voices are easier to understand over short-wave broadcasts because the higher pitched frequency is transmitted more clearly.

You probably have experienced the fallacy of pitch stereotypes when you have met people with whom you only have spoken over the telephone. Most likely their actual physical appearance didn't match the image you created. To help your listeners form the best mental image of you, it is important to know how to control the pitch of *your* voice.

Each person has a pitch range of approximately two octaves. The pitch of men's voices lowers dramatically after puberty. Women, however, also add three or four lower tones after puberty. These tones add depth and maturity to the voice. To maximize the effective range of your voice it is important to determine your **optimum pitch**. Your optimum pitch is usually about one-third of the way between the lowest and the highest notes you can sing. You can find your range on a piano keyboard: First sing *down* the scale to the lowest note you can reach. Then, sing *up* the scale to the highest note you can reach. You have marked out the perimeter of your voice range. Now, travel up the scale five notes from your lowest tone. You will find yourself at or near your optimum pitch. This is the pitch you should be using most often when speaking.

Now that you have your optimum pitch, you should compare it with your **habitual pitch.** This is the pitch you normally use most often when speaking. Choose some copy and record yourself reading. Play back the recording, and find the note on the piano that is closest to the average pitch of your reading. You may find that you are speaking several notes higher than your optimum pitch. You probably also will discover that you don't use all of the notes above your optimum pitch to the top of your voice range. Your voice pitch and range give life and vitality to your voice.

Inflection is the change in pitch and stress that occurs within a word while you are producing sound. Speaking in a monotone creates audio wallpaper and bores the listener. The upward and downward inflection in delivery keeps the listener's attention. Inflection adds *melody* to the voice, but the inflection *must have meaning*. The inflection in your voice should coincide with the meaning of the words you are saying and should stress the appropriate points in the sentence.

Inflections that are not tied to the meaning of the words simply create a "roller coaster" or "singsong" effect and detract from your message.

Iverson Warriner, a drama coach from Louisville, Kentucky, illustrates the use of inflection and stress in sentences with this chart:

LEVEL 4	**Special Emphasis**	high in voice range
LEVEL 3	**Primary Stress**	up slightly in range
LEVEL 2	**Home Base**	optimum pitch
LEVEL 1	**Finality**	low pitch

Level 2, "Home Base," is the pitch for your natural speaking voice. This is the pitch that you should use for most of your message. **Level 3**, "Primary Stress," is the pitch you should use for key words or points in the sentence. Your voice will go up several notes from home base to warn the listener that this is the main point. Level 3 also should be used at the end of an interrogative sentence. **Level 1**, "Finality," is the pitch to use at the end of sentences or ideas. It is down one or two pitches from home base. **Level 4**, "Special Emphasis," is very high in pitch and probably won't be used much unless you are a sportscaster. This is the level at which you indicate extreme agitation or excitement. Cheering for your favorite team or screaming "Fire!" take place at Level 4. The following examples outline a simple use of this system:

Statements of fact and command:	*"Now tell him."*	2–3–1
Interrogative sentence:	*"Is he ready?"*	2–2–3
Questions with interrogative words:	*"Where is it?"*	2–3–1
Fright or excitement	*"Fire!"*	4

Rate and Tempo

Your message determines the rate and tempo at which you speak. Serious messages are delivered slowly, with thoughtful pauses. Complicated or technical subject material also should be delivered at a slower rate to allow the listener more time to understand the concepts. Light, humorous messages are spoken much more quickly.

You can measure the *rate of speech* by counting the number of *words spoken per minute (w.p.m.)*. There will be some variance because of the different length of words, but it will give you a rough estimate. Oral reading rates can range from 140 to 180 w.p.m. A slow reading rate, 140 to 160, can become tedious if the listener is familiar with the subject matter. There are regional differences in the rate of normal conversation. The fastest speakers—180–190 w.p.m.—are usually from the Northeast. The slowest speakers—150–160 w.p.m.—are from parts of the South. The rest of the country averages between these two.

It's useful for anyone working in radio to be able to **talk to time**. This skill takes practice. Many people read too fast because they are nervous. Choose a prose selection from a book or newspaper. Read it aloud for a minute. Stop and count the number of words you have read. This will give you a measure of your normal speaking rate. Now select a serious story and a humorous story. Read each story for two minutes. Stop and count the number of words you read and divide by two. This will give you the words-per-minute rate. Does your rate vary between the two stories? The content of different types of stories will affect your rate and pitch. If you start a newscast with a story about Congress but end with an obituary, you will vary the rapid pace of the hard news story to a slower, more sombre tone for the obituary. If the last story is a light, humorous story, you will read faster and play with the pitch and pacing. If you are speaking conversationally and delivering meaning, this will be natural.

Tempo in speech is related to tempo in music. In music, the beat reflects the timing of a composition, and divides the music into equal units of time. In speech, words-per-minute is similar to the beat in music. The musical tempo determines the pace of the music—how fast or slow the beat will be played. In speech, the tempo is determined by the meaning of the words. The tempo gives the emotional interpretation of the content. Tempo in speech comes from the phrasing of words, duration of the syllables, and the use of pauses. We often stretch the key words in a sentence to increase the attention drawn to them. Tempo creates the unpredictable quality of human speech that makes it interesting. A concerto could have 72 different tempos. A radio story also should have different tempos that match the interpretation of the words being spoken. Varying the tempo and "playing" the pauses is necessary for the life of both a musical and a spoken composition.

Volume

The volume or loudness of your speech depends on several things: the acoustics of your environment, the microphone, the recording equipment, the style and atmosphere of the story, and the style of your radio station. Achieving an appropriate volume level is seldom a problem in broadcasting if you have proper microphone placement. You will need to place yourself close enough to the microphone to be in its pickup pattern. Always talk across the **axis** of the microphone, not straight into it. Maintain the same microphone placement throughout the recording. (See Chapter 12, "Field Recording: Techniques," for more detail on microphone placement; see Chapter 14, "Studio Production," for a discussion of perceptions of loudness.)

Read the story copy aloud to preset the level for the microphone. Deliver the story in the style that you will use when you are recording. Inexperienced announcers often say *"Test 1, 2, 3,"* to check the mike level. This gives a false volume level for the voice because it doesn't reflect the copy or style of the performance. The preset mike level is often lower than the actual level you will use when recording and could cause distortion. If you are recording with music or natural sound in the background, you are likely to talk louder. Preset your voice level while playing the music or natural sound in your earphones to prepare for the recording. Remember, your volume level should reflect the intimacy of the conversational style of radio.

Writing is the Key

Writing is the most important component of delivery. "For me, being conversational comes from my writing," says Lynn Neary. "When I'm reading an introduction written by another person, I may change the writing to make it more natural for me. For instance, if someone gives me copy with long sentences, I usually break it down to shorter sentences. I find shorter sentences more conversational." You may even want to read your copy aloud as you write. It will show you if you are creating any delivery traps. Wendy Kaufman, an NPR correspondent in Los Angeles, says she reads her copy aloud up to five times before going in the studio. "If I stumble over a word or phrase more than once, it isn't written well for the radio. I'll rewrite the copy because the writing really dictates the delivery."

The pacing and speaking style of the tape in the story also affects delivery style, so be sure to write your copy while listening to the tape, and matching the style and even the phrasing. Listen to the tape cuts while recording your tracks whenever possible. "If you have tape cuts that are slow, expressive and emotional, you can't come out of the tape cut delivering rapid-fire facts," says Kaufman. "You need to balance your tone of voice and pacing with the person on tape."

Mark your script so you will remember where to emphasize, where to slow down, where to speed up, and so on. Underline words you want to stress; use slashes to indicate pauses; spell out difficult words phonetically so they are easier to pronounce. "It takes a lot of energy to sound natural," says Neary, "but too much energy can also sound phony. Commercial radio usually sounds too frenetic, and NPR style is often too laid back. The best delivery may be somewhere between the two styles."

The most important thing is to know your copy. If you read it with meaning, you won't sound singsong.

Warming Up

Before any recording session, it is wise to use some vocal warm-up and relaxation techniques. Begin by taking several deep breaths from your diaphragm.

Relax your shoulders and slowly roll your head in a complete circle three times to the left and three times to the right. To improve the circulation in your face, open your eyes, mouth, nose, ears, and throat as far as you possibly can. Hold that extreme position for a few seconds. Then constrict the same muscles as tightly as you can and hold for a few seconds. Exaggerating facial expressions will add energy to the voice. It doesn't matter what you look like as long as you sound animated.

If needed, drink some warm water with a slice of lemon before going into the studio. The warmth releases the tension in the muscles and restores moisture to the mouth. The lemon cleanses your mouth and dilutes the saliva. Don't drink soft drinks with sugar before recording. The sugar coats your mouth and increases mouth noise. You might also want to try some vocalizations. Inhale slowly and exhale the sound *ahhh* very slowly several times. Say the sound *"eee"* on a scale from the highest note you can reach to the lowest and then back up again. Next, try some tongue twisters to improve your diction. Voice-over actress Susan Blu suggests *Good blood, bad blood* and *Red leather, yellow leather* as two phrases that exercise your mouth, lips, and tongue. Repeat each phrase five or six times, increasing the speed and exaggerating the delivery.* Voice coach Marilyn Pittman suggests repeating all of the consonants, "cacaca, dadada, fafafa, gagaga, etc." to warm up the articulators. Use other phrases that exercise your diction weak spots. Any voice and diction book will have a variety of exercises from which to choose.

This warm-up will help you release the "fight or flight" symptoms that come during a performance: When the body is frightened, it sends blood to the arms and legs and stops the digestive process. That causes your mouth to dry up and your arms and legs to quiver. Deep breaths can slow down the adrenalin and refocus your energy. Breathing is a key to sounding natural and relaxed. Each exhalation will release the tension. Use yawns and sighs to help relax the body. Mouth noise comes from dry lips and tongue smacking while speaking. Drinking warm water or placing a flat cough drop between the cheek and gum can help relieve mouth noise by increasing saliva in the mouth.

Q-TIP

Teddy Handfield uses the acronym "Q-TIP" to help her students remember the elements of good delivery. *quality, timing, intensity,* and *pitch* are necessary to transfer the appropriate meaning to the listener. Carl Kasell says: "You want to

---

*Susan Blu and Molly Ann Mullen, *Word of Mouth* (Los Angeles, Calif., Pomegranate Press, Ltd., 1987), p. 23.

read and take the ink out of it and put yourself in its place so you find yourself expressing ideas simply by talking to another person."

Practice "cold readings" to improve your spontaneous delivery. A cold reading is simply reading, without practice, copy you have never seen before. Listen for the meaning of the words. Are you tempted to slip into a melody not related to the meaning of the sentence? Is your rate appropriate for the content? Do you vary the tempo spontaneously? Is your voice concerned or connected with the listener?

Finally, there are three *"P's"* that are necessary for good delivery. The first is *pronunciation*. It's important to pronounce all words, especially proper names, correctly. Many parts of the country and the world have idiosyncrasies in the spelling and pronunciation of names. I worked as a newscaster for the Wisconsin network and learned this lesson the hard way. There are many Native American names for towns in northern Wisconsin. I encountered the town, *Shawano*, in copy one day and said *Sha-wah-no*. The phones began to ring because the correct pronunciation is *Shah-no*. Be sure to check the pronunciation of any tricky words before going on the air. The wire services usually distribute a daily pronunciation guide for difficult names in news copy.

Another *"P"* is *performance*. You are performing each time you record your tracks. Edward R. Murrow majored in speech and theater. Undoubtedly, this training helped his broadcast journalism career. Taking a speech class or an acting class may help improve your performance skills.

There is no substitute for the final *"P," practice*. Reading aloud every day is the best practice. Recording your reading will give you a chance to critique your performance. Save these recordings and review them. I save samples of recordings from all points in my career. They show the way the voice matures and the changes in interpretation that come from practice. You will be encouraged by the improvement you have made when you review your work. Maintaining good vocal delivery, like staying proficient at playing a musical instrument, requires continual practice.

Karen Kearns is a professor of radio, television and film at California State University, Northridge (CSUN). She has been a producer for L.A. Theatre Works and KCRW in Santa Monica on the radio adaptation of Frank Norris' novel, McTeague. Before teaching at CSUN, she worked as a newscaster for ALL THINGS CONSIDERED *and as associate director of NPR's Education Services Department. She has won a George Foster Peabody Award, three CINDY Awards, and a Golden Mike for her work at NPR and KOST-FM in Los Angeles. She has also worked as a newswriter for Voice of America. Kearns received an M.A. in communication arts from the University of Wisconsin and a B.A. in theater and an M.A. in speech communication from Southern Illinois University.*

Part III

FEATURES

8

Conceiving Features: One Reporter's Style

Robert Krulwich

Every feature begins with an idea, and developing that idea for the radio is much more than a writing job. For me, the writing part—sitting at the typewriter and knocking out a script—comes second to last. My features go through five stages:

1. Finding the Idea
2. Creating an Outline
3. Isolating the Tape
4. Writing
5. Refining

Finding an Idea for a Feature Story

There are basically two ways to do feature stories: find them yourself, or follow up someone else's story.

When editors assign features, they usually take the second approach. Often they ask reporters to get the "local angle" on a major news story, so if the United States has just landed a man on the moon, editors across the country will want to know if anyone in their towns, or any relative of someone in town, was part of the effort. These stories are called **sidebars, soft pieces,** or **color stories.** Seasonal stories, "Area Jews Celebrate Passover," are in the same category. Follow-up features are generally more fun if you think them up yourself; that is why it's best to read the morning paper before you get to work and hold on to any story that makes you so curious you want to know more.

So, if you read in the paper that 17 out of the 18 lawyers the governor nominated to be judges were not approved by the state legislature, you might wonder how the 18th lawyer got through. Or, if you see a story announcing, "Paul Smith has been appointed president of the Hills School, replacing John Jones, who held the job for the last four months," you might wonder what happened to Mr. Jones, and why the school has such a high turnover. If this doesn't come naturally, pick out a few stories, and force yourself to think of some aspect that the paper overlooked.

Another tip: If you read the morning paper and discover that you know a central figure—or better, someone who is friends with, related to, works with, or bowls with that figure—you've got yourself a **source**. Give your source a call, if possible, before you see your editor. Then ask your source, "Your son was at the Hills School when John Jones got there. Was Jones a good principal? Why did he leave?"

The other way to get feature story ideas is hard to explain. Some people can get up in the morning and, by the time they get to work, they have seen something odd in a store window, overheard a suspicious conversation, or met a man whose wife is about to be named ambassador to Trinidad. Good reporters are always making mental notes. They never stop reporting. The littlest thing can get them going:

• A friend mentions that a friend of hers is training a) to become a pilot; b) to become a shoe salesman; c) to stop smoking. And the reporter thinks maybe there are features here. . . .

• The local movie theater has been showing the same film for nine weeks; there are only 30,000 people in town. Everyone who wants to see the movie has seen it. A reporter may wonder: Why is it still there? There must be some explanation. . . .

The key is, *anything that makes you curious could turn into a feature. Anything.* Suggest your idea to your editor or news director. If you have thought the story through and are excited about the material, you will have a good chance of selling others on your idea.

Here are a few do's and don'ts:

• *Do follow up a lead*. A friend of yours says in passing, "Strange, but that's the third boy to get leukemia in the same neighborhood. In fact, they live on the same street." If you think there may be more than coincidence involved, ask for the boys' names, the name of the street, the hospital they went to, and write the information down. *Don't trust your memory.*

- *Do check out stories promptly.* Don't sit on a lead. Call right away. Someone else could get the story.

- *Don't quit a story because the first interview goes badly.* If the person you talked to was abrupt, insulting, confusing, or gave you too much information, that is not a reason to stop. Don't let yourself be intimidated. Try one more call. The second call is almost always easier.

- *Don't be embarrassed to ask the friend, relative, or acquaintance for an interview,* even if asking is awkward. Being a little pushy is part of being a reporter. You will constantly be amazed at how many doors can be opened just by asking forcefully (but politely). Reporters are forever imagining privacy difficulties that don't materialize. If you have ever been interviewed, then you know the experience: At the start, you are nervous and careful, but, as the conversation warms up, you find yourself saying all kinds of things you never expected to say, and only afterward do you wonder, "What came over me?" Whatever it is, it comes over almost everyone. This does not mean you should betray confidences. Some exchanges, even if they would make good stories, are really **off the record.**

- *Don't trust newspaper accounts.* They are not always accurate. Before assuming a statement to be true, check it out yourself. "Mrs. Lesko, the *Chronicle* says your collie dug up $48 in the front yard. Is that right?"

Creating an Outline: How To Organize a Feature Story

A straight news story offers facts in order of importance; the classic structure of a hard news story will cover who, what, when, where, why, and how over the course of the piece. These questions will be answered with appropriate supporting paragraphs in the appropriate order. But features flow any way they have to to hold an audience. So I cannot tell you how to structure a feature. But you must have a structure.

Features require a peculiar way of thinking common to reporters and storytellers. Experience has to be turned instantly into narrative outline. For example, suppose my editor tells me he had heard that a famous music magazine has decided to change its name from *Crawdaddy* to *Feature*. He wants to know why. "Check it out," he says.

The beginning reporter is likely to rush over to the magazine without further thought. The reporter will arrive on the scene, find the person in charge, and say something like, "Excuse me, I hear you are switching names. Tell me about it." This doesn't work very well. Asked a general question, a source will usually give a general answer like, "Yes, we're changing names. The new one comes out next month." This lets your source shape your story, and it may not be until you are back in the office that you will notice a small remark that could have been the focus of your story, if only you had followed up on it. A better approach is to try to imagine a possible shape for your story *before* you start interviewing.

Scene I: Publisher notices two newsstands downtown where *Crawdaddy* has been put next to the sports magazines. It sits between *Trout and Stream* and *Reel 'n Rod*. He wonders why.

Scene II: Publisher gets a marketing report that says two out of every five newsstand dealers think *Crawdaddy* is about Southern fish.

Scene III: Publisher sends colorful mailing to 10,000 news dealers saying that *Crawdaddy* is about music, and belongs next to *Rolling Stone* and *High Times*.

Scene IV: Nothing changes. Publisher decides to get a new name.

Scene V: News dealers react.

Not one word of this has been verified. It is probably entirely untrue. But, with an outline, however imaginary, I have something that gets me going and guides my way. I now have a better sense of what to do next.

First, the story line (as I imagine it, anyway) seems a little nutty, so I am excited. This is important. If the editor's suggestion had triggered a dull scenario, I would have argued that it was a dumb idea, and I should be assigned something else. But I like it. So I am motivated. Second, my five scenes suggest a definite line of questioning: What was wrong with the name *Crawdaddy*? Who discovered the problem? Why change to *Feature*? Were there competing alternatives? How will they explain the change to customers? Third, I can guess at a short list of people to talk to: a) whoever discovered the problem; b) the person(s) who decided to change the name; c) readers; d) maybe news dealers, if my hunch is correct.

Now I am on my way. I make calls, ask questions. But let's suppose that my first interview, with the publisher, goes terribly. Let's assume that he is dull, frightened, and monotone. Unfortunately, he was the one who discovered that *Crawdaddy* was, indeed, placed with the wrong magazines on the newsstands— not the fishing magazines, as it happens; it was stacked alongside *Teen Scene* and *Teen Age* and the comic books. *Crawdaddy* is intended for 16- through 35-year-old readers, not the 8–14 set, so the wrong people were seeing it. I also learned (again from my dull, monotone publisher) that he ordered an investigation and found that when news dealers looked at the cover design and the funky name *Crawdaddy*, the magazine so resembled other teen/fan magazines that the dealers just assumed they belonged together.

Yes, there was a meeting, but the publisher says everyone who was at the meeting is too busy to talk with me. Yes, they decided to make the magazine look more adult. Yes, that is why they dropped *Crawdaddy* and chose *Feature*. *Feature*, he says, has definite adult appeal. End of interview.

What to do? My original scenario assumed a colorful, bright narrator who would tell the magazine's story. Then I would talk to readers and news dealers. But my narrator is a drag, and no one else on the staff has permission to talk on tape.

I know my original outline won't work. If I let the publisher tell his story for three or four minutes and throw in the news dealers at the end, the audience will never stay with the piece—too dull—and if the dealers are any good, all my strong tape will come in a jumble at the very end. So I decide on a new outline that will introduce the dealers earlier in the story. I imagine:

Scene I: Publisher sees magazine in the wrong place.
Scene II: Dealers say they thought it was a teeny-bopper magazine.
Scene III: Publisher redesigns cover; changes name.
Scene IV: Dealers react.

That feels more lively. It depends less on the publisher, and it switches back and forth from the executive to the newsstand. It won't be dull. So with this substitute outline in my head, I go to interview the news dealers. I tell them what the publisher has said, and ask them to react, step-by-step, to his narrative.

They are marvelous. One tells me yes, he put *Crawdaddy* with the comics, but he knows they are changing the cover, and from now on *Feature* will be where it belongs—with the literary magazines. That is what he remembers being told. The other dealer says *Crawdaddy*'s problem is not its name. "It stinks. It won't sell if they called it *Newsweek*," he says.

As we are talking, I can feel the story falling into place.

Scene I: Publisher sees his magazine in the wrong place.
Scene II: Dealers say they thought it was a teeny-bopper magazine.
Scene III: Publisher redesigns cover; changes name.
Scene IV: Dealer No. 2 says it won't work. The magazine stinks.
Scene V: Publisher talks of plans to "educate" dealers.
Scene VI: Dealer No. 1 tells me from now on it goes with the poetry journals.

Because I have a working outline in my head, I walk away from those dealers with a story that is almost finished. I don't have to dub off the full interviews, only the parts I need. Walking back to the office, I can start composing the introduction in my head. When I am up against a short deadline, having that outline constantly on tap is a terrific help.

However, I must be careful. Because I begin most interviews with a preconceived outline, it is easy to miss a better story if one should come along. Should one of the dealers mention that *Feature* is going to cut its price in half, and so is *Rolling Stone*, bells should go off. If I am alert, I must immediately switch scenarios:

Scene I: *Feature* starts a price war among music magazines.
Scene II: *Rolling Stone* reacts and drops its price.
Scene III: So does *Record World*.

Now I have a business story. I don't completely ditch my earlier *Crawdaddy* scenario. I can go back to it if the business story proves uninteresting, or incorrect, but I decide to switch gears. Also, I have to be willing to let my outline become more complicated. My initial scenarios are often fairy-tale simple. The characters always tell the truth.

Suppose, however, that some of the dealers tell me that they hear *Feature* may never be delivered. The magazine, they understand, is too deeply in debt and is about to go under. If they are right, I am going to look very foolish talking for four minutes on the radio about a name change when the product itself is about to disappear. So, I have to check their story, and, if the publisher won't deny it, then I would ask my editor whether we want to run the story at all. We would have to restructure the outline to include the magazine's financial problems—which could get unwieldy.

But, if I had gone from person to person with no structure in my head, I could never have controlled my interviews as effectively. I would have been less certain about what to ask, what to emphasize, whom to talk to, and, most of all, when to stop. And once I stopped, with no structure in my head, I would have to re-listen to all my interviews and superimpose an outline. That takes too much time. To make deadlines, reporters have to be efficient.

Isolating the Tape

This part is easy. When I am interviewing somebody, I always know when I have just had a good moment. Sometimes it is a concise answer that fits perfectly into my outline (or creates a good alternate outline). Sometimes it is a funny exchange that will be easy to listen to. Sometimes (and these are best), it is a remark that is perfect as a cap to my story and will fit wonderfully at the very end (I can hear myself signing off immediately afterward). As soon as I have such a moment, I think, "I can use that," and it goes into the outline that is building in my mind. When I am walking back to the office, I play that moment back on my cassette recorder to hear if it was as good as I thought.

Beginning reporters too often feel compelled to use tape segments that contain official or "important" statements. For example, the mayor intoning in his official voice, "This was the worst earthquake we've had in eastern Michigan in

50 years." In fact, you can say that just as well yourself, in your script ("Mayor Jones called it the worst earthquake. . .").

You will find you can usually convey information more succinctly than the person you interview. The tape that is best is the tape that conveys mood, emotion, involvement, or context—things you can't convey as well yourself.

A word of warning, however. Since vivid tape (or good pictures) is so helpful to broadcast reporters, we often structure our stories around those moments, even if we have to take a weird detour to make them fit. This is dangerous. I have a weakness for nice tape that is as strong as the next fellow's, and I don't like to let a good moment go, but I know that I must not distort a point or break a narrative flow just to accommodate a few seconds of flashy tape. Sometimes, tape must go. I have found that if I postpone the surgery to a later stage (the "writing" stage that follows), it is much less painful.

Therefore, after I have finished my interviews, I select all the "best moments"—even the ones that don't quite fit my outline. I arrange them in order of probable appearance, as suggested by my outline, on a single reel. Each moment is separated by **leader tape** (colored or paper tape that cannot be recorded on, used for visual identification of parts of a reel; see Chapter 13, "Tape Editing"), so when I play the reel through I can hear my story in rough outline, minus the connecting, scripted parts. I listen through at least once, mentally "writing in" the connecting material. Then I sit down to write.

Writing

As I said earlier, for hard news, the form is all important: hard news always begins with the hard lead, followed by supporting material, spoken in the neutral, natural voice. Features, on the other hand, can have a personality. The reporter can become a character in the story by allowing his or her personality to be heard, or give a minor player a major voice, or let the scene play itself exactly as it was recorded. The choices are so varied that I cannot lay down hard rules for feature writing, but I can offer some tips.

You are allowed to use "I." When I write a story about an experience I had, I choose the first person form. I try to write my script as though I were talking to a friend across a table.

I compose out loud. I sit at a typewriter, write a paragraph, and then speak it. If it sounds like me talking, I move on. If it sounds like my written self, I try again.

I am not offended by laughs, grunts, snorts, giggles, and sighs—my own or anyone else's. It is okay to make human noises on the radio. When appropriate I will give myself a stage direction in the script, "Sigh here."

When is that appropriate? I find that when I am writing out of tape that finishes with lots of people laughing, it is sometimes correct not to break the mood. If they were laughing at a joke, I may keep the laughing going for an instant more, or at least speak my next lines smiling.

A mood or tone established on tape does not have to end just because the tape runs out. That is true before a tape cut too. If I have a bad scene on tape that begins with a woman crying, I anticipate the mood. My words may look neutral on paper ("I met Janet Jones in her apartment. The door was open and I just walked in. . ."), but I know what's coming. This is going to be sad, so I put a little sadness in my voice ahead of time. A mood is established that makes the transition smoother. That way, the audience is not distracted when I move from script to tape, and the story flows more easily. I do change moods, but only when it fits the narrative.

There is a tendency, especially among beginning reporters, to draw too clear a line between tape and script. Tape and script are not separate entities, standing side by side; they must sound like two interdependent parts of a whole.

Suppose I go out and do a feature on acute depression. It is my first feature, and I get an interview with a famous psychiatrist, who has just written a book on the subject. He says there are four types. He describes Type A beautifully; he is brief, clear, and to the point. On Type B, he has a stuttering attack, which makes him nervous and hard to follow. On Type C, he is so-so and Type D takes too long.

I come back to the office. My outline is obvious. I will report on all four categories of depression. Since the tape on Type A is good, I will use it. To avoid the stuttering episode, I throw away the tape on Type B and script that section. I have to have more of the doctor in the story, so I go back to the tape for Type C and I write up Type D.

I end up with a story that moves like a fox trot; four steps, tape-script-tape-script, each separate, each equal. Boring. When a story moves in so predictable and regular a rhythm, the audience knows what is coming, and, if listeners aren't that interested in the subject, they will nod out. Each segment is self-contained, like unfriendly neighbors in an apartment house. Each makes its point, then ends. Novice reporters often fall into this pattern.

There are other options. You could start with tape segment A, where the doctor does well, then roll into segment B, still on tape, until the doctor begins his stuttering fit, and then just pick up in script after his second or third stammer. That way, the reporter appears to be rescuing the doctor. That adds a dimension to the story (it is interesting when a psychiatrist stutters), but, more important, it is a more lively transition from tape to script.

When you finish describing Type B depression, you don't have to go back to the doctor for Type C. Begin describing the third category yourself, and pass off to the doctor only when he was at his best in that segment, even if you give him just two or three sentences. A short tape cut is okay. There is no such thing as too long or too short for tape or script segments. I have inserted a one-word cut of tape that lasted one second. I do whatever suits me, as long as it moves the story along, keeps the audience listening, and is faithful to the material.

Remember, there are all kinds of ways to alter the rhythm of a story. Not everyone agrees about these techniques, and not everyone can make them work. The first suggestion I am offering tends to be controversial. Make sure you know the opinion of your editor before cutting too much tape. Here are some suggestions for altering the rhythm of a story:

1. **Start a sentence in the script and have someone on tape finish it.**
   Script: "Yes, doctors say they are working on a cure . . ."
   Tape: "But we won't have one for another 10 years . . ."
   Script: ". . . says Dr. T. B. Gross."

2. **Don't return to script between each cut of tape. Go from script to several consecutive tape cuts.**
   Script: "Doctors say they are working on a cure . . ."
   Tape of Dr. Jones: "Yes, but that's a long way off . . ."
   Tape of Dr. Smith: "I'd say 10, 11 years . . ."
   Tape of Dr. Gray: "At least that or maybe more. . . ."

(Notice that each tape cut is quite short. This works best if the three voices are very distinctive. So it would be nice if Dr. Smith were a man, and Drs. Jones and Gray women, so the voice changes would be obvious.)

3. **Start the story in a specific location (a hospital laboratory) and then leave the scene. The change in, or absence of, atmosphere will alter the rhythm.**
   Tape Ambience: hospital/hospital/hospital/hospital/studio/studio/studio/studio
   Script: "The doctors are still looking for a vaccine. But, they are out of money."

4. **Use tape to punctuate a script. Take a single word (an enthusiastic "yes!"), or a short sentence ("yes! yes!" or "Oh no!"), and drop it in to break up your script.**
   Script: "He drew the line in . . . slowly . . . and then he saw the fish. . . ."
   Tape: "YES!"
   Script: "It was a beauty!"

   Script: "She says she looked up, and that was when she saw him."
   Tape: "Oh no!"
   Script: "He was hanging off the balcony. . . ."

Refining

It is time to make my final cuts. Now that I have completed the first or rough cut, my story will get much shorter. In this last review, precious moments on tape hit the floor. Beautiful lines drop away. I am editing for a consistent, even pace.

I not only cut, I sometimes add. I might mix in some new sound recorded at one of the places I visited—background sound of people playing or street traffic—because I find that a **bed** of non-studio sound can pull a section together.

This can be a dangerous time, too. I sometimes get so carried away tightening and cutting that I will chop out a minor, but important, detail so that a complicated idea becomes too simple, and the story is no longer as precise, or as clear or honest as it should be. So I have devised a test. It is the last thing I do before I go into the studio to record.

The 'Squirm' Test

I ask myself, "Can I bring all the people I interviewed for this story into this studio and read this script and play this tape right in front of them without shame, and when I finish, can I look them in the eye (all of them) and defend everything I have just said?"

If I can, I go in and record.

Robert Krulwich is a business and economics correspondent for CBS Television and a regular contributor to public television. He developed his speciality—explaining complex economic, legal, and diplomatic news in a style that is clear, compelling, and entertaining—on radio. Before joining CBS in 1985, Krulwich was business and economics correspondent for National Public Radio and NPR's national editor. He still contributes to NPR's WEEKEND EDITION. Krulwich has won numerous awards for his reporting, including Gainsbrugh Awards from the Economics Broadcasting Association, a Champion Award from the Amos Tuck Business School, and PBS's special award for programming excellence. He covered the Watergate hearings for Pacifica Radio and was the Washington bureau chief of Rolling Stone magazine. Krulwich has a B.A. in history from Oberlin College and a J.D. from Columbia University School of Law.

9

Writing for the Ear:
A Personal Approach

Scott Simon

Several years ago I was part of a documentary team a well-regarded and civilized producer took to a spot in the western part of this country. We were to produce a one-hour program that would leave the listener with an accurate and compassionate sense of the community that we'd inhabited for one week, and an appreciation for a way of living that was odd and unknown to most of our audience. We taped everything, soaking up sound with shotgun microphones, hand-held microphones, wireless microphones strapped into improvident places, microphones strung out of trees and over tanned, hard and mostly soundless prairies. "What I'd like to do," said the producer, "is create a whole hour of sound that will communicate this story with no script at all. I guess that's something we always shoot for."

After several months of difficult stereophonic production, the documentary was ready. I listened to it while kneeling on the rug, my ears purposefully trained at the identical height of the woofers (or was it tweeters?). A great deal of it I liked. But sound spattered unexpectedly; squeals, jangles, chimes, and commotion bustled across the speakers and tramped over my mental interior, as if I were overhearing an intruder and trying to determine exactly where he is in the house and what he's stealing. After a while, it was only tedious.

What was missing from the mix was good writing: a voice that could have poked about, implored, queried, become friendly or abrasive, empathetic or instructive. The voice of a piece, which is what your writing becomes, is what provides the vision to a story. It is the eyes of the audience—and the nose, the fingers, the mind. Good writing can give unexpected worth (even if it's just the shine of style) to a piece that is otherwise unremarkable. It can turn good reporting into memorable reporting. Bad writing can leave brilliant reporting in ruins.

Nothing can offer identifiable character to your work as well as your good, sensitive, imaginative writing. It is the first skill most of us are told to master in this craft, yet often the first one sacrificed—to the crunch of deadlines and the constraints of air time.

Getting Started

There is a tendency in the news business to define a story according to certain italicized designations: *hard-news, soft-news, profile, personality, investigative, retrospective*. The hazard in this is in believing that writing technique and writing standards change from category to category. I do not believe they do. Our minds don't have switches—on/off, humorous/serious—that we throw one way or the other, depending on the story. When you want to highlight humor, you should remember that you still want to respect the facts and use the language well. When you have to be unrelievedly serious, remember that small glints of good feeling, if not outright humor, can help the listener weigh the seriousness of the situation.

Be wary of developing one style for reporting on an audition of chickens for a role in a Broadway show (one of my first assignments, by the way) and another for an analysis of logistics during the Gulf War (a more recent one). The same voice should be recognizable in both. Soft news stories need to convey information no less than hard news; profiles should be investigative; hard news must have enough retrospective to lend context; and so on.

Defining the story. Little else is worth worrying about in writing a story until you've answered this question: What is the story?

The story may seem too obvious to worry about defining it, such as

Mayor Proposes Tax Increase.

However, the real story is found in the questions underneath the headline: Is the mayor increasing taxes because of budget deficits, or to fund an increase in certain city services? If new taxes are necessary, who will be affected most by the proposed ones? Does the increase represent a reversal of campaign promises? Is the city forced to compensate for the loss of federal or state revenues, or has it just been overspending?

For the sake of example, let's say that federal revenues have been shrinking while city crime has been growing, and the mayor has promised to hire more police. The story then gets more complicated:

> *Despite reductions in city revenues caused in part by a loss of federal aid, the mayor wants to hire more police, so she has proposed a tax increase.*

To get from the more complex question to actually writing the story, try this: Identify three points in a story you want listeners to know if they absorb nothing else between distractions. In our example, the three points might be these:

1. The city needs more money to hire more police.
2. Sources of revenue are shrinking.
3. The mayor seemed short-tempered.

Some of these points will seem obvious; others unexceptional, but perhaps telling. Don't be reluctant to include the latter type in your short list. During the war in the Persian Gulf, I wrote an essay about waiting with the troops for ground combat to begin. The three points I wanted most to communicate were:

1. Intelligence estimates said that ground combat would be necessary to spur large Iraqi surrenders.
2. Soldiers were anxious for ground combat to begin soon, because they saw it as the quickest way to be done with the war and return home.
3. Many soldiers eat Froot Loops breakfast cereal.

Now I am confident that most listeners understood and comprehended all three of these points. But I still hear from people who remember the Froot Loops—and nothing else. It may have seemed like the least critical point, but it easily was the most memorable, because it seemed to symbolize the youth of the soldiers and the concept of their fortifying themselves to die.

Outline. After you have determined your three points, outline the way you think the piece should sound. An academically correct, categorized and subcategorized outline is not necessary, but some black-and-white scribbling of the themes and points you want to make, the scenes and details you wish to describe, will help you plot the proper approach. Too many radio reporters care for little more than those parts of a story that can be acquired through the business end of a microphone. If you rely solely on information that can be recorded or remembered, you may be cheating the audience out of the benefit of a reporter's practiced, firsthand observations.

Isolate and Characterize

Some large, endlessly unfolding stories (wars, economic crises, political campaigns) can be made fresh and worth hearing by isolating a smaller element from them and using that to suggest the contours of the whole event. An example of this is a story I filed before the Persian Gulf ground war began in 1991. The story, which was about the U.S. logistics operation, tried to convey a sense of the overwhelming amount of materiel and personnel accumulating in the desert for lethal purpose:

Simon: Operation Desert Storm has brought American-style truck convoys to the remote northern desert on roads laid down like pipelines in the scattering sand where Saudi Arabia runs up against Kuwait and Iraq. *(Natural sound of music up full, then under.)* An American lieutenant pins the pedal of a jeep above 120 and cranks a country-music tape above the buzz of the emergency alarm for much of the 10-hour drive toward the border. There is no rush hour and no letup along this highway. Trucks, troop carriers, missile launchers, and ammo vans loaded up and lashed down with all the war commodities of today's armed forces. Quarter-of-a-ton artillery shells, some already inscribed, at the factory or dock, "Eat this Saddam." Bags of holiday candy sent with the best wishes of American and British school children, Tow Missiles, and tampons. The man who is overseeing this methodical expansion of so much American resources is Army Major General William "Gus" Pagonis.

Pagonis: Well, it's probably the largest logistical operation deployment, reception, armored movement, and sustainment ever done of a force in history. And it was done in an extremely rapid, short period of time.

Simon: General Pagonis was one of the first ranking American generals to arrive in Saudi Arabia. A notably short, silver-haired man, he plays basketball with his staff several times a week, which may seem a surprising enthusiasm for a man his size except, say his aides, the game they play consists of passing the ball to the general for him to take shot after shot. General Pagonis, however, seems more generous in passing off credit for such an apparently rapid and effective deployment. He likes to tell about the time last fall when he ordered a young lieutenant to design and install Vietnam-style latrines.

Pagonis: Well, immediately I could see by the expression on his face he had no idea what I was talking about. Then I realized: At his age, he probably didn't participate in Vietnam, which is obvious. And then he looked at me and—a very aggressive kid—he said, "Well, I saw the movie *Platoon*, and I saw the latrines. Is that what you want?" And I said, "Absolutely!" So he went out and within 24 hours designed it, had the Saudis design a prototype, and they were off the production line within three days. It's fortunate he saw the movie.

Simon: During that last major American war, the Vietcong used to ridicule American soldiers for what was taken to be their inability to make war without sit-down latrines, the latest music tapes, and familiar snack food. But General Pagonis believes that attending not only to the needs but the comforts of American soldiers—delivering fresh fruit and hot shower tents into the field, as well as artillery shells—will make them stronger and better motivated than most of the Iraqi soldiers across the border.

Pagonis: Our medical and sick rate here is the lowest in the history of any war. It's even lower than peacetime. So according to our Article 15, which is our Uniform Code of Military Justice, it's the lowest it's ever been . . . court martials, everything. The morale of the troops is high. Well, to keep morale high you have to provide them those services that will help keep their morale high and their sanitation and everything else.

Notice the way the *details* accumulate to tell the big picture. Mentioning together items as large as Tow missiles and as small as tampons gives the listener an understanding of the scope of the American logistical effort much more vividly than raw tonnage statistics. Describing the fact that the general, who is not tall, plays basketball—and how he plays it—tells as much about the man as several paragraphs of psychological speculation, especially when it's combined with the story about the young soldier and the latrines.

Often we believe that if we simply pile on statistics—hard facts—we will convey the whole story. This is not so. The late Chicago journalist Ben Hecht used to complain that his analysis of courtroom cases was outdated and forgotten the morning after a verdict. Maybe so. But his picturesque descriptions of defendants, his rendering of the interplay of judges and defendants—all of that survives as a human story we take pleasure in reading today.

Using Tape

Of course, in most of your pieces, a substantial portion of your script is already in existence before you start writing: on tape. Your words must bounce off and between the words of those you have interviewed or taped in some proceeding. With the possible exception of traffic reports, all scripts we write must set off, expand, or integrate the words of others. Indeed, this is where *real* radio exists: conversation, verbal wordplay, the sound of people running through their thoughts or reliving moments.

Log your tape. Know what's there. Sometimes, what you *think* you heard is *not* there. Machines malfunction. The mind misremembers. More pleasantly, sometimes something you did not hear *is* there, waiting to be heard, discovered, and used.

So for feature writing I prefer the method of carefully auditing and logging each second of tape recorded for a story—taking care to star (*) those moments that stand up best, then deciding which tape to use, and in what order—rather than scripting before locating tape to fit.

Let the tape tell the story. I prefer tape that is active and expressive, something that contains the sound of thinking, musing, recollection, or events actually unfolding. In some rare instances you may interview people whose sense of self and narrative is so complete and entertaining that your log is lined with stars. In such cases let the tape play, and apply script only sparingly, as a highlight rather than a base. Here's a segment of a piece we did on a telephone answering service in New York City, featuring its founder, Clifford Harris:

Harris: (into phone) Can I help you? . . . Yes, I can, who is this? . . . What do you want, Lena? . . . Well, you can't have messages. No one calls you. You're not pop-u-lar. *(ringing phone)* Well, look, I gotta run. I'm being made famous. OK, bye-bye. *(to Simon)* Anyway, what was the question?

Simon: One thing I can't help but think about, and it does hearken back to that old Judy Holliday movie about an answering service. She became infatuated with one of the clients. . . . Does that happen?

Harris: Yes, it does. The problem is, you build up these crazy fantasies in your mind about them, over the phone. And they never quite live up to what you expect them to be, so it's not really fair to them, because I meet them, and after a half an hour I'm very disappointed with them, and I think that they can tell it. And no one wants their answering service to, like, be disappointed in them.

Simon: As you may have gathered, this small office off of Broadway, with a window that fronts on an alleyway, is actually an interesting place from which to watch New York—or a part of it. And Clifford Harris likes that about it—that, from a telephone on a scarred desk, he can clue together an idea of the kinds of people he services. But still, he speaks of leaving the business.

Harris: It's just the fact that I'm tired of taking other people's messages. I want to go out and make my own. The first thing I'll do is go and get my own answering service, and I will drive them insane. You kind of, like, find out what other people are doing in the city while you're sitting here doing nothing. You realize that there are a lot of things that go on in this city—a lot of people who are just, like, out on the fringe.

Simon: And everywhere around the room, cellophane-taped from the ceiling to the baseboard, there are thousands of pictures of his clients, 8-by-10 posed publicity glossies that are sent to agents and directors by those looking for work. Their names and telephone numbers run beneath their set smiles. And Clifford Harris can find this sad.

Harris: Because this is just, like, a small part of it. There are many, many more actors and actresses than this. And very, very few of these people will be even able to make a living at it, much less obtain any kind of status. *(ringing phone)* It is kind of, well, it's real sad. I'm depressed already. Excuse me. . . . *(to phone)* Can I help you?

Simon: This is Scott Simon in New York City.

Harris: (continuing into phone) Oh, we are always sharp this early in the morning. You sound like you're better than you were . . . *(fades out)*

This piece rendered into script underscores the point that's too easily forgotten: *The tape of a piece and your script are equal partners in the ultimate product.* Dull, witless actuality debases, rather than enhances, good writing. Dull, witless, thoughtless, or uninspired writing only frustrates good tape.

The benefits of careful and imaginative writing are most apparent, I think, in those stories in which good writing illuminates good tape and makes it whole; words, sounds, phrases that might be puzzling and incomplete if left to themselves can be lifted up by good writing. Here's an example: a summer evening in 1979 I spent in the emergency room of an animal hospital in New York City.

(Traffic sounds)

Simon: The New York City Animal Medical Center sits just below the bridge at 59th Street looking over the East River into the borough of Queens. And at night you cannot see the traffic, really, but you hear it . . . iron sounds rattling out from under the girders . . . *(sounds up full, then under)* An emergency room facility at a veterinary hospital is unusual, . . . and here, the waiting room winding off of the second-floor ramp looks like something between a *New Yorker* cartoon and a more ordinary trauma center, with some dogs sitting primly in plaster splints or gauze muzzles . . . families struggling to leash in their St. Bernard from lunging at a cocker spaniel . . . and a pair of women grinding tears from their eyes, the lid of an empty cat-carrier thumping onto their chairs. The chief of staff in the emergency room is Dr. John Cave.

Doctor: So what's up?

Woman: She's growing weak, and for about the past three days, she hasn't hardly eaten a thing.

Doctor: She's about 15 now?

Woman: Yeah, well, she's in her 16th year.

Doctor: OK, what about vomiting?

Woman: Well, no, not that I know of . . . *(fading under)*

Simon: The cat is named Cassandra. Her fur is ticked brown, black, and white, and she seems quite slender, peering around the doctor's fingers as he presses the palms of his hands in carefully below her ribs. *(tape up full)*

Woman: She's very weak. She couldn't jump up on the table today by herself. *(tape under)*

Simon: Dr. Cave seems quietly, clearly concerned over the condition of his patient, who slumps without complaint as he takes her temperature, but squirms her face away from the cradle of his elbow as he tries to feed her beef liver baby food from the tip of his finger. Most alarmingly of all, Cassandra has not groomed herself in several days, whether from weakness, the summer heat, or advancing disinterest. The human equivalent of that might be a man so dispirited he refuses to rub the sleep from his eyes each morning. *(tape up full)*

Doctor: (fading in mid-sentence) . . . I can't foreclose anything. I'm reluctant to give her a clean bill of health. That's not really legitimate in a cat her age . . . *(fading under)*

Simon: And as Dr. Cave leaves the room for the paperwork to admit Cassandra, the woman who's lived with her for 16 years holds the cat's ear against her cheek.

Woman: (consoling Cassandra) I love ya . . . even if you do smell bad.

This example suggests how your writing can be used to expand the scope of a scene. The conversation between the doctor and the pet owner may be compelling on its own. But it is the writing that conveys the greater feeling—the look of the waiting room, the beef-liver baby food and the fingertip of a gentle doctor, the cat running short of interest in life, the woman whispering into the ear of a loved one. These details increase our understanding of that single line at the end: "I love ya . . . even if you do smell bad."

Balance between tape and script. Some people recommend an arbitrary ratio of tape to script. I can't. Some pieces—**news spots,** obviously, but also many essays—will be entirely script. Others, like brief sound portraits, may be entirely tape. The point is: Engage, inform, and even entertain listeners with whatever ratio is required.

Nevertheless, there are some general guidelines from which you can deviate when the story dictates. Straight news pieces commonly run about 65 percent script, 35 percent tape. Features commonly run closer to 50/50, or even the reverse of straight news—that is, 65 percent *tape*, 35 percent script. If it works, fine. Reporters who are more comfortable with tape-editing than with writing usually will use a higher proportion of tape; reporters who are more confident in their writing are likely to apply more prose. Either approach can accomplish the task.

But do not assume—as many radio professionals do—that the audience somehow listens to tape more intently than to script. My own experience over the years has been that the audience hears what is most listenable. An Andrei Codrescu commentary can draw a deeper response than a sound-portrait. Radio, remember, uses the sounding board of our minds for resonance. The first great radio pieces—by Edward R. Murrow, Eric Sevareid—are *still* enthralling to listen to, although they do not begin to meet our contemporary expectations for tape. The elements of drama and rhythm are there—in the writing.

Elements of Writing

Strive for rhythm in your words. There may not be a more difficult concept to convey about writing than this one. It has to do with bringing a balance, harmony, even a certain melody to your scripts. It is not "moon, June, spoon" writing. It *is*, I have become convinced, the way the human mind most abundantly absorbs words.

Thomas Paine's, "These are the times that try men's souls," sticks with us because of the alliteration of the *t*'s. Would it have been correct to write, "These are difficult times"? Well, a good many people have. But we *remember* Paine.

Winston Churchill could have said something like, "I'm not saying it's over, but the first phase might be drawing to a close," rather than, "It is not the beginning of the end; but it may be the end of the beginning." I like to think of some bright counselor telling him, "Oh, no, minister, too obscure," but Churchill himself knowing that the alternative also would have been more ordinary and forgettable.

Of course, we cannot—and should not—write news spots with a rhyming dictionary nearby. And even if such constructions occur to us naturally, too much use becomes abhorrent—as in Spiro Agnew's (actually, William Safire's) "nattering nabobs of negativism." But vivid, harmonious language succeeds best in the spoken word.

Describe. Probably the most surprising, best-obscured virtue of radio is what it provides to the eye. The mind's eye can be stimulated by vigorous writing, directed and filled with selected detail, which might not be noticed on film or video. It can offer the powerful sensation of "being there," by offering, in close-up phrasing, the small glints of detail that can reflect the feel and texture of an event. Describe. Here's an example from an early 1980s piece about the offices of the City News Bureau of Chicago. I think you might almost be able to re-create sections of an artist's drawing from the opening description of the inner-city wire service:

(Newsroom noises)

Simon: The City News Bureau occupies the corner office on a floor 15 stories up from the street. It hangs like an opera box over the tracks of the West Loop elevated train. . . . And in this confusing period of Chicago spring, as the afternoon warms, windows are wrenched open to the clatter of trains, sprinting past. There are no video displays in this newsroom; the desks are glazed in grime. And reporters type, sometimes listing to the side, so as not to sit on the bared inner coil of a desk chair.

(Sound of Teletype)

Simon: There are actual iron Teletype machines in here that slug, swipe, and slam out words, not squirt them quietly in inky whispers as on more contemporary units. The sound, the swelter, the crunch of soot, cigar ash, and coffee grounds aren't intended to make employees of this organization entertain the idea of spending a comfortable career here.

Royko: Most people who worked at the City News Bureau, at least in the years I was there, recall it the way Marines recall boot camp.

Simon: Pulitzer Prize-winning columnist Mike Royko, who began as an editor at City News. . . .

Again, look for the details that tell the larger story. If you're profiling an individual, it's often good to begin by scrutinizing the distinct traits of physical appearance, especially as they seem to bear on character or career. Here's the way I began an election-year profile of Timothy Hagen, the former "boss" of the Cuyahoga County (Cleveland, Ohio) Democratic organization:

Music: ("Happy Days Are Here Again")

Hagen: (into phone) Hello, is Ethel Kennedy in? Tim Hagen from Ohio.

Simon: Something used-up and unpleasant can come into the face of someone at the close of a long political campaign. It's a skin-bleaching, really . . . a bloating of the cheeks, neck, and eye sockets . . . a swelling collar of pastry, glazed doughnuts, acid-sour coffee, room service hamburgers, and dulling, late-night drinking all swallowed in full stride between engagements. Tim Hagen has been campaigning, more or less full time, for 12 years.

Hagen: Ethel? . . . How are you? . . . I don't know, did the senator call you last night or yesterday at all? You're scheduled to come into Toledo on Sunday. . . . Do you know that yet?

The odd point about that passage is that you would still find it difficult, despite the metaphors and similes, to recognize Tim Hagen on the street. My description nowhere mentions the color of his hair, his eyes, his height. But this is one of those times that radio pictures can tell more than real pictures; in the real pictures, the visual details can get in the way. For the mind's eye, I hope, my description of Tim Hagen told the listeners more than they ever could see in an 8-by-10 color glossy.

Particularize. If something is large, how large? If small, is it small as a Pekinese dog? Small as a child's tricycle? Small as a baby elephant, which, in turn, is much larger than a baby ferret? The point is to detail descriptions and actions not only for their narrative worth, but in the interest of precision and accuracy in telling a story.

In all your writing, however, be careful: It is possible to be excessive. Here's what I wrote for a piece on Quebec's then-Premier René Lévèsque:

Simon: Amiable, animated, Napoleon-small, an incessant smoker, the ash from a cigarette sprinkling onto his shoulders often, as he pulls back twines of his concrete-gray hair horizontally across the half-crescent of his head before public appearances . . . René Lévèsque's last major rally of the referendum campaign was held this weekend in a hockey stadium in Verdun West on Montreal Island. He was introduced thunderously, looking fuzzy and indistinct through the veil of flame-blue cigarette smoke, like an ill-tuned television picture. The premier seemed exhausted, wan, his skin a mottled nicotine orange under stage light.

"By the time you were done with him," said my editor, "I didn't know if he was blue or orange or what-the-hell color he was." He preferred a phrase I had used in describing a rancher from western Canada who had urged Premier Lévèsque to stay within the Canadian confederation. I said the rancher had come to Quebec with "his newly learnt French pinching like a pair of tight boots." "It's the difference," said my editor, "between the rich tapestry of an Elizabethan work, and the isolated beauty of an uncluttered Japanese flower arrangement."

Use a thesaurus, and don't feel you need to keep it hidden. Using it should be no more a cause for embarrassment than a physician's occasionally referring to *Gray's Anatomy.* The English language, as we have noticed, is rich and subtle and varied; you cannot be expected to remember all of it. But having all of it available for your discriminating selection can make your writing stronger.

Write the way you talk. A radio script is spoken language. This is not an excuse for ill-considered, sloppy language, but a conversational tone often helps to communicate. Therefore, use "don't" instead of "do not" except where the latter is needed for emphasis.

Avoid the overly complex sentences and hyphenated phrasing that sometimes finds its way into newspaper writing: "Mikhail Gorbachev, the precedent-setting Communist apparatchik-turned-reformer, today conceded his obvious slippage of public support in the rapidly dissolving former Soviet Union and resigned the presidency of a nation that no longer legally exists since the formal establishment of the new Confederation of Independent States by Russian President Boris Yeltsin and 12 other leaders of former Soviet republics."

That summarizes the story (although I know many print editors who would rework that kind of newspaper prose, too). But if ears could gag, they would do so on such clotted phrasing. Talk that way *aloud* (go ahead—try it), and people will likely say, "Good grief, get with it!"

Read while you write. As you write, read your words aloud to test the rhythm, the sense, and the ease with which you can read your words in a studio. I once worked at a desk just 15 feet behind a local sports reporter who bellowed as he did this, chanting and barking out scores and predictions. Unfortunately, he had three sportscasts scheduled each day, and it was a bit like trying to write while seated beneath the amplifier-speaker at a commuter railroad station. A soft, just scarcely audible reading to yourself should suffice—and help maintain friendly relations with those around you.

Get bogged down. If we tell ourselves, "I'll go back and get it right later," too often we never will. That's too much like leaving certain struts and braces out of a building until it's topped off, then trying to return and install them in a completed structure. To build rhythmic sentences that flow from one to the other, get your first draft as right as you can. Then you can return to your script to revise for clarity and conciseness and to smooth out rhythms.

This was the opening of a piece we did on the 50th anniversary of Twinkies snack cakes:

(Sounds of unwrapping, munching, and chewing, down for voice-over-sound.)
Simon: There may not be a more familiar, friendlier-looking insignia of American life than these tiny, twin, almost-orange confections sealed into cellophane wrap . . .

Voice: *(chewing)* I dunno . . . Twinkies . . .

Simon: They're sold over the counter in snack-shops, supermarkets, gas stations . . . in the vending machines of car washes, at cigar stands along Park Avenue . . . where they teeter over copies of the *Wall Street Journal* and *Paris-Match*. . . . They're with us always, Twinkies . . . like elevator music . . . sold, we're told, in the PX of Army camps in Thule, Greenland . . . plastic-wrapped ambassadors . . . in their way . . . from the abundance of American life. . . .

The words are meant to strike off one another in a certain order. It is necessary to have "familiar" before the phrase "friendlier-looking insignia of American life" to balance the sentence. "Tiny, twin, almost-orange confections sealed into cellophane wrap" builds from the alliteration of the two *t* sounds, into the assonance of "almost-orange," into the play of *s* sounds in "sealed into cellophane wrap." It would have been perfectly accurate, of course, to write something like "small, paired, reddish-brown baked goods wrapped in cellophane"—but not, I think, as interesting.

A Final Caution

If you begin to develop a distinctive style—a separate and identifiable voice in your work, which is your own—you may also begin to invite imitation, or, somewhat less welcome, parody. Or, worse, self-parody. This is the opening passage of a piece we did purporting to report on the success of a scientific program researching communication between homo sapiens and coho salmon:

Simon: As the spring drifts to Warnock, Wisconsin, the winter's overlay of ice, like a great white goose-down quilt spread out like the robe of a thoroughbred horse over the shoulders of Lake Michigan, begins to recede . . . and deep beneath the moss-colored cover of the lake, coho salmon begin to swirl, as the lake, slapping sloop and shore, begins again to take on life.

That is, of course, pure crap. But to those not listening with great attention, it *sounded* plausible; it sounded, unfortunately, like *me*. That, of course, is distressing. It is, however, a risk worth taking. It is the easiest price to suffer for trying to be original.

Scott Simon is host of NPR's WEEKEND EDITION *on Saturdays. During the first two months of 1991, he covered the Persian Gulf War for NPR. Simon joined NPR in 1977 as chief of its Chicago Bureau. Since then, he has reported from 49 states, covered presidential campaigns and three wars, and reported from Central American, Africa, India, the Middle East, and the Caribbean. Simon has received numerous honors for his NPR reporting including a George Foster Peabody Award for his 1989 radio essays, a Robert F. Kennedy Journalism Award, a CINDY Award, and a Major Armstrong Award. Simon also hosts public television series, including the quarterly newsmagazine* American Pie. *He holds a B.A. from the University of Chicago.*

10
Producing Features
Deborah Amos

A radio story is a shared experience between you and the listener. Preliminary research is as important as taking notes in the field, but your tape and your script tell the story and give this shared experience a beginning, a middle, and an end. The tape and the script allow the listener to share not only *your* experience but also the experience of the people involved in the story.

How do you turn hours and hours of tape into a finished radio story? This chapter will explore some of the ways to do that. There are plenty of approaches to producing a radio piece, almost as many ways as there are producers, but some techniques are common to all productions. Take what you can use, and invent new techniques as you go along.

It all begins with the tape—what you record in the field or the studio. You can engage listeners in the story only if they can identify with the people involved. Even if the story is about *something*, rather than someone, you must find a way to put a person in the story. It is that simple. Every something affects someone, and people must be heard talking about your subject. The more complicated the story is, the more this holds true. The writer John McPhee, in his book *The Curve of Binding Energy*, made nuclear engineering understandable and interesting simply by telling the story of one nuclear engineer. In one scene, McPhee had his subject explain atom-splitting as he and McPhee were playing billiards. It was a concrete metaphor that worked wonderfully. Of course, the same scene would work in a radio story, too.

A Thanksgiving Goose Story

There are many different ways to prepare a story, but there are some general approaches that are common to all of them. To illustrate them we'll use a good radio technique: We'll focus on one specific assignment—a story about goose hunting at Thanksgiving—as a way of explaining the broader principles.

Let's go back to the beginning of the assignment. For a Thanksgiving Day ALL THINGS CONSIDERED we were assigned to produce a documentary on goose hunting on the Eastern Shore of Maryland. Every winter nearly a million geese fly south to nest in the corn fields and ponds of Maryland. Thousands of hunters come to the area during hunting season; many take home a bird for Thanksgiving dinner. The story was to be about hunting.

Story preparation begins on the phone. We called the local newspapers to find out when the season opened. One newspaper had run articles about goose hunting in Maryland with the names of hunters, so most of the research was already done for us—including leads to sources (hunters, guides, etc.). Some books about hunting pointed out that: 1) hunting dogs were important; 2) hunting guides were a skilled part of the hunt; and 3) a duck/goose blind would probably be a pretty noisy place. From this research we compiled a list of all the types of interviews and sounds we would like to gather for the piece.

Before You Leave

Before leaving on an assignment, have a few interviews set up. Work the phone hard before you leave, and even harder after you get to your destination. Ask all the people you interview for names of others you should talk to. If the story is controversial, ask them who their most worthy opponents are, and then interview the opponents. Talk to officials and professionals and shop clerks and parking lot attendants. Know what you must cover, and cover those subjects with a number of interviews. It is better to have too many than too few choices back at your editing station—better to be in a position to use only your best interviews in the finished piece and to discard the others. Remember, if you just go out to fill in the blanks of a story you have already done in your mind, you won't have the story—*not the real story*.

When you are in the field and sense the story starting to evolve, that's the time to trust your judgment and to follow the flow of the story. When we asked a couple of hunters to name their most worthy opponent, they directed us to the "meanest" and strictest federal game warden in all of Maryland. We called him for an interview. We had expected a dry discussion about the law and law enforcement. Instead, he talked about the personality quirks of hunters, and he filled our tape with stories of agents hiding in a corn field all night to document hunters breaking the law. His stories were as passionate as the hunters' stories. We knew we would use this interview in the final production.

We interviewed many hunters for our goose hunting story, but one man seemed different from most of the others. He had spent most of his life training hunting dogs. He talked about his animals with a warmth and sincerity that could be heard in his voice. When he called to his dog during the interview, the dog walked over to the microphone and whimpered just loud enough to be recorded. It was a lovely moment, and it captured the contradictions of the hunter—a person who loves the outdoors, nature, and animals, but who shoots beautiful birds out of the sky.

We had recorded many hunters but used only this interview in the final story. It was a great find. The other interviews didn't go to waste, however, because each interview gave us a few more details about hunting, which we used as research. You can never do too many interviews, but don't be afraid to leave the bad ones on the editing room floor.

Location Recording

The principle of sound recording on location is simple: *Get it all, get everything*, keeping in mind that you only use 10 or even 5 percent in your completed production. Remember that each interview has a distinct environment, and the listener should be able to hear that place. The sound you record on location will set the stage. When you are in a quiet room interviewing the mayor, record the sound of the room. Use that sound under your narration. When interviewing the local elementary school principal near a playground, record some extra sound on that playground. Record the playground without the principal speaking. These pieces of sound are called **ambience beds** or **ambience tracks**. Because no foreground voices are recorded, these pieces of sound are like pictures, and they can be used as a source of sound mixed under your script. It places you and the interview in a place—the school yard, a quiet office—and it gives the listener a picture of where you are.

Record long ambience tracks. Look at your watch as you record an ambience track: Whether 30 seconds or five minutes, record as much as you may need for a long script passage, and then record some more. It is often the sound you didn't bother to record that turns out to be the sound you really need.

For the opening of the story about goose hunting, we needed to use a lot of descriptive copy to set up the premise of the story, and we wanted to bring the Eastern Shore of Maryland, the hunters, and the geese to the listener. Here's what we did:

The day before the hunting season opened, we set up our microphones in a cemetery. This cemetery serves as a bird sanctuary, and 10,000 geese were spending a quiet Sunday feeding, chattering, and flying about. We recorded more than two hours of "ambience." During those two hours of taping the wind blew, a car drove by, an airplane flew overhead, and all the geese decided to fly up in the air in an enormous swell of sound.

In the editing room we located about two minutes of useable goose squawking without wind noise or cars or airplanes. We also had the lovely piece of tape with the sounds of birds flying up in the air. We mixed the birds with sounds of shotguns being loaded and of shotguns being fired. Two pictures, the hunters and the birds, made a third picture when mixed together—a picture of the Eastern Shore of Maryland during goose hunting season. We had the opening of our story.

During our trip to the Eastern Shore, we discovered a goose-calling contest at the local high school. We recorded hours of tape at the contest. We recorded from the stage, with the microphones close to the contestants and the announcer on stage. We recorded the audience applauding a winner. We recorded the auditorium from the back of the hall and the hubbub of a crowd of people waiting for the event to begin. When we got the tape back home, there were plenty of possibilities. After the production was finished, there was also plenty of tape on the editing room floor. *The more angles you try in the field, the more choices you will have when it's time to edit the tape.*

Listening in the Field

Listening sessions in the field are also essential. It's the only way to be really sure you got what you came for. Listen to all of the material on good earphones while you're on site. If something isn't working, record it again. Better yet, to cut down on technical mistakes in the field, always wear headphones when you are recording. Most interviewees won't feel uncomfortable when you slip on the headphones if you explain they are necessary to make everything sound right. In fact, most of the people you interview want to be as helpful as they can and want to sound as good as they can—they'll do it again for you if they have to.

Finally, if you have time to listen, **log** the tape while you're in the field. Mark the good parts, and build on them for your next interview. A gap in the story may occur to you in the afternoon as you're listening to an early-morning interview. You will still have time to fill in the gap.

Early one morning, in a duck blind with two hunters, a dog, and a hunting guide, we recorded a flock of geese coming toward the blind. The guide was calling the geese closer to the hunters, and the hunters stood and shot at the birds. They missed, and the birds flew away. Tension subsided in the blind.

Much later, in the afternoon, we were to interview the hunting guide, so we had time to listen to the sequence recorded that morning in the duck blind. We decided it was probably going to go into the final piece and fashioned our afternoon interview to tie in with our morning sound recordings.

When we finished all the interviews, it was time to head home with the tape. Some words of caution here. *There can be no excuse for not getting the tape back safely.* A lot of time, effort, money, and emotional strain is on those tape reels or cassettes, so label them clearly, number them in the order they were recorded, put all of them into one bag, and *never let go of that bag*, except to have it *hand*-inspected by airport security. There is some disagreement over the relative safety of X-rays and audio tape, but I believe it is always best to play it safe.

Cataloging Your Material

Some producers like to start right in working on the story they've just recorded in the field. Others want time for the experience to settle. This should be a personal choice, but deadlines usually dictate the decision. You should try for at least enough time away from the tape so that the material is fresh again.

All the material should be logged. Use a stopwatch, or the tape counter in your recorder, to keep running times or location references for material on the tape. Make detailed notes on the content and quality of each segment of tape. Put some kind of mark next to the notes on the tape you may want to use. Some producers transcribe verbatim everything that was recorded. Some producers write little at all. Whatever you do, in the end you will need to know what you have and where it is so you can retrieve it. When it comes time to listen, you'll find you have three distinct types of tape: 1) **hot tape**, 2) **explanatory tape**, and 3) **sound tape.**

Hot Tape

Remember our hunter? All of his interview was **hot tape**. He told hunting stories, old hunter stories, and good dog stories, and it was hard choosing the best of the best tape for the finished story. But the best tape came by accident: our hunter, sitting in his chair, calling his dog. It was a moment most listeners can share because they can hear how it feels.

Hot tape makes the story interesting. Hot tape grabs your ear. It can be emotional—a strong statement spoken with energy and feeling—or, like the hunter and his dog, sensitive. Hot tape sounds like people are involved with the story.

When looking for hot tape, forget editorial aspects for a moment. What you're listening for are statements made interestingly, with humor, with passion, with pathos. This is not to say that every good radio piece has to contain tape of people crying. Emotion is easy to use and can be just a quick and cheap way to tell a story. Hot tape answers the question, "How did it feel?"—without asking the question itself, which often can be demeaning.

There are many ways to get the answer. You will hear it *after* the premise, especially if you have asked people to tell you stories that *explain* the premise. You will hear it if you have asked them to tell you the best story they've ever heard that explains why such and such is so. Always keep in mind that the premise can usually be *written* better and more concisely than it can be done extemporaneously on tape.

Explanatory Tape

Explanatory tape is a close cousin of, but not the same as, hot tape. It is tape on which a person explains the premise of the story, what the situation is, what the situation means, or gives an opinion about the issue. Explanatory tape is needed to present the premise in someone else's voice. For explanatory tape to work, the premises must be stated in complete thoughts—sentences that are complete and do not need lots of script to explain or string together. Sometimes, entire features can be put together with just the people involved in the story, and without use of a reporter/narrator. (It's much easier to do this with features than with news reports, and, as Scott Simon points out in Chapter 9, it carries some risks.)

The explanatory tape in the goose hunting piece came from the federal game warden. He told us the laws a hunter must obey, the number of geese a hunter may legally kill, and the kind of work a game warden does.

Sound Tape

Sound tape is the ambience bed. When listening to this kind of tape, it's important to have a stopwatch and to make careful notes about what sort of sound you have. You must know what ambience beds you need and how long they must run. If they are too short, you'll have to budget production time to double, triple, or infinitely **loop** the sound. (See Chapter 14, "Studio Production.")

Listen for the quality of the ambience material. Sometimes authentic ambience will not work behind your interview because it is acoustically too dense or too thin. For example, you wouldn't use an alarm bell under a narrator. Some sounds are just too heavy to use as voice-over ambience. A woman's voice will not sound right if placed over ambience of other women talking in the background; the frequencies will compete, and the ear will become confused.

We recorded many hours of ambience tape for our goose hunting production: geese at a sanctuary; the street ambience of downtown Easton, Maryland, during the annual Water Fowl Festival; a goose-calling contest; a hotel lobby with hunters milling around at 4 a.m.; a small ferry carrying cars full of hunters; a restaurant kitchen where wild goose was being prepared; the CB radio in the game warden's office. We gathered a lot and used very little, choosing only the very best sound tape and matching it with the best interviews.

It may help to think in cinematic terms. Take notes of your **full-up** (or foreground) sounds: A train whistle, a loud dog bark, a car door slam, a gun shot are like close-ups in film. They convey single images, and the listener must be able to recognize them without being able to see the image and without narration to describe it. You can use these sounds to make transitions or to end scenes. You should also note full-up sounds that can possibly be used as ambience beds.

Don't forget that once you have recorded something in a **long shot,** from a distance, you can't expect to be able to use it up front in the mix. It just won't be strong enough. But if you record as close as you can, it's then easy to place the sound in front. Occasionally, close-up sound can be mixed up in the background, using echo, equalization, and level reduction to simulate a background.

Our full-up sound in the goose piece included a goose-calling contestant practicing in a hallway, a telephone conversation between a hunter and a guide, a clock in a hotel lobby striking 4 a.m., a hotel clerk making wake-up calls to sleepy hunters, a crackling fire, a series of shotgun shots, a gun reloading, a conversation among hunters, a truck door slamming followed by the hunters driving away on their way to the blind, and a hunting dog sniffing at our microphone.

You should devise your own system for keeping records of what tapes you've brought back. The system should be keyed to plans for including the tape in the production. Repeated listening and note-taking will make you familiar with the material so that ideas for structure, and especially for links and transitions, will start to come into your mind—even in your sleep. Let it work for you: Find a quiet moment, and juggle the material around in your head. A natural starting point will become clear. Eventually, the ending will become obvious as well. When stuck for a beginning, ask yourself, What is the best piece of tape I have from the field? Put it first. Try to grab the listener right at the beginning, and structure the piece from there. (This doesn't always work, of course. News pieces, for example, are structured by the logical pattern of information.)

During this process of reviewing your raw tape, you should check your notes and research material because you are into the difficult phase of deciding how much weight to give a piece of tape, a sound, a fact you've learned. This is the time to put a lot of tape on the editing room floor. If it doesn't fit, if it's not important, if it takes away from the main points of the story, don't use it.

There is always the danger of emotional involvement in the story, of liking a piece of tape too much. You may really think it is super material, needing just some editing and an introduction and a little script at the end to sum it all up. But you may really need to let go of it for the sake of the overall story.

Outline Structure

One of those people who weighs such things once said, "There are no good stories, just good ways to tell stories." But how are you going to do it? You have now separated your tape into three categories, picked the best interviews, and stored everything else on an outtake reel. You now face a radio jigsaw puzzle.

One way to start is at the end. Find, in your tape or notes or research, an ending. In radio, the last thing is often the most important, because it sticks with the listener. It's the stopping point, the "and so," the summation, the element that pulls everything together. But make your ending a good one, not one that starts *"And so, as the sun sinks slowly in the west, the issue is still undecided, and only time will tell. . . ."* And if you have to restate what has been told in the rest of the report, then something is drastically wrong. At the end of our goose hunting piece, we used the sound of the killing of a goose.

Now back to the start. A simple way to structure production was developed at the Canadian Broadcasting Corporation (CBC) as a means of training print journalists to be radio producers in a hurry: *Structure a piece in three-element sections—sound, script, interview.* The first element, the sound, is always a full-up sound—a school bell, for example. The second element, the script, read over the ambience (such as the fading school bell or a schoolyard), is the issue of controversy. And the third element, the interview, would be the teacher, explaining why it's necessary to hit the kids when they won't pay attention.

It is possible to put together long news features using no other structure than this simple, three-element device. And, if you have to work very fast, not having to think about the structure can help a lot. Just do those three elements at a parent's home, and then do another three outside on the playground talking to the kids. It's a formula, but one that works if it's not overused.

Perhaps the **CBC style** is not your style, but do you have a style? Just when you figure out how to do a piece one way, you should be trying to figure out another way and then another. Keep on trying until you have a repertoire, a trick bag you can choose from to fit the material. Remember: *Content always determines structure and style.*

The best way, I think, to study structure for radio is to study other media. The opening and closing scenes of movies translate wonderfully into audio devices.

Short story scene-setting tricks can come from television commercials. These are often made by good people working in other media who are doing (every day and very well) exactly what you're trying to do in your radio story. *Tell the story; tell it right. But make it interesting, moving, and memorable.*

When the story's done, edited, written, and almost finished, put it away for a while if you can. Go read a book or see a movie, or work on another project. And then, without listening to the tape again or reading the script over, go over it with your editor.

This is your first chance to test the material on a listener. Read the script and play the tape cuts in your final production. You know the story well, but your editor, like a radio listener, is hearing the story for the first time. Talk about the piece. Does it explain the story? Is the tape interesting? What is missing? Is anything unclear? Is the presentation too long or without details? Your editor's first impressions are important. Use those first reactions to clarify the story.

Putting It All Together

The goose hunting story was assembled as a series of scenes. We began by stating the premise of the story: Every year thousands of geese come to the Eastern Shore of Maryland from Canada. Thousands of hunters come to the Eastern Shore every hunting season to walk in the woods, sit in a cold, dank duck blind all day, and test their skill in bringing home a goose. Next we presented the high school goose-calling contest. It explained that goose calling is an art in that part of the country.

We then used the interview with the hunter to explain why dogs are important to the process. Our hunter also gave a little insight into the character of the hunters, the locals, and the outsiders. Then it was on to the lobby of a local hotel as the hunter and his buddies gathered at 4 a.m., talking about the geese and the day's hunt. Next, the game warden revealed more about the character of the hunters and the conflict with managing natural resources.

The last scene took place in the duck blind with the hunters, a hunting guide, a dog, a couple of dead geese, and a beautiful morning sky. We used the sound of shooting and an interview with the guide.

The production was a team effort. Noah Adams prepared the script and narrated the piece, Flawn Williams recorded the sound in the field and mixed the tape in the final production, and I cut and structured the piece.

You are at the end of the process. You have structured your piece, cut it, mixed it, written and recorded a script, and had the piece edited. You're ready to put it on the air.

Listen to the way it sounds on the radio. It's always different from the way it sounds in the studio. If someone liked it, ask what was wrong, what could have been done better. There are usually methods for improving even a very good story.

The final test should only come two or three months later. Get the tape out and listen—you'll probably like what you hear.

Deborah Amos is based at NPR's London Bureau. She covered the Iraqi invasion of Kuwait and the Gulf War and often works as NPR's Middle East correspondent. Since joining NPR in 1977, Amos has reported from Poland, Afghanistan, Lebanon, Israel, China, and many other countries. She also has worked as a documentary producer and as director and producer of weekend All Things Considered. *She has received numerous awards for her work, including the International Prix Italia, the Alfred I. duPont-Columbia University Award, and the Women, Men, and Media "Breakthrough Award" for her coverage of the Gulf War. In 1991–1992, she was a Neiman Fellow at Harvard University. Her book on the Gulf War,* Lines in the Sand: Desert Storm and the Remaking of the Arab World, *was published by Simon & Shuster in May 1992.*

PART IV

RECORDING, TAPE EDITING, AND PRODUCTION

11

Field Recording: Equipment

Flawn Williams

Technical advances in portable tape recorders over the past decade have made it much easier to get good field recordings. But field recording is still inherently less predictable than studio recording. It requires that you pay attention to *where* you're recording, *how* you're recording, and *what* your listeners will hear from the tapes you make.

This chapter and the next one will describe a kit of basic equipment for field recording, how to operate it to your best advantage, how to analyze the acoustical environment you're recording in, and how to spot problems and know how to deal with them. The kit consists of a portable tape recorder, one or more microphones, and some helpful accessories and supplies. The kit should be small enough to fit into a briefcase or shoulder bag, to keep you truly portable.

Because most news reporting is monaural, we will concentrate on basic mono tape recording techniques for the reporter or producer. Stereo recording adds complexities best saved for another day.

Portable Tape Recorders

What's a portable tape recorder? For the purpose of your work, it is one that weighs less than five pounds, can operate on battery power, and can record and play back sound on tape with good fidelity.

129

Some portable tape recorders use **open-reel (reel-to-reel)** tape, while others use **cassettes**. Recording on open-reel tape has some advantages: its wider tape and faster recording speeds offer better fidelity, and you can edit the original tapes on studio machines. In contrast, field recordings made on cassettes must be **dubbed**—that is, transferred in the studio to open-reel tape before editing.

Digital audio tape (DAT) cassette recorders can make even better field recordings, although with these machines, as with standard audio cassette recorders, you'll still need to transfer material to open-reel before splice-editing is possible.

But for the radio producer on a budget, standard **analog** cassettes are probably the way to go. They make satisfactory recordings. Analog cassette recorders are lighter than open-reel recorders. And they are easier to operate, cheaper, and use less power than open-reel and DAT. So we will concentrate on helping you get good field recordings with a portable cassette recorder. Most of what is said here, however, should still be applicable if you use a portable open-reel or DAT recorder.

Basic Features of Portable Cassette Recorders

Although the exact operating details will vary from machine to machine, almost all portable cassette recorders share some basic features:

- A *PLAY* button, a mechanically interlocking button for playing the cassette (you can't press *PLAY* and *STOP* or a fast-motion button at the same time).

- Another mechanically interlocked button marked *RECORD* for recording on the cassette (often you have to engage both the *RECORD* and *PLAY* buttons).

- Buttons for fast-winding the tape back toward the beginning (*REWIND*, sometimes marked *REVIEW*) or toward the end (*FAST FORWARD*, sometimes marked *CUE*).

- A *PAUSE* button or switch for interrupting the tape motion momentarily while recording or playing.

- A *digital counter* or aid in locating particular sections of the tape (not a minutes-seconds readout, just a relative numerical reference).

- The ability to use *disposable batteries*, and also (often with optional accessories) house power, rechargeable Nicad (nickel-cadmium) batteries, or the electrical system in a car or a boat.

- A *jack* to plug in an earphone to monitor what's going on during recording or playback.

- *Volume and tone* controls to adjust the loudness and crispness of the sound during playback.

- A *small loudspeaker* for field playback (not found on most smaller cassette recorders).

Not all portable cassette machines offer adequate recording quality or the necessary features to make tapes for broadcast work. You can expect to pay $200 or more for a decent broadcast-quality portable cassette recorder. And what will you get that's different from an inadequate machine? Here are some features to look for.

There should be a jack (typically marked *MIC* or *MIKE IN*) for connecting a separate microphone to the cassette recorder. Some recorders only permit recording with a built-in microphone. This might be acceptable for transcribing meetings, but it is not good enough for broadcast. We'll describe later what types of microphones you should use, but make sure at this point that your recorder has a jack for a microphone.

There must be some means of controlling the volume level of what is being recorded. If the recording is made at too low a volume level, the noise of the tape (hiss) will be objectionably loud compared with the recorded sound. If the recording is made at too high a level, the louder sounds will be distorted and unusable for broadcast. In portable cassette recorders, there are three methods for controlling recording level:

- *Automatic Level Control (ALC)* monitors what's coming in from the microphone or other sound sources and automatically adjusts itself up or down to ensure a safe average recording level. This is a good system for avoiding distortion and noise when you can't pay much attention to the recorder during recording. But there's a drawback: The resulting sound isn't as "natural" as with other techniques. The background sounds are constantly getting louder or softer in response to the nearer, louder sound. This constant variation also makes tapes recorded with ALC harder to edit unobtrusively. (On some machines this function is called automatic gain control, AGC.)

- *Manual Level Control*, found on better portable cassette recorders, leaves the control of recording level up to you. The recorder provides a meter to show how loud the sound being recorded on the tape is. Your job is to set the record level knob at the proper position so that the loudest sounds you're recording move the needle on the meter to its highest recommended position, and no farther. Some adjustment of the record level knob during recording may be necessary, but if you can find a good setting and leave it set for the duration of the recording, the resulting tape should sound more "natural" than one recorded with ALC.

- *Manual Level Control with Limiter* is available on some of the better recorders. This offers sonic advantages of manual control, with an added protective feature. The limiter senses any sounds that would be loud enough to distort the recording at the record level you've set, and it lowers the recording level very briefly, just long enough to prevent distortion.

The most useful recorders for broadcast field recording offer a selection of level control options. You can choose ALC for situations in which you have to be away from the recorder and can't monitor what's being recorded, but when you're able to monitor, you can make better recordings using the manual or manual-plus-limiter feature.

Other Convenient Features of Portable Cassette Recorders

Some portable cassette recorders offer other features, like these, that are useful for making field recordings:

- *Automatic Shutoff* or *End-of-Tape Alarm.* This lets you know when you've run out of recording tape. Some recorders even warn you a few minutes before you run out of tape.

- *Variable Playback Speed (Varispeed)* can save some crucial recordings. If you record something when your recorder's batteries are weak, the tape may run at slower-than-usual speed during the recording. Played back later with normal power or good batteries, the tape will run at normal speed, and the recording will sound faster and higher-pitched than it should. With Varispeed, you can slow down the playback speed to match the errant recording speed and transfer the recording to another tape at proper speed. Varispeed is also invaluable for saving time by speeding up tapes while playing them back.

- *Cue and Review* are features that let you listen to what's on the tape during fast-forward and rewind, respectively; this helps locate a particular section of tape quickly.

- *Off-Tape Monitoring* lets you listen to the sound you're recording a fraction of a second after it gets recorded on tape. With an ordinary cassette recorder, the sound may seem fine during recording, but if there's some problem with the recording process or with the tape itself, you may not know it until you replay the tape. If your cassette recorder has off-tape monitoring, you can listen to what's actually recorded on the tape, while the recording is going on. "Three head" machines have this feature.

- *Noise Reduction,* such as Dolby or dbx, is helpful in making recordings with less of that objectionable tape hiss. Typically, noise reduction is available only on stereo cassette recorders. These machines can, however, be used for monaural recording too. Some are equipped with a stereo/mono switch that places one microphone input on both channels. Remember that to get good natural sound and less noise, the noise reduction must be turned on during both recording and playback.

- *Ability to Use Higher Quality Cassette Tapes.* If you've been shopping for cassettes, you've already run into a wide range of different types of tape. Greatly improved recordings can be made on premium tapes, but only if your cassette recorder is capable of recording properly on them. Check your recorder to see whether it has selector switches for different tape bias or EQ settings. (These are explained in greater detail in the next section.)

Decent quality portable mono cassette recorders with most or all of the above features are available for $200 to $300. And for those seeking excellent performance from cassettes, higher quality stereo units are available for $300 to $800. By comparison, a portable open-reel tape recorder might cost from $2,000 to more than $8,000, and portable DAT decks run from $700 to $10,000.*

Once you have acquired a portable cassette recorder, read the instruction manual carefully. Follow the step-by-step directions for inserting a cassette, for playback and recording of tapes, and for checking battery strength. You should be familiar enough with the "feel" of the recorder to operate its mechanical controls without looking at them.

Cassette Tapes

The "Compact Cassette" was developed by Philips Electronics in the 1960s. Its case measures 2.5 inches by 4.0 inches and is 0.5 inches thick; it uses tape that is .150 inches wide, commonly referred to as 150 mil tape. (More recently, an even smaller analog cassette, called a "micro-cassette," has been introduced for dictation and note-taking use. Generally, recorders using these smaller cassettes do not make broadcast-quality recordings and should be avoided.)

The plastic housing encloses two spools. The one on the left is the **feed spool,** and the one on the right is the **take-up spool**. When you begin recording on a cassette, the tape should be on the feed spool. As recording progresses, the tape unwinds from the feed spool and passes by a series of open slots in one of the long sides of the cassette (see Figure 11.1). First, the tape passes over the **erase head** of the cassette recorder (where any previously recorded information on the tape is obliterated), then over the **record** and **playback heads** (which are

*These are 1992 prices. The price of DAT machines will probably go down as their numbers increase.

often a single head). The tape then passes between a metal rotating drive-shaft of the cassette recorder called the **capstan** and a rubber roller called the **pinch roller**. When the tape is pressed against the capstan by the pinch roller, it is propelled at a constant speed. The tape then winds onto the take-up spool.

When all the tape has been shuttled from the feed spool to the take-up spool, the cassette can be ejected from the recorder, flipped over, and reinserted with the other side of the cassette facing up. Now the tape is once again on the left-hand spool, and recordings can be made on the other half of the tape (referred to as a "side" of the tape, even though sides are recorded on the upper and lower halves of the same surface).

If you've made a recording on Side A of the cassette that you want to protect against accidental erasure, find the small plastic tab on the back edge of the cassette, on the feed-reel, or left side (as viewed from Side A). Breaking out this tab will prevent the cassette recorder from being put into record mode when that side of the cassette is loaded into the recorder. If, later, you want to record new material on Side A of that cassette, place a piece of adhesive tape over the open slot where the tab was; the cassette should now record properly. The same procedure applies to the B side.

There is, on most cassettes, a small scale of dots or lines marked 0–100 just beneath the clear plastic central window. This is a rough scale for locating positions on the cassette, and is not a reference to minutes or any other accurate estimate of time or tape length remaining.

Cassettes vary in the type and quality of tape they use, duration of recording time, type of housing, and quality of construction. What's best for your purposes? Here's a guide to some of the variables.

Tape Types

There are three different types of tape currently being manufactured: Naturally, they are called *Types I, II,* and *IV. (Type III,* ferrichrome, didn't have enough advantages of its own and eventually was dropped by the tape manufacturers.)

To achieve good recording results, each type of tape must be used with a recorder that is capable of handling it properly. Most portable cassette recorders are only capable of handling *Type I* tapes, but many of the better recorders have switches or automatic sensors to select the proper recording characteristics for *Type I, Type II,* or *Type IV* tapes.

Type I: Referred to as *normal* or *standard,* also as *low noise* or *high output* tape. Requires normal bias (*see below*) and normal (120-microsecond) equalization (EQ) (*see below*). Uses ferric oxide particles.

Type II: Often referred to as *chrome type,* since most tapes in this category are made with chromium dioxide (CrO_2) particles. Requires high bias and 70-microsecond equalization.

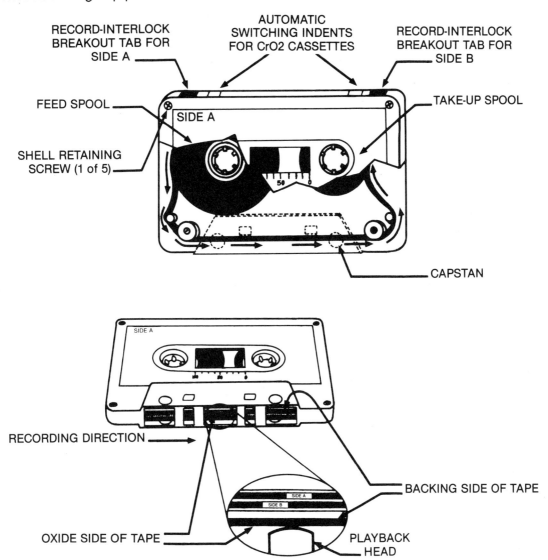

Figure 11.1. The Anatomy of a Standard Phillips-Type Compact Cassette.

Type IV: The newest, called *metal*, requires yet another combination of bias and EQ, and higher-than-normal recording power, which only the most expensive machines can provide. Uses particles of pure metal instead of oxides. The higher recording power also consumes batteries faster than recording on Type I or II tape.

Bias refers to a high-frequency signal added to the sound during recording to make the magnetic patterns flow more smoothly onto the tape. **Equalization,**

or **EQ,** refers to an electronic manipulation of the sound, which must be done in both recording and playback functions. Each of the three types of tape requires different bias and equalization settings.

If your cassette recorder does not have a switch for using different types of tape, you will have to use Type I tapes. But if it does have a switch, you can substantially improve the quality of your recordings by using one of the Type II or Type IV tapes. Although Type II tapes cost more than Type I tapes, the difference in quality is worth it. Remember, too, that you can reuse cassettes many times, so the cost-per-use of good tape isn't much more than that of mediocre tape.

Tape Lengths

Cassettes have a standard labeling system for length. The number is twice the recording time available on one side of the cassette. The most common are C-60 (30 minutes per side) and C-90 (45 minutes per side); other common lengths are C-30, C-46, C-100, and C-120.

It's hard to pack so much recording time into such a small package. To get their extra recording time, the C-90, C-100, and C-120 cassettes use thinner tape than the other cassettes. While results are usually good with cassettes up through C-90, cassettes as long as the C-120 are more prone to jamming, tape tangling, dropouts, and other mechanical problems. Avoid them.

Cassette Shell Construction

Some cassettes are held together with five small screws, while others are welded together. This isn't all that important—until your tape breaks or tangles and you need to get inside the cassette to repair or retrieve the tape. You'll find the job to be much easier with the screw-type shells. Screw shells are also an indication of better overall construction quality.

Cassette Quality

For use with most portable recorders, the best type of tape may not be necessary, but you should still stick with the better name-brands. Each makes tape of all types. The local drug store ads are always offering cassettes at ridiculously low prices, but you can be sure that the quality is just as ridiculously low. High-quality, name-brand cassettes don't cost much more, when you weigh the increase in sound fidelity and the decrease in heartache.

Tips on Using and Storing Cassettes

- *Avoid recording on the first 30 seconds or the last 30 seconds of each side of a cassette.* These areas are the most likely to have wrinkles or other problems in the tape surface, which cause momentary dropouts in the sound.

- *Erase old recordings that are no longer needed before reusing the cassette.* You can do this with an accessory called a **bulk eraser** (also known as a **de-gausser**), or by running the cassette through the recorder set in the "record" mode, but with no sound being fed in. Either way, erasing tapes helps avoid a lot of confusion when you begin a new recording.

- *Store cassettes in a cool, dry location when possible.* Cars are not a good place to keep cassettes because of heat, vibration, and dirt.

- *Don't try to splice cassette tapes, except in a dire emergency to repair a broken tape.* When you need to edit the material you recorded on a cassette, transfer it to an open-reel tape. (See Chapter 14, "Studio Production.")

Microphones

The microphone is one of the most critical components of your portable recording system. You may have to go to a bit of trouble to get a good professional-quality microphone to use with a cassette recorder, but the better recordings you get will justify the trouble.

What's a microphone? It's a **transducer**, a device that changes mechanical vibrations (sound) into electrical signals (or vice-versa, as with loudspeakers). In this sense, the microphone acts just like your ear, which translates the mechanical energy in sound waves into electrical impulses that your brain can understand. Like your ear, the microphone can pick up nearby sounds and more distant ones as well.

Many different microphones are available. Some are useful in a variety of situations; others have specialized uses. They can be divided several different ways: by *pickup pattern*, by *transducer type*, by *impedance*, and by *special features*.

Microphone Pickup Patterns

The **pickup pattern** of a microphone describes the direction in which the microphone is most sensitive to sound. Some microphones are equally sensitive to sounds from all directions; these are referred to as **omnidirectional microphones.** If you drew a picture of an omnidirectional microphone's sensitivity, you'd see something like Figure 11.2A, roughly spherical.

Another popular microphone pickup pattern is **unidirectional**. Mikes with this characteristic are most sensitive to sounds coming from the front and sides, and least sensitive to sounds arriving from the rear. If you drew a picture of a unidirectional microphone's sensitivity, you'd see a shape like Figure 11.2C, roughly heart-shaped. This gives us another name for the popular unidirectional microphone: **cardioid,** from the Greek word for heart.

There are other pickup patterns, too. **Bidirectional** or **figure-eight** microphones are sensitive to sound from front and back but not from the sides. **Hyper-cardioid** microphones are even more sensitive than cardioids to sounds coming only from directly in front. **Shotgun** or **line** microphones have extreme directional sensitivity.

Pressure zone microphones, also known as boundary microphones or **PZMs,** are the newest family of mikes. These are typically used on a flat surface area such as a table, wall, or floor, and have a hemispherical pickup pattern with a very coherent 'sound' for distant recordings. But they're not as good as conventional cardioid or omnidirectional mikes for close-miking voices. For the basic field recording kit, the most versatile and dependable mikes are omnis and cardioids.

Microphone Transducer Types

Microphones can also be described by the way they convert sound waves into electrical signals. Most common is the **dynamic** microphone, which consists of a metal diaphragm moving in the field of a magnet. The small movements caused by sound waves striking the diaphragm induce an electrical signal.

Also fairly common is the **condenser** microphone, in which two metallic membranes (one of which is electrically charged) are suspended very close to each other. Sound waves striking one membrane cause it to move toward or away from the other membrane. This movement creates a variation in the electrical charge of the other membrane. This tiny electrical signal is then amplified in the microphone. There are two types of condenser microphones. Both require power from a battery or other source to run a small amplifier in the microphone. But **regular condenser** mikes also require external power to charge the membrane, while **electret condenser** mikes have a permanently charged membrane.*

The only other type of microphone transducer you're likely to run into is one you've already been using for years: A **carbon** microphone. Never heard of it, you say? Well, that's the kind of microphone used in most telephones. Sound waves going into a carbon microphone cause the particles of carbon to jostle around and strike each other, modulating an electric current passing through them. We'll go into more detail about working with telephones in Chapter 12.

---

*You may occasionally see **ribbon** or **crystal** microphones. Ribbon mikes are generally too delicate for field recording work, and crystal mikes are extremely low in sound quality.

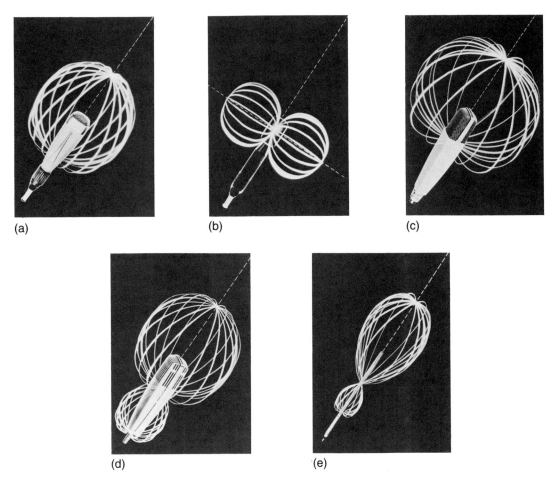

Figure 11.2. Three-Dimensional Representations of Microphone Pickup Patterns. (a) The omnidirectional polar pattern. (b) The bidirectional or figure eight pattern. (c) The unidirectional or cardioid pattern. (d) The unidirectional hypercardioid pattern. (e) The shotgun or line pattern. Photos courtesy of the Sennheiser Electronic Corporation.

Which microphone is best for your needs? There are many tradeoffs involved, and so far no one has built the perfect microphone. Some of the problems you'll encounter are:

- **Wind and blast noise.** Microphones are built to sense the tiny motions of air molecules caused by sound waves. When air strikes the microphone too hard—wind blowing across the microphone, or a blast of air from someone pronouncing a "P," "B," or other plosive consonant into the axis—the microphone produces a distorted signal, causing a loud noise on the tape, which obscures the sound you're trying to record. Dynamic mikes are better than condenser mikes for outdoor recordings where wind is likely to be encountered. Omnidirectional mikes are less sensitive to wind and blast than cardioid mikes. In addition, some mikes are built with metal mesh or plastic foam screens to help break up wind. For extreme situations, you can get an extra foam wind screen to slip over the mike.

- *Handling and contact noise.* Moving your hand around on a microphone, or placing the mike on a surface where it can pick up vibrations or concussive sounds, will cause noise. Both dynamic and condenser mikes share this problem; it is a little less severe with an omnidirectional mike than with a cardioid. Some microphones are built specially to minimize this problem. Their pickup elements are shock-mounted within the microphone casing.

- *Recording in a noisy environment.* In this situation, the cardioid mike can give you much better results than the omnidirectional. By pointing a cardioid microphone at someone who is speaking in a noisy room and getting to within a foot or so of the speaker's mouth, you can get more direct sound from the speaker and less of the general room noise. To get the same ratio of direct-to-background sound with an omni mike, your mike would have to be within a few inches of the speaker's mouth, which might be close enough to make the speaker uncomfortable. It is the cardioid microphone pattern, not its type (dynamic or condenser), that makes it more suitable in noisy environments.

So far, we've presented a mixed case for choosing an omnidirectional or cardioid mike for your field recording kit, and a fairly strong case for choosing a dynamic mike over a condenser mike. Condenser mikes, in general, have greater sound fidelity than dynamic mikes, and better high-frequency response, but they are more difficult to use in the field. If you are limited to acquiring one or two mikes for field recording, get dynamics. As to the choice of omni or cardioid, both are useful. If your budget can handle it, you should get one of each. But if you're restricted to one microphone, the omni is the safer, more versatile choice.

Other Characteristics of Microphones

There are still some details to know about your prospective microphone. One is its **impedance,** a measure of its electrical "resistance" that must roughly match that of the tape recorder input. Most microphones you'll come in contact with are **low impedance** or **LO-Z** mikes; typical values you'll see range from 50 to 500 **ohms.** But there are some mikes that are **high impedance,** or **HI-Z,** which have values from 10,000 to 50,000 ohms. These will not function properly with most cassette recorders, so you should avoid them.

Another factor is whether a microphone's output (the signal it is producing) is **balanced** or **unbalanced.** Most professional microphones are capable of operating in either a balanced or unbalanced mode; this has to do with how the mike is internally wired and externally connected to the tape recorder, not with how the mike responds to gravity. Most portable cassette recorders' microphone input jacks require unbalanced signals. Figure 11.4 shows how to connect a balanced-output mike to the unbalanced-mike input jack of a cassette recorder.

The last characteristic we'll examine is the type of support a microphone requires. The most versatile mikes are designed to be hand-held, or attached to a stand or other support with an accessory clamp. Some mikes are so large and awkward, or susceptible to handling noise, that they should be used only when attached to a stand. And some specialized mikes are designed to be attached to the person whose voice you're recording: 1) **lavalier** mikes hang by a strap around the speaker's neck, dangling at chest level; 2) **tie-tack** mikes can be clamped onto a tie or other clothing. These mikes are usually omnidirectional and can give quite good results when used as designed, but they are not versatile enough for other field recording needs. Lavalier mikes are familiar to viewers of TV newscasts, where they are valued for their unobtrusive visual characteristics. However, to get a good intimate recording for radio, you'll do better with a hand-held mike.

It's possible to make almost any of the microphone types discussed in this chapter into a "wireless mike" or "radio mike." In essence, the mike is attached to a small, battery-operated radio transmitter; then a special radio receiver can pick up that signal, and you can feed the received audio into your recorder.

This equipment is very popular in TV and film work, where it's helpful not to have a cable tether connecting the mike to the camera/recorder, or where keeping the mike invisible is a high priority. But even the best quality wireless mikes add noise and distortion to the sound, and if they are not carefully used and monitored, they can cause complete loss of sound. For most radio reporting needs, avoid wireless mikes.

The Importance of Using Quality Microphones

When you get a cassette recorder, it often comes equipped with a small, built-in condenser mike, for which the manufacturer often makes great claims. Or a separate condenser mike may be offered as an optional accessory, for which even greater claims are made. But for the exacting requirements of broadcast recording, most of these microphones are inadequate. Your field recording system requires a rugged, versatile, dependable microphone, and those qualities don't come cheap. Professional microphones offer:

* *Good sound quality*, with sensitivity to a wide range of sounds from low bass to high treble. This is called "good frequency response." Response should be

both wide (covering almost the entire audio range, 50–15,000 Hz) and flat (without much variation through the range of frequencies).

- *Ruggedness,* in order to take the punishment of field work. Most professional mikes are made from die-cast aluminum or other metals, not from plastic.

- *Protection* from some of the problems of wind, blast, concussive noises, and distortion. Most good mikes will have enough protective screening built in to protect against plosives, although they probably will need an additional foam wind screen for outdoor work.

- *Versatility,* the ability to put them where you need them and to record what you want your listeners to hear. A versatile mike can be hand-held, placed on a table stand or floor stand, attached with a clamp to other objects, hung in midair— wherever you judge to be a good listening perspective. This also may involve the use of long extension cables so the mike can be placed at a distance from the cassette recorder. A professional low impedance mike is best for this purpose.

Connecting the Microphone to the Cassette Recorder

Most professional microphones sold in the United States do not have a permanently attached cable to connect the mike to the equipment with which it is being used—a tape recorder, a mixer, or an amplifier. Instead, the mikes use a particular type of built-in jack, which has three pins arranged in a triangular pattern and surrounded by a metal collar. The corresponding plug on the cable, which "mates" with this jack, has three holes in the same triangular pattern. The plugs and jacks are called **XLR connectors**. They're also sometimes referred to as **Cannon connectors**, referring to the original manufacturer, but many companies currently produce plugs and jacks that are compatible with the Cannon XLR series (see Figure 11.3A). Plugs or jacks that have protruding pins are called *XLR male*; plugs or jacks with holes are called *XLR female*. XLR plugs and jacks are sturdy and safe. When connected together, they lock with a spring latch, so that it takes positive action to disconnect them. They are also suited for carrying balanced connections (which require three wires, including a ground/shield wire), or unbalanced connections (which require only two wires).

Unfortunately, no cassette recorder under $300 has a corresponding mike-input jack of the XLR type. Most cassette recorders' mike-input jacks are of the type that accept only "mini" or quarter-inch phone plugs (see Figure 11.3B and 11.3C).

To compound the problem, few stores carry the adapter cables you'll need. The manufacturer of the microphone will generally include a cable with the proper XLR plug on one end and bare wires on the other. Once you know what type of mike-input jack your cassette recorder has, you'll need to purchase an appropriate plug to attach to the bare-wire end of the cable. This requires soldering the bare wires onto the terminals inside the plug. If you don't have the

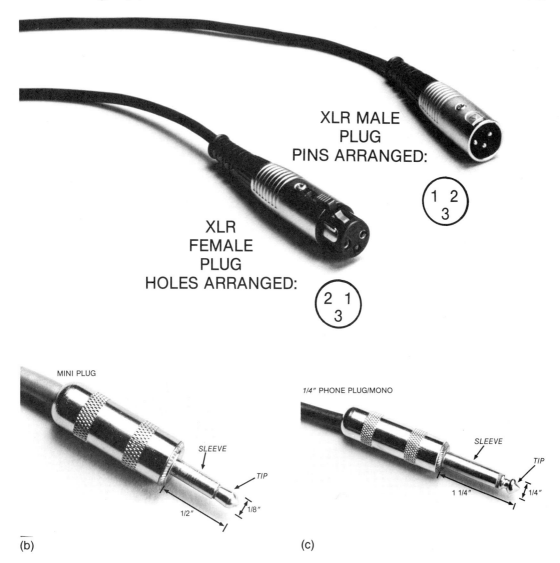

Figure 11.3. Plugs Commonly Used in Connecting the Microphone to the Cassette Recorder. (a) XLR or "Cannon" Connection. (b) Mini Plug. (c) Quarter-inch Mono Phone Plug.

proper tools for this job, or don't want to attempt it, you can ask an audio repair shop, broadcast maintenance engineer, or radio hobbyist to make one—plus a spare—for you. (See Figure 11.4 for the details of wiring the cable.) Often the adapter cable is made from scratch using a retractable "coily cord" with the appropriate connectors attached to each end. Once you have this adapter cable, your life will be much easier. If you need to move the microphone farther away from the cassette recorder than the adapter cable can reach, you can use additional cables with XLR plugs on both ends between the microphone and your adapter cable to extend the cable run as needed. These cables *are* readily available.

Using More Than One Microphone

You can record some events better if you use more than one microphone. But the typical monaural portable cassette recorder has only one microphone input jack. It is physically possible to construct a cable that can connect two microphones to one input jack; it looks like a "Y" and is called a **Y-adapter.** This technique has many disadvantages. It alters the sound quality of both microphones. It doesn't give you a separate record level for each microphone. And it's prone to pick up buzzes and other spurious noises.

A better idea, if you need to use two microphones, is to get a **mixer.** There are a wide variety of mixers available, from the small, simple kind, which can mix two to four mikes, to the semi-portable ones, which can mix 20 or 30 mikes. Basically, they all perform the same function. You connect the mikes you want to use to the mixer and adjust a separate level control on the mixer for each mike. The mixer then combines all the mikes into one signal that you can connect to the **auxiliary** or **line input** of your cassette recorder.

Another way to record two mikes on one cassette recorder is to use a stereo cassette recorder. The stereo recorder will have a separate mike input jack for each of the two channels. You can connect one mike to each jack and record them on separate channels. Later, when you get back to the studio, you can mix the two channels of the stereo cassette down to one monaural sound. This gives

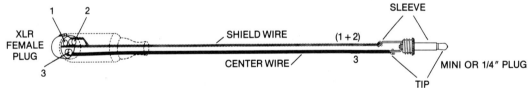

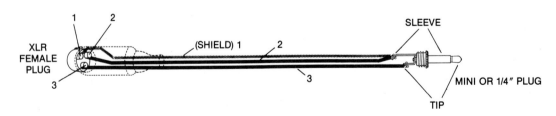

Figure 11.4. Wiring for Cable Connecting Mike and Cassette Recorder. (a) XLR female plug connected to mini plug or quarter-inch plug using single-conductor shielded cable. (b) Same plugs connected using two-conductor shielded cable.

you the additional flexibility of being able to vary the relative levels of the two mikes in the studio after the event, instead of worrying about getting an exact sound balance between the mikes while recording. There is one drawback to this method. The tape noise on the two channels of the recorded cassette will add together when the two channels are combined to make the monaural mix.

Storing and Transporting Microphones

Even rugged professional microphones will last longer and make better recordings if you take proper care of them. Keep mikes away from extreme heat, humidity, smoke, dust, and especially iron filings (remember, there's a magnet in every dynamic mike). Whenever you don't need to have the mike handy and connected, put it away—in the box supplied by the manufacturer, in an old sock, a pouch, or some other protected place. If you're carrying a briefcase or shoulder bag for accessories and supplies, set aside a protected corner for your microphone.

Accessories for the Recording System

The following items will help you make better use of your cassette recorder and microphone(s) when you're in the field:

Accessories for the Microphone

- The all-important *adapter cable* to connect the mike to the recorder. Don't forget to make and carry a spare adapter cable.

- A *desk stand*, which is a small support for the microphone. It's good for recording someone sitting at a table. Some look like small tripods, while others have a wide base and small pole.

- The *stand adapter clip* supplied with the mike by the manufacturer lets you attach a mike to a desk stand or other support.

- A *clamp* is used to attach the microphone to a podium or other upright support. Some excellent clamps are made for supporting cameras (one is marketed by Rowi), and can be adapted to support a microphone.

- A *gooseneck* can be used to extend the height of the desk stand or clamp. It's a flexible metal tube, generally six to 18 inches long.

- Extra plastic foam *windscreens* will protect against wind noise or vocal blast.

- A *floor stand* and *boom arm* won't fit into the standard briefcase kit, but they can come in handy for recording situations where you don't want to have to hold a microphone for a long time. Also, a mike on a stand placed close to someone is not as disturbing as a mike held close by someone. The inanimate stand doesn't violate personal space the way an arm does.

- A *microphone mixer* is useful for situations where two or more mikes are needed to get a better recording of an event.

Accessories for the Cassette Recorder

- *Extra batteries.* You should know how many and what size your recorder uses, and how long one set of batteries will last in the machine (in the record mode).

- A *rechargeable battery pack* is needed for longer trips when there's time to recharge between recording sessions.

- An *AC power cable* or *external power supply* for the cassette recorder, plus an AC extension cord, will help preserve batteries.

- A *car/boat power adapter* is useful if your work includes driving or boating.

- *Earphones* are used for monitoring during recording and later private listening.

- A *shoulder strap* and *carrying case* will protect and support the recorder if you're not carrying it inside a briefcase or shoulder bag.

- *Accessory cables* for special needs include a mini-plug-to-mini-plug cable or an RCA-stereo-to-RCA-stereo for connecting your cassette recorder to another cassette recorder for copying cassettes, and a mini-plug-to-alligator clips cable for connecting your cassette recorder to a telephone. (See Chapter 12, "Field Recording: Techniques.")

- *Extra cassettes.* Pack up to twice as many as you think you'll need. Make sure they're the proper type for your machine.

General Accessories

- *Pad* and *pencil.*

- *Adhesive tape,* such as the metallic-gray *gaffer's* or *duct tape,* for securing microphone cables, and such.

- *Blank cassette labels* are helpful when you're reusing old cassettes.

- A *briefcase* or *shoulder bag* large enough to carry the cassette recorder, microphone(s), accessories, and supplies. Make sure you leave room for printed matter and other materials you'll pick up in the course of making field recordings.

Maintenance of Your Cassette Recorder

The only item in your field recording kit that needs frequent routine maintenance is the cassette recorder. Check the recorder's instruction manual for exact maintenance details. However, here's a set of general guidelines and procedures applicable to most recorders:

Cleaning the Tape Path (after every 10 hours of use)

This small bit of maintenance can make the difference between noisy, distorted recordings and good ones.

- Use cotton swabs and denatured alcohol, which are available at drugstores. Ordinary rubbing alcohol contains water, which could cause heads to rust.

- Remove the cassette from the recorder, then lock the recorder in the *PLAY* mode for better access to the heads and other components.

- Clean everything with which the tape comes in contact—heads, guides, pinch roller, capstan.

- Don't use the so-called "head cleaner cassettes," which claim to clean the heads and tape path while running in the machine. They don't live up to their advertising.

Demagnetizing Cassette Recorder (after every 25 hours of use)

Heads and other metal parts that come in contact with the tape can become gradually magnetized. This can lead to loss of high-frequency sounds and eventually to gradual erasure of tapes that are played many times.

- Obtain a small hand-held demagnetizer.

- Disconnect the cassette recorder from the power source, and remove the batteries; then lock the recorder in the *PLAY* mode for better access to heads and other components.

- Following the instructions supplied with the demagnetizer, plug it into power while still a few feet away from the cassette recorder. Slowly bring it as close as possible (without touching) to each metal part in the tape path (heads, guides, capstan). Pass over each part and withdraw the demagnetizer. Disconnect from power again when you are a few feet from the cassette recorder.

- Take care that you do this procedure properly. Otherwise, you may wind up with heads more magnetized than before you started!

Maintenance to Refer to a Technician

Your recorder should be checked at least twice a year (sooner if audible problems develop) by a qualified service technician. If you work at a radio station, the engineering staff there may be able to handle these needs. Otherwise, cultivate the friendship of a repair person at your local stereo store. Things that should be checked include:

- *Record bias and equalization.* Give the technician a sample of the particular type and brand of cassette you've decided to use. Have the technician optimize the recorder's performance for that tape, then continue to use that type and brand of tape for the best results.

- *Head alignment.* Often severe loss of recording quality can be traced to misaligned heads.

It's a good idea to buy a repair manual for your recorder to help you or the person handling your maintenance know what's going on (or what's gone wrong) inside the recorder. They're available from the manufacturer for a few dollars.

Other Suggested Maintenance

- Clean the metal contacts of your connecting cables periodically with denatured alcohol.

- Tighten set screws on XLR connectors on mike cables.

- Check adapter cables for loose connections.

- Check cable insulation for damage, and replace damaged cables.

- Tighten external screws on the outside of the cassette recorder.

- Remove batteries before storing cassette recorder or microphone.

Flawn Williams has been a technical producer and instructor for NPR since 1978. His field recordings and studio production have enhanced many award-winning documentary features. He was technical director of All Things Considered *from 1983 to 1985. He is now the bureau engineer in NPR's Chicago Bureau. He has also produced more than 70 folk and traditional music albums for various labels from his live concert and studio recordings. He's written for* TV Guide, Radio World, Broadcast Engineering, *and* NPR's Engineering Update *magazines, and taught workshops at public radio stations across the country.*

12

Field Recording: Techniques

Flawn Williams

If there is one word that can guarantee you a better chance of success in field recordings, the word is *practice*. This involves not only the rudimentary practice of familiarizing yourself with how your tape recorder and microphone work, but also simulating interviews and other recording assignments. Draft a co-worker or friend to serve as a guinea pig, and stage a mock interview. This will give you a better sense of what it takes to pay attention to both the interview and the recording process. And, if you listen carefully to your recordings of these mock interviews and pay attention to the sound, you will learn to improve your technique.

Recording Checklist

Here's a list of reminders and helpful hints to prepare you for recording in the field.

Before you leave for the recording assignment:

- Load tape into the tape recorder.
- Attach the microphone to the recorder.

- Put the recorder in *PLAY* mode, and check the battery strength.

- Put the recorder in the *RECORD* mode, and check the record meter or other visual indicator. Also, listen to the recording with earphones.

- Play back the test recording, and listen to it through the built-in loudspeaker or earphones.

- Rewind the tape to the beginning; then move the tape past the leader, zero the index counter, and turn off the recorder. You should now be ready to record.

When you're ready to start recording a real interview:

- Set up the recorder as before, plugging into AC power if it is available.

- Start recording about 10 seconds before you're ready to start asking questions. This gives you a bit of the "ambience" of the recording location. And if you're recording with Automatic Level Control (ALC), it gives the ALC sensor time to sense what the average loudness of the recording will be. (Never hide the fact that you're recording. Tell the person you're interviewing when you're about to "roll tape.")

- During the recording, if you're not recording with ALC, check the record level meter or other visual indicator, and adjust the record knob to make sure the highest meter readings fall within the range advised by your recorder's instruction manual.

- Monitor the recording with a good pair of earphones, listening for cable-banging, mike-handling, or other concussive noises—wind blast, popping P's, etc. If necessary, adjust the mike position to eliminate the problem.

- Look at the tape occasionally to confirm that it is still moving.

- If your recorder has a separate playback head that allows "off-tape monitoring," occasionally throw the switch and monitor the tape to confirm that something is actually being recorded.

- At the end of your interview or the event you're recording, let the tape run on for an additional 30 seconds or so with the mike held in the same place, but with no conversation. This gives you "clean ambience" or "room tone," which will help you when assembling the final produced tape in the studio.

After you complete the recording:

- Rewind the tape a bit, and listen to the last part to confirm that the recording was satisfactory.

- If you're recording on cassette and wish to protect the new recording from accidental erasure, break out the protection tab on the rear edge of the cassette. (See Figure 10.1.) DATs also have a protection tab on their rear spine. It slides, so it can be reset more easily.

- Load fresh tape into the recorder before putting it away, so you can be ready to record again quickly if the need arises.

Recording Ambience in the Field

When you're making field recordings, "ambience" is the "sound" of the space where you're making the recording. Often, it's an important part of the story itself, a way of telling your listeners something about a place or an event without using words.

When you're in the field, listen for characteristic sounds of the environment—airplanes, machine noises, birds, children playing, church bells, barking dogs, etc. Record these sounds with no conversation or interview going on nearby, and do it from various distances and perspectives. Think in the jargon of film or television; get **close-ups**, **medium shots**, and **long shots.** You can use the close-up recordings of a sound to focus the listener's attention on a location, environment, or mood. You can mix in medium- and long-distance perspectives of the same sound behind the narration or interviews. But you can't do any of this if you don't record different perspectives of the ambient sound in the first place.

When recording voices in their natural ambience—that is, someone speaking with audible background environment sound—it's difficult to get a good balance between the voice and the ambience. If your mike is too far away from the speaker's mouth, the background sound may obscure what the speaker is saying. Also, editing the speaker's words may be more difficult, because the listener will hear abrupt jumps and changes in the background ambience at the points where edits are made. One solution to this problem is to record your interviews, monologues, and narration in a quiet location, and mix them later with the sounds for the story. (You should never make people appear to be someplace they are not or otherwise mislead the listener, but careful use of sound can bring the listener closer to the story.)

Always record more ambience than you think you ever could use. Look at your watch when you record, or you may not record enough. It's better to have too much when you're ready to assemble the piece than to have too little. Be sure to bring enough recording tape and batteries, and allow yourself enough time to make recordings of ambience as well as voices.

Controlling the Environment

In many instances, you won't have any control over where something you want to record takes place. News events happen where they happen, or where the newsmaker wants them to happen. But you can have some influence on where you conduct an interview. Paying attention to the acoustic environment can result in tapes that sound much better and are easier to edit. In general, conduct the interview in the quietest, "deadest" place you can find. If the local sound is important to telling the story, record that separately and mix it in later. Here are some acoustic traps:

- *Fluorescent lights* emit a buzzing or humming sound that may not be distracting when you're in the room. But you'll hear it when you play the tape back in the studio. Buzz or hum makes sound harder to edit unobtrusively, and the constant noise is tiring to your listeners' ears.

- *Air conditioning* (or forced-air heating) makes a great deal of background noise, which again is fatiguing to your listeners' ears. Is it possible to turn off the blowers for the duration of the interview? Similar problems occur with office machines, refrigerators, space heaters, computer hard disks, and other appliances that use motors or blowers.

- *Wind noise* can be a problem if you're recording outdoors. Try to find someplace that is sheltered from the wind, such as the leeward side of a building.

- *Traffic* is a bigger problem if you're recording outdoors. Cars, trucks, trains, and airplanes may all be a part of your story, but they can be disruptive in an interview. Recording inside a moving car also creates problems, because the pitch and volume of the engine will change noticeably during the recording.

Be cautious also about recording indoors in rooms with lots of hard surfaces: uncarpeted linoleum or wood floors, stone, cinderblock or plaster walls, drapeless windows, etc. The sound will reverberate, and one spoken word will carry over into the next. This makes for noticeable jumps in sound if you attempt to edit out words or phrases. Music from a radio or stereo in the background also makes jumps noticeable when you edit.

Paying attention to the recording environment and seeking out a quieter place to record an interview has another benefit: It can give your guests the impression that their particular interview is important to you. This can make them feel more important, and you may get a better interview as a result.

Microphone Placement and Handling

Much of your recording work will consist of holding the microphone in one hand to record your own voice, someone else's voice, or appropriate sounds. When "miking" your own voice, try to find a place to hold the mike that is close enough to make you sound "on-mike" but not close enough to cause "popping" when plosive consonants like P, B, or T are pronounced. If you're using an omni-directional mike, you may be able to bring the mike as close as two or three inches from your mouth. In any case, don't hold the mike directly out in front of you; instead, hold it below your mouth and a bit to one side. Keep it close to your chest, pointed at your mouth (see Figure 12.1 A). This will help minimize breath noise.

When miking someone else in a situation where you and the other person are standing or seated together, many of the same rules apply. You'll be searching to find a happy middle ground between getting too close (where you'll get popping P's, breath noise, etc.) and too far away (where the voice will sound distant, less distinct, "off-mike").

Social distance problems also affect mike placement. (See Chapter 4, "Interviewing," for more detail on social distance.)

The only remedy is not to be afraid to place the mike in the best place for good sound. Push the limits of social distance a bit if you need to. If you keep the mike low and pointed up, rather than straight at the speaker, it will be less intrusive.

Don't hand the microphone over to the interviewee to hold. You will relinquish control over the interview. Interrupting to ask questions or changing the direction of the discussion is more difficult if you don't have control over the microphone.

One decision you should make before starting any particular interview is whether you need your questions on tape. If you don't, you can concentrate on keeping the microphone aimed properly at the person you're interviewing, thus producing a stable aural perspective that is easy on the listener.

Unless you're really certain that you won't need your questions in the final version, though, it's much safer to record both your questions and the interviewee's answers with equal quality. You'll have to move the mike back and forth. When doing this, you need to be even more conscious of social distance. You'll have a strong tendency to hold the microphone closer to you than to your interviewee. Try to err a bit in the opposite direction by overcompensating to make the interviewee sound a little bit closer than you. With practice, you will find the right balance.

When recording with a hand-held mike, watch out for noises caused by moving your hand on the mike or bumping the mike cable. They often can occur when you move the mike back and forth between you and other speakers. But by listening with good earphones while recording, and by checking your tapes afterward, you

(a)

(b)

Figure 12.1. Miking Techniques. (A) Try miking from this angle, close to the mouth with the microphone off-axis relative to the mouth. (B) But *not* this angle—this position is the most likely to accentuate plosive pops and other breath noises. (Photos by Anthony Buttitta.)

can train yourself to hold your microphone without making these distracting noises.

Recording with Stationary Mikes

When you can choose a quiet place to do a "sit-down interview," you can avoid most of the noise associated with hand-held mikes by mounting the microphone on some stationary object before starting the interview. When recording with just one mike, this technique is useful for getting a good recording of just the interviewee. If the interviewee is seated at a table or desk, use a desk stand for your mike; have the person talk while you test a few positions to find the best-sounding spot for the mike. If the person is seated in a chair or couch, you may be able to use a clamp and gooseneck extension bar to position the mike where you need it. In this situation, a floor stand with boom arm can also be helpful. Keeping the mike in one position will avoid any jarring shifts of acoustical perspective on the tape. But be careful that the person you're interviewing doesn't move away from his original position or "talk around" the mike instead of into it.

If it's necessary to have both you and the interviewee on tape, and you have only one mike, this stationary miking technique will not work. But if you can set up two separate mikes—one for yourself, another for the interviewee—you can record both of them and get good results. Two mikes can be combined with a mixer and then recorded on a monaural recorder. Or two mikes can be recorded on a stereo tape recorder, and the resulting two-channel tape mixed together to mono later in the studio. (See "Using More Than One Microphone" in Chapter 11 for details.)

When two mikes are used, try to position yourself and the interviewee farther apart than you would if you were conducting an interview with a single hand-held mike. As a rule of thumb, *the distance from your mouth to the interviewee's mike should be at least three times the distance from your mouth to your mike, and vice versa* (see Figure 12.2). Even more distance would be helpful, so that not too much of each voice is picked up in the other person's mike.

When recording two speakers with two separate microphones, the distance of the far microphone should be at least three times the distance of the close microphone. From the interviewer's perspective, "B" should be at least three times "A"; from the interviewee's perspective, "D" should be at least three times "C."

Lavalier or tie-tack microphones can also be useful in this kind of two-mike sit-down interview. If you use this kind of mike, you still need to separate yourself from the interviewee by at least that three-to-one ratio of distances. Also, listen for noise from the microphone or cable rubbing against clothing and for the sounds of the interviewee fiddling with the mike cable. Lavalier mikes are notorious for these problems.

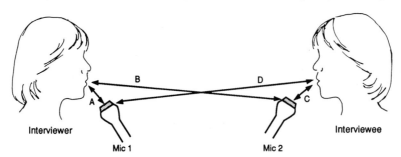

Figure 12.2. Distance Ratios for Recording with Two Mikes.

Recording a Speech or News Conference

Generally, in this situation, one or more people will be seated at a table or standing at a podium. If this is true, you should be able to get your mike relatively close to the person speaking by using a desk stand or mounting clamp. Often you will need a gooseneck extension to get the mike into the best location.

Add microphone extension cables to your mike if necessary, so that you can keep your tape recorder with you where you are sitting. It's awkward to have to get up and run to the podium to change tapes, and if you have to leave the recorder at the podium or press conference table, it's impossible to monitor the recording and make notes of index counter readings.

Occasionally you'll need to record someone giving a speech who is not standing at a podium or seated at a table. The only way to get a good recording of this event is to get the mike close to the speaker. Try to convince the speaker to wear a lavalier or tie-tack microphone, which you supply, or, if you must, have the speaker hold your microphone. If there is little need for movement, the speaker might be willing to talk into a stationary, floor-stand mike, but if the speaker is going to move around, the lavalier or tie-tack (with enough extension cable) will give better results. In any case, make sure the speaker is aware that the microphone is for recording purposes, and not for the **public address (PA)** system. Otherwise, your tape of the event will begin with those immortal three little words, *"Is this on?"* If there is a PA system, locating your recording mike near the PA mike (by clamping or taping) is essential (see "Recording From a Public Address System," below).

If none of these options is practical, you may be able to get a usable recording using a highly directional microphone such as a hypercardioid or shotgun microphone from a relatively long distance. You would probably need to hand-hold the microphone and track the speaker's movements with the mike.

Recording from a Public Address System

Recording a speech, press conference, or other event can be helped or hindered by the presence of a public address system (also called a "sound reinforcement system"). A PA system usually consists of a microphone, amplifier, and loudspeaker designed to reinforce a voice or other sounds so that large numbers of people can hear what's going on.

In many cases, the presence of a PA system will mean that the people who are speaking will tend to stay close to the mike for the PA system, so if you can position your mike next to the mike that is connected to the PA system, you stand a good chance of getting a usable recording. But a PA system may also cause the same kind of problem as a reverberant room: The sound bounces around the room and takes a long time to die away, and some sound from one word will be lingering when the next word is spoken. This makes the recording difficult to listen to and to edit. *The closer* YOUR *mike is to the speaker, the less of this unwanted background sound you'll get.*

In some cases, if you can locate the person operating the PA system, you may be able to attach your tape recorder directly to the PA amplifier. The mike for the PA system thus becomes the mike for your recording as well. You'll need an adapter cable with one end having the proper plug for your recorder's *AUX* or *LINE IN* jack (*do not plug this feed into your recorder's mike jack*) and the other end having the proper (and probably different) connection for the PA system's record output jack. Most PA systems use a **quarter-inch phone connector** or **RCA phono connector**. The person operating the PA system may be able to help you make the connection.

If you're using a direct connection from the PA system to make your recording, be sure to make a test recording to check the sound quality you'll be getting. Watch out for electrical buzz or hum, often a problem with direct connection to a PA system.

If you can't attach a mike near the PA system's mike, or make a direct connection to the PA system's amplifier, try putting your mike close to one of the PA system's loudspeakers. If necessary, you can use a clamp, stand, or adhesive tape to attach the mike to the loudspeaker. You won't get a perfect voice quality with this method, but you'll often get a more intelligible sound than with certain other techniques, such as holding a mike somewhere in the audience.

Recording from a Mult Box

When an event is being covered by many reporters, a **mult box** (sometimes called a **splitter box**) often will be set up by one of the media organizations or by the organizers of the event. This allows the newsmaker to speak into one microphone that is connected to a large box with many jacks on it. Each reporter can then connect a tape recorder to one of the jacks on the box and receive a signal from the microphone. This saves the reporters the trouble of having to set up their own mikes and reduces the visual clutter of a forest of mikes in front of the newsmaker.

When mult boxes are designed to provide your recorder the same kind of connection and the same kind of electrical signal as a normal professional quality microphone, the boxes are referred to as "operating at mike level." So you should be able to plug into the mult box with the same cable you'd use for your mike (the mult box replaces the mike). Sometimes mult boxes will have different connecting arrangements, so it's a good idea to bring along a variety of adapter cables, such as those you'd use for hooking up to PA systems. You may want to check with the event's organizers in advance to find out what type of equipment, if any, will be available.

Mult boxes can be a source of added noise, hum, or buzz in your recording. So check the audio quality of the feed you're getting from the mult box as soon as you arrive at the event. If there's a problem, let the mult operator know about it. And if the problem persists, be ready to be assertive about putting your own mike on the podium to circumvent a bad-sounding mult box.

Recording the Output of Another Tape Recorder

If you have the proper connecting cables, you can transfer sound directly from one tape recorder to another. This provides much better quality than, for instance, playing a tape on one machine and aiming a mike from another recorder at the loudspeaker of the first machine—a practice definitely *not* recommended.

The direct connection is accomplished by plugging a cable into the *EARPHONE* or *LINE OUT* jack of the machine playing the tape, then plugging the other end of the cable into the *AUX* or *LINE INPUT* jack of the machine on which you want to make the copy. Adjust the playback level and tone controls on the first machine to somewhere in the middle of their range; then adjust the record level control (if any) on the second machine to get proper peak readings.

Note that, in this arrangement as well as when recording from a PA system, you must connect to the *AUX* or *LINE IN* jack on your recorder, not to the *MIKE* jack. This is because output signals from amplifiers and tape recorders are much stronger than the signal from a microphone. If you plug an amplifier or tape machine's output into a tape recorder's *MIKE* input jack, the resulting recording will be grossly distorted.

You should, of course, listen to a sample recording—making whatever adjustments are necessary—before proceeding to record an entire event from a **line-level** source.

If your tape recorder doesn't have an *AUX* or *LINE IN* jack—if it has only a *MIKE*-level input jack—then in order to be able to connect your recorder to line-level sources such as the ones described above, you'll need a special cable called a **level-dropping** or "attenuating" **cable**, which is available from electronics specialty stores. The cable will allow you to plug line-level sources into the *MIKE* input jack of your tape recorder.

You can also use the technique of connecting the input of your recorder to the output of another recorder to help get good recordings of events in an emergency. Let's say you arrive at an event and discover that you don't have enough microphone extension cable to reach all the way from the podium, where the newsmaker is speaking, to the area where you need to sit. But another reporter has already set up a mike on the podium, run her cable over to where you both will be sitting, and connected the cable to her tape recorder. If she's willing, and if you have the proper adapter cable, you probably can get a satisfactory recording by connecting from the *EARPHONE* output jack of her recorder to the *AUX* or *LINE IN* jack of your recorder. *It is always best, however, to have your own microphone up on the podium as close to the speaker as possible.* Your colleague may stop recording or have technical problems or otherwise be unable to provide you with satisfactory sound.

Transmitting Tape and Voice over the Telephone

For breaking news stories—where it's important to get what you've taped on the air as quickly as possible—it may be worth trading a loss of some sound quality for speed of transmission back to the studio by using the telephone. Telephones have a restricted frequency response (about 300 Hertz to 3,000 Hertz)—hardly high fidelity. Much bass, treble, and intelligibility are lost. There is also a lot of background noise and substantially more distortion than you'd get if you took the tape back to the station. But, in many cases, time is of the essence, so your station should have some way of taping what comes in on its telephone lines.

Head for the nearest telephone. Don't attempt, except in the direst of emergencies, to send sound over the telephone by holding its mouthpiece close to the tape recorder's loudspeaker. The inferior-quality carbon microphone in the telephone adds distortion; background noise from the room where you're using the telephone will leak in; and the resulting sound that reaches the radio station over the telephone will be virtually unintelligible.

Instead, you should play your tape directly into the phone. Here's how to do it:

- Have a cable that can connect your recorder's *EARPHONE* output to a pair of **alligator clips** (spring-loaded clips) (see Figure 12.3).

- Unscrew the mouthpiece of the telephone. (Note: You can't do this with many styles of telephone, including pay phones whose mouthpieces are sealed. Go find another phone if you can't remove the mouthpiece.)

- Remove the loose disc inside the mouthpiece. This is the carbon microphone. Underneath it should be two exposed metal posts.

- Connect the proper end of the cable to the tape recorder, and connect the alligator clips on the other end of the cable to the posts. It does not matter which clip goes to which post.

- Play the tape in your recorder. Listen through the telephone earpiece and adjust playback volume and tone controls for the loudest, clearest sound without undue distortion.

   You may also be able to read live narrations through this setup with better quality than by using the carbon mike in the telephone. With the tape recorder connected as described above, put blank tape in the recorder. Plug your mike into the recorder, set the recorder to *RECORD* mode, and activate the *PAUSE* control. If your recorder has "feed-through" capability, your voice should be heard down the telephone line.

   Modern technology is blessing (or cursing) us with a wider variety of new telephones. With most of these, it's harder to use the alligator-clips feeding method described above. But other options *are* becoming available:

- *Modular connections*. It's now possible to buy adapter boxes that will plug into the small modular port that normally connects a telephone's handset, letting you send and/or receive sound through a direct cable hookup. Or you can use a modular adapter to hook up one of these boxes in parallel with the phone set, similar to connecting an answering machine.

- *Cellular phones.* If you or your station are investing in cellular phones, make sure you get the type that have a modular connector built in. This will allow you to hook up your tape recorder's output directly to feed tape and voice to the station. Many broadcast-supply houses sell a variety of accessories for hooking up ancillary gear to cellular phones.

- *New dial-up services.* For those situations where you file frequently from a particular location, such as city hall or the county courthouse, phone companies now offer dial-up digital circuits, which carry much more information than a standard phone line. By installing one of these "switched 56" circuits and some digital audio encoding equipment, you can file reports back to the station with sound approaching full FM-radio quality, for a dial-up charge only about twice the cost of a normal phone call.

Conclusion

There isn't enough space in this book to describe all the different recording and feeding situations you'll run into as a radio journalist. But if you've prepared your equipment and practiced with it, you should be ready to solve problems as they come your way. And if you pay attention to the recording environment, and keep your ears open for the sounds that tell the story, you'll communicate your story in an effective and listenable way—and avoid many problems during the production process.

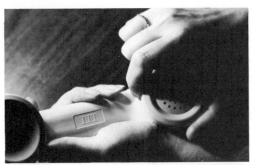

Unscrewing the receiver mouthpiece by twisting it counterclockwise. (Note: Many pay-phones are permanently sealed, and will not permit this.)

Removing the mouthpiece cover, revealing the carbon microphone.

Removing the microphone by lifting it out of the receiver.

Attaching the first alligator clip to one of the receiver's "tongues."

The alligator clip is attached in this fashion to provide the firmest connection. Its teeth grip tightly *across* the edges of the "tongue," rather than gripping the flat, smooth surface, from which the clip could slide off.

The second clip is attached in a similar manner. It doesn't matter which clip goes to which tongue, as long as the clips don't touch each other.

To prevent the clips from touching each other, rubber or plastic sheaths are recommended. This receiver is now ready for "phone-feeding."

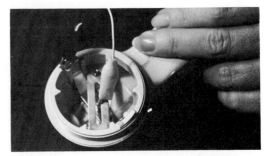

In some parts of the country, GTE style ("Automatic Electric") phones are found. They use two bars instead of "tongues."

Figure 12.3. Playing tape through the telephone.

13

Tape Editing

Jonathan ''Smokey'' Baer

Broadcast journalism is not a process of transmission as much as one of synthesis. You may spend three days on a story, record more than an hour of tape, and have to distill the entire experience into a five-minute report. Real time is different from *radio time*. And in radio, there is no more useful tool in packaging information than skillful tape editing.

When Scott Simon produced his award-winning report for ALL THINGS CONSIDERED on an American Nazis' rally in Chicago, he condensed a six-hour event into 17 minutes. He selected the telling details—not necessarily the obvious ones. And by using short snippets of tape gathered in the crowd, interspersed with well-written, highly detailed narrative, Scott gave the listener a sense of what it was like to be at the rally. Just as a painter or photographer carefully selects what to include inside a frame, he constructed a picture of that event.

But people don't have entire days to immerse themselves in all the stories and issues pertinent to them. They must rely on media to transmit information to them in short, digestible bits.

Radio time is compressed time. Translating real time to radio time necessarily compresses information. When I worked on a program about the Americans held hostage in Iran, I selected a passage of tape acquired from an American who'd been living in Tehran at the time of the Iranian revolution. He'd recorded his thoughts as he stood on the roof of his apartment building surveying the revolution in progress. The sound of people shouting in the streets could be heard underneath his voice. This segment of tape provided little practical information, such as economic or religious explanations for the Iranian revolution. What it *did* provide was *an environment for the listeners,* a context for understanding what was to follow in the program and an emotional experience to which they could relate. It ushered the listeners into radio time; it engaged their intelligence and imagination and prepared them for the "harder" segments that followed.

Imagination is the key to radio time. Radio takes place in the mind of the listener. Humorist Stan Freberg once developed a promotion for a national radio-sales convention that answered the question, "What can radio do that television can't?" He created an audio gag about how Lake Michigan had been drained and filled with hot chocolate. Then he brought in a 500-foot mountain of whipped cream and had the Royal Canadian Air Force drop a 10-ton maraschino cherry on top, all to the cheers of 25,000 screaming extras. "Try that on television!" was the tag line.

While *editing tape* is a physical task (cut the tape, join it together again), *tape editing* is a creative process that is as demanding and rewarding as fine writing. Like a writer attending to grammar, a tape editor must be careful to make clean splices that leave the listener unable to distinguish edited material from unedited material. An editor must also take professional (i.e., ethical) responsibility for content. The power to change someone's comments and leave listeners with the impression that what they heard is what the speaker said is awesome and easily abused. A good editor can listen to a passage, understand what is being said, and then present the passage in an easy-to-understand manner with the least possible distortion of the sense of the original material.

Introduction to Tape Editing

Just as you can cut and paste and rearrange written words on a page, you can also manipulate audio information with tape editing. Words, sounds—even breaths and pauses—all have locations on magnetic tape. A trained editor can mark the location of a sentence, word, or syllable and remove it.

Tape is not as easy to edit as the printed word. That's because tape editors must preserve the qualities of speech that linguists call *suprasegmentals,* the cadence and inflection of the voice. This is audible information that you can't see in a transcript but that is picked up and processed by the ear and the brain. Just listen to a bad edit. The text makes perfect sense, but your ear knows something is amiss. There may be no breath where the speaker should have taken one, or there may be changes in background sounds, or the speaker may have abruptly moved far away from the microphone.

Unfortunately, no written guide to tape editing can show you how to make an edit. But this chapter will introduce you to the process. And if someone with knowledge of editing can give you a 10-minute demonstration, you can sit down and practice on your own to become an adept tape editor.

The Tape

Audio recording tape is made of plastic. It is ¼-inch wide, and usually 1.5 mil (.0015 inch) thick (see Figure 13.1). Each side of the tape—the **backing** and the **oxide**—has its own distinct function and appearance. The backing provides structure for the tape. It holds the oxide and carries the material that actually stores the audio information. The oxide side faces the playback head, which senses the magnetic flux contained in the material on the tape.* Though the two sides have different appearances, the variety of tapes on the market makes it difficult to give an absolute rule for determining which side is which. For Scotch 176, the backing side is shiny brown, and the oxide side is dull brown. For Ampex 406, the backing is a dull flat black, but the oxide side is a shiny brown.

The tape winds onto reels of 5, 7, or 10½ inches in diameter. The largest reels are the best to use for editing because their **hubs** (centers) have the largest diameter. This makes them easy to rock back and forth. When all the tape is on one reel, you say it is either **heads out** (that is, the beginning of the tape is on the outside of the spool) or **tails out** (the end of the tape comes first, so the tape must be rewound before it can be played back). Blank tape is assumed to be heads out because it is placed on the **feed** or **supply** (left) **hub** of the tape recorder.

The Machine

The first step in making the tape machine work is to thread the tape (see Figure 13.2). Put the reel of tape (if it is heads out) on the left-hand, or feed or supply hub. Put an empty **take-up reel** on the right-hand hub. Thread the tape around the **idler arm** and **idler wheel**, past the **tape heads**, between the **capstan** and **pinch roller**, and finally around the take-up reel.

When the tape is secured in this fashion, the buttons will operate the machine if the **tension arm** (which activates an interlock) is in the "up" position. Sometimes when you press *PLAY*, this arm will drop too low and the machine will automatically stop. Be sure that the tape is threaded tautly and that the tape tension switches are correctly set. Professional machines have controls for adjusting the tension on the threaded tape. These controls select tensions for small reels (5 or 7 inches), large reels (10½ inches), or a combination of the two. It is always

---

*Sometimes, tape gets twisted and the backing side faces the playback head. You recognize this because the sound of the tape is "bassy"; there are no higher frequencies. You can correct this by simply untwisting the tape. In the unlikely event that the entire tape is wound on the reel incorrectly, just put a twist in the tape and wind it onto another reel, so the tape rolls up with the backing side facing the outside of the reel.

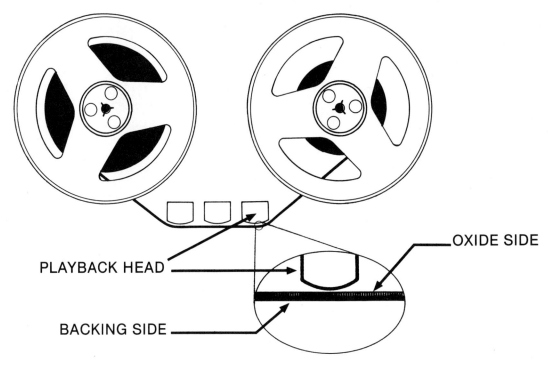

Figure 13.1. Tape Structure.

best to use the same size reels on both the supply and take-up reels. Proper tension settings will prevent stretched or broken tape.

Besides the tension-select switches, modern professional tape machines have buttons that make the machine play, stop, run at fast-forward, rewind, and operate in the **edit mode**. The functions of the first four buttons are obvious. The edit button puts the machine in the play mode, but instead of the tape winding onto the take-up reel, it spills onto the floor. Essentially, this button disables the take-up reel motor, engages the capstan and pinch roller, and overrides the tension arm switch. This function is convenient when you are deleting long portions of tape.

Reproduction of Sound

Reproducing sound from tape is made possible by the motion of the tape past the playback head. The playback head senses the magnetic information stored on the tape. Professional machines have three heads (see Figure 13.3). From left to right, they are the **erase head,** the **record head**, and the **playback head**. When you are editing, you will be dealing with the playback head.

Again, moving tape past the playback head is essential to the reproduction of sound, and the speed at which the tape passes the head is critical. Seven-and-

Figure 13.2. Tape Path. (Photo by Pheobe Chase Ferguson.)

a-half inches per second (ips) is the broadcast standard speed of ¼-inch, reel-to-reel tape machines. Other speeds occasionally used are 3¾ ips and 15 ips. The slowest speed is not normally used because it produces sound that is too poor in quality. The highest speed is easier to edit because there is twice as much space between words, but you use twice as much tape. At 15 ips, an hour-long program would require two 10½ inch reels—and a reel change during broadcast. For speech, 7½ ips is an economical and convenient speed for recordings. When working with music, where fidelity tolerances are more exacting, 15 ips is highly desirable.

Finding the Edit Point

Let's say you have these three sentences on tape, and you want to remove the middle one:

President Bush spoke about the energy situation. His manner was grim but optimistic. He indicated there would be no gasoline shortage once the price per gallon reached two dollars.

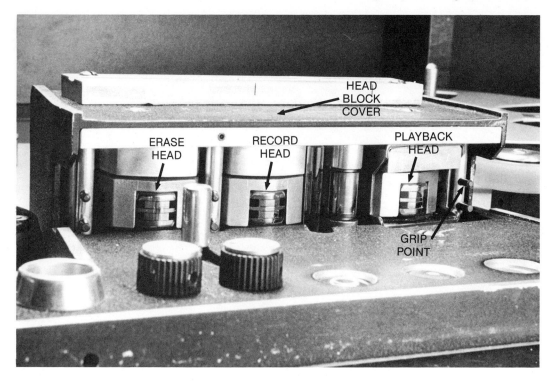

Figure 13.3. Tape Machine Heads. (Photo by Pheobe Chase Ferguson.)

Assume that between each sentence is a breath and that the recording was made in a quiet studio.

Every sound you hear played back has a physical location on the tape. Since the tape head is in a sense "reading" the tape, you know that the instant you hear a particular sound, the point at which that sound is located is at that moment passing across the center line of the playback head. If you stop the machine when the speaker begins the second sentence, you probably will stop in the midst of the *h* sound in the word "he." This is not the edit point, *yet*. There are two important skills you must develop to determine the exact location of the edit point: *rocking the tape* and *identifying phonetic sounds at low speed*.

Rocking the tape enables you, in a sense, to take a magnifying glass to the passage you're editing. To do it, place one hand on each reel, then twist both reels first in a counter-clockwise then clockwise direction. This moves a small portion of tape forward, then backward past the head. It'll take a while to become comfortable with this motion. Practice it often. First, rock the tape slowly, and the words will sound like murky sludge. As you speed up the motion, whole words become clear: ". . . situation. His manner . . ." and then the same words backward.

BECOMES

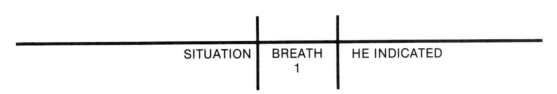

Figure 13.4. Sample Edit Point.

This brings us to the second skill: recognizing phonetic sounds at slow speeds (and backward too). In general, hard consonant sounds (B, D, K, etc.) are the easiest to locate and cut between. Softer sounds, particularly vowels, are often more difficult. There is no simple trick for recognizing phonetic sounds. Experience is the key.

There are some pitfalls to avoid. The most common error in rocking the tape is to be too cautious and too intent on finding the sound. You will slow the tape down too much and the sound will become lower in pitch, less distinct, and eventually inaudible. The best motion is one that is quick enough to make the phonetic sounds recognizable and yet slow enough to isolate the sounds. In terms of our example, instead of rocking slowly between the words ". . . situation. His manner . . ." the best motion would focus the rocking to only the point between the *n* in "situation" and the *hi* of "his." The *h* should then reveal itself as a distinct sound after the breath. Since you've narrowed the possible changes in sound (between the *n*, breath, and *h*), the one after the breath must be the *h*. It also helps to look at the tape as you're doing this. Eventually you will sense the relationship between the sound and the space it occupies on the tape at a given recording speed (see Figure 13.4).

Marking the Tape

Once you've found the edit point, you will want to mark that spot on the backing side of the tape so you can remove the tape from the head and still know where the edit point is. For this, you need a **grease pencil**. This is really a china marker, a type of pencil capable of leaving marks on slick surfaces (any manufacturer model 164T or equivalent in a light color). They are available at art supply stores. Be sure to use a bright color, white or yellow, so the mark contrasts against the dark tape backing.

To make the mark on the tape, you need only lightly touch the grease pencil to the back of the tape, leaving a small dot, or draw a small, vertical line perpendicular to the edges of the tape (see Figure 13.5). Don't press too hard. The cumulative effect of pressing hard against the playback head with a grease pencil is substantial and could alter the critical alignment of the head relative to the tape. Pressing hard also leaves excess marker material on the tape, which can get on the capstan and the oxide side of the tape as it winds on the reel. Too large a mark will leave marker material on the playback head and reduce its high-frequency response, harming the performance of your machine.

An alternate method of marking the tape, which is better for the maintenance of the tape machine but may be slightly less accurate, dispenses with the grease pencil. Once you find the edit point, grasp the tape between your thumb and index finger at what is called the **grip point**, a location that is always the same distance from the head. The edge of the head block makes a convenient grip point. You can calibrate your edit block by making a mark on the edit block that is the same distance from the cutting channel as the grip point is from the center of the playback head. Once you've grasped the tape at the grip point, move it to the edit block, being careful not to allow your fingers to slide along the tape. Place the tape in the tape channel, positioning that part of the tape gripped by your fingers at the calibrated mark on the edit block. This should position the edit point in the proper location for cutting. Be careful not to crease the tape.

Making the Edit

The **edit block** is a sort of miter box for carpenters of tape, a piece of machined metal with a specially designed channel that holds tape in place (see Figure 13.6). Across the channel, at differing angles, are two or three slots, which guide the razor blade as you draw it across and through the tape. The edit block was designed many years ago by Joel Tall, a CBS radio engineer during the early years of magnetic tape. Under his license, one manufacturer markets the EDITall, one particular brand of edit block. Mr. Tall's invention makes tape editing a simple, quick process, which makes possible all sorts of programming alternatives that might not have existed without it.

Looking at a cross-section of the edit block (see Figure 13.7), you notice the channel that holds the tape is narrower at its top than at its bottom. This allows the block to hold the tape in place. To put the tape in this almost clamp-like affair, place the marked portion on top of the tape channel, backing-side up, and,

Figure 13.5. Marking the Tape with a Grease Pencil. (Photo by Pheobe Chase Ferguson.)

with one finger, gently press the tape into the channel. Then, sliding your finger along the entire channel, just press the rest of the tape into place.

Once the tape is secured in its channel, maneuver the edit point in line with the appropriate cutting channel. If you use a grease pencil, you can slide the tape to line up the cutting channel directly underneath your mark. If you don't use a grease pencil, place the tape on top of the tape channel with your thumb at the calibrated mark on the block and press it into the tape channel carefully so you don't move the tape to the right or left. If you do this properly, the edit point should be located over the cutting channel.

Edit blocks wear down. If a tape won't stay secured in the channel, you may need a new block or one of a higher quality.

Many edit blocks have more than one cutting channel. There is always the ordinary cut, made at 45 degrees across the width of the tape. But older blocks also have a vertical cut, 90 degrees across the tape. You should not use this cut, even for tight edits where there is little or no space between words. When you cut tape, you also are cutting **bias tone**, which you can't hear but which is recorded along with the audio frequencies. If you cut this bias tone at the 90-degree angle, you run the risk of leaving an audible click on the tape.

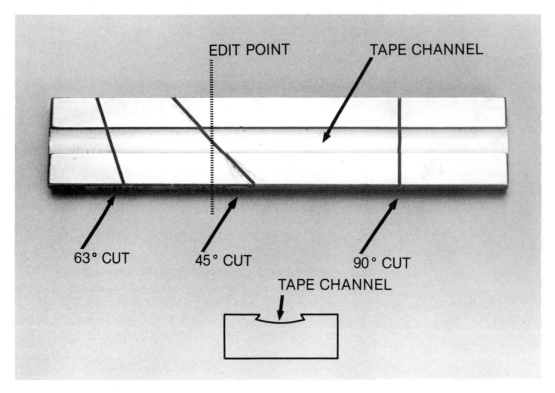

Figure 13.6. The Edit Block.

Besides the standard 45-degree cut, newer blocks have a **stereo cut** 63 degrees across the width of the tape. This allows you to cut tape with two channels of audio information (see Figure 13.8). Even if the tape is monaural, it may be **two-track**, meaning audio information is recorded along two strips (upper and lower) of the tape. If the information is identical, the tape is mono. If the information corresponds to right and left sides of a stereo field, the tape is stereo.* (Occasionally, a tape will have completely different materials on each track, effectively doubling the amount of information that can be recorded on a given reel. Cutting tape with this *half-track* configuration also cuts the other track at an arbi-

---

*The stereo cut is useful when editing two-track tape because it reduces the amount of "lag" or "lead" between tracks at the point where the edit hits the playback head. On a 45-degree angle, the material on the lower track arrives at the head an instant before the material on the upper track. Since each track is usually sent to a discrete speaker, the ear hears one channel of sound ever so slightly before the other channel. If you're working with stereo speakers, a 45-degree edit might seem to move from one speaker to the other. For headphone listeners this effect can be distracting. Cutting along the 63-degree angle, however, reduces the lead or lag to the point where the brain can no longer distinguish it on recordings made at 15 ips.

Figure 13.7. Placing Tape in the Tape Channel. (Photo by Pheobe Chase Ferguson.)

trary location. It is therefore impossible to edit such a tape without first dubbing each track onto a separate tape or section of tape.)

At this point, with the tape properly placed in the edit block, you can reach for a single-edge razor blade and draw it through the slot provided. It should cut the tape very easily if you hold it at a 45-degree angle to the surface of the tape (see Figure 13.9). Don't saw the tape. If it binds or doesn't cut cleanly, you may need a new blade.**

To join the two sentences into one paragraph on tape, you use **splicing tape**. Like household tape, splicing tape is sticky on one side and slick on the other. It is slightly narrower than its corresponding-width magnetic tape, making it very easy to apply the splicing tape without having it slop over the sides of the magnetic tape. Before applying the splicing tape, you must bring the two ends of the

---

**Whenever you throw a razor blade out, cover the sharp edge with a piece of masking tape. This protects those who have to empty the wastepaper basket.

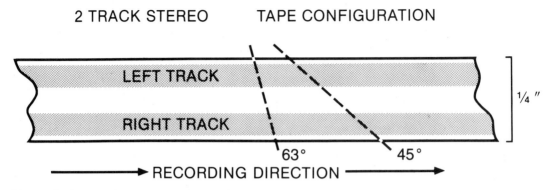

Figure 13.8. Two-Track Stereo Tape Configuration

Figure 13.9. Cutting Tape. (Photo by Pheobe Chase Ferguson.)

recording tape together with no space in between them. Apply the splicing tape centered left-to-right over the splice. Some people stick the splicing tape on their razor blade and use the blade as a lever for proper positioning (see Figure 13.10).

You can check the splice by inspecting the oxide side of the tape to make sure the pieces of tape are touching. Then, to be certain the splice is strong, rub your fingernail over the splicing tape until all the air is forced out of the space between the adhesive and the tape backing. You'll know this has happened when the color of the splicing tape resembles the color of the tape itself (see Figure 13.11). If, for any reason, the splicing tape is not aligned with the recording tape and parts of the sticky side spill out over the sides, start again. To pry apart the splice, hold the tape, oxide side up, forming an upside-down "U" with the tape, then rock the tape with your fingers so the apex of the "U" rides back and forth across the cut. This should force loose one of the edges of the cut and give you enough tape to hold to pull the splice apart.

Never reuse splicing tape. It's not worth the risk of a splice breaking. If, when new splicing tape is reapplied, some adhesive from the first splice remains on the tape, be sure to remove it by rubbing it off with your finger. (Or press some masking tape on the back of the magnetic tape, and remove it quickly.) When wrapped on a reel, the adhesive could wind up on the front side of the tape and gum up your machine.

Organizing Tape

A far more important question than *how* to edit is *what* to edit. The standard joke is, *Take out the bad and leave in the good.* By definition, it is a subjective process. But here are some hints that can help you decide:

The Outtake Reel

Some people make initial decisions the first time they hear the tape—and start cutting right away. Others listen first and take notes. **Logging tape** is more time-consuming, but for some people it may shorten the effort in the long run. It helps if your tape machine has an electronic counter; otherwise, you always will have to stop and start the tape and your stopwatch simultaneously. Jot down particular phrases, questions, or ideas along with the time into the tape at which they occur. When you're done, you have a rough outline of the tape. Using the log of your tape, it should be easy to pick out, locate, and order the segments of tape you want.

Whether you log the tape depends on the amount of time and patience you have, and is ultimately a matter of personal style. But whatever you do, don't be afraid to cut the tape for fear of locking yourself into an idea you may want to

Figure 13.10. Applying Splicing Tape with a Razor. (Photo by Pheobe Chase Ferguson.)

change. One of the wonderful things about tape editing is that you can always change your mind. The key to avoiding problems is *don't throw away those sections of tape you think you don't want*. Put all these **outtakes** on a separate reel. This way, when you're done with the first listen, you can edit the **keeper reel** to tighten, rearrange, and simplify the content. But if you find you've edited yourself into a corner or left something important out, you still can reclaim material from your outtake reel.

The outtake reel can also be a great aid during the final editing process. Sometimes you need a pause, breath, or even a sound (like an off-mike telephone ringing) to throw into your tape to make an edit sound right. Consider your outtakes a reservoir of room ambience and speech effects (coughs, *uhms, ahhs*, etc.) that you can use to maintain the natural cadence of a person's voice. You can't necessarily mix outtakes, though. The ambient sound of a certain place is closely related to microphone placement. A person's voice recorded, say, during a tour of a very large room, might change timbre as he or she moves through the room. Taking a breath or a phrase recorded in one part of the room and editing it into a portion of tape recorded in a different location may or may not work. Let your

Figure 13.11. A Complete Splice.

ears be the final judge. If it sounds natural, leave it in. If it doesn't work, take it out and look for another section of tape to help you solve your problem.

An outtake reel is also a defense against the most common error in editing—**upcutting**. An upcut results when you've cut off a bit of the sound or word you intended to keep. "He," for instance, might sound like "e" if you upcut the *h*. This is easy to repair, as long as you've kept what you cut out. Simply resplice the *h* you saved from the original material to the *e* on the keeper reel.

Of course, you don't need to keep every last bit of tape you remove from your keeper reel. Outtake reels are probably only used if you're working on something quite long and you'll be removing sections of tape that are 30 seconds or longer. Once you have your tape pared down, and the bits you're taking out are short sentences and phrases that you're certain you don't want, just toss the material in the garbage. But make sure every cut works before you throw away any tape.

Frequently, you'll be undecided about a clip of tape. If it's long, put it on the outtake reel. If it's short, you can use masking tape to stick it to the wall or some other convenient place, such as the tape recorder top. Be sure to stick the masking tape at the "heads out end" and on the backing side of the tape so no adhesive gets on the oxide side. You can label the clip on the masking tape.

Pacing and Cadence

Not enough can be said about the value of maintaining the pace and cadence of a speaker. This does not mean that everybody on the radio should speak flawlessly. On the contrary, they should speak *characteristically*. The editor should be sensitive to a speaker's speech pattern and work to preserve it, despite editing. Listen to where speakers pause, how often they say "ahh." Do their sentences run on? Are they given to multiple metaphors? Taking advantage of a speaker's traits can help you hide an edit. A well placed "uhm" can make a shift in conversation seem absolutely normal. If the interviewee tends to jump around conceptually in real time, you can use that to your advantage when editing real time to radio time. If the speaker builds arguments with tight logic, then the editing must reflect that. You can't leap to a conclusion after cutting out the keystone of a person's argument. The most important thing to remember is *let your ears be the judge*. Experiment until the tape sounds right. Your worst enemy is boredom. Tape is a lot of fun to work with, so don't let yourself become bored. Use your imagination to find the answers to editing problems.

Special Effects

Tape editing does not end with interviews and reports. You can edit music, sound effects, and background sounds. Creative editing can produce an abstract whole from diverse sounds and words. Once you become comfortable with editing, you'll probably start to play games with it. For a lark, splice together coughs, uhms, and ahhs. Cut together in rapid succession people's responses to a single stimulus—like an audio pie-in-the-face. Create a narrative by cutting together a series of sounds. When you can edit tape well, you can arrange time in ways to suit your fancy—within the constraints of journalistic ethics.

Music editing is probably the most exacting kind of editing. Shortening a song or lengthening it to fit your production needs is difficult to do without leaving an audible sign that you've been there. The key is staying with the beat. Like speech, every song has a rhythm. This rhythm cannot be violated. The best way to follow the beat is to concentrate on the drum track of a song (for pop music). You can usually hear the downbeat and drums provide sharp, clear edit points. The problem, of course, is that other instruments are playing at the same time, often overlapping the beat you can cut. Sometimes you can just concentrate and hear the drum. Other times you may have to follow a different instrument. The piano is a good one. Editing music is so complex that my best advice is to record some music onto tape and practice. Your ears are the best guide.

Tape loops are endless circles of tape. You can take a sound, music, or even a sentence, splice the ends of the passage together so you have a loop, and play it, round and round, continuously. The section of tape must be long enough to fit around the head assembly, but once threaded around the heads and between the capstan and pinch wheel, all you have to do is keep tension on it so it is tight and flat against the playback head. Hold the tape outstretched, but in the same plane as the tape deck, with a pencil.

Loops are particularly useful in lengthening background sounds for mixing under interviews. Just be sure the sound is nondescript or your listeners will notice that it is being repeated. Music can be looped, too. You can transform a particularly catchy four-measure phrase into a rhythm bed for something you want to lay on top of it. (See Chapter 14, "Studio Production," for more on tape loops.)

Housekeeping

Leader Tape

Leader tape is used for visual identification of sections of a reel of tape, such as the head, tail, or internal sections. Leader tape has no oxide, and thus cannot be recorded on. It is manufactured in several colors (e.g., white, yellow, and red), or in white and colored stripes. Each production facility has its own convention for the meaning, if any, of the different colors. One common convention:

Color of Leader	*Denotes*
White	head end of reel; or internal tape segment
Red	tail end of reel
White with red stripes	head end of stereo reel

NPR stores tape tails out (even temporarily), uses white head leader, no tail leader, and narrow red adhesive tape to attach the tail end of a reel to one outside face of the reel. The possibilities are endless. Establish whatever conventions you need and stick to them.

Reusing Tape and Reels

It is best to use only virgin tape and new reels when recording. Obviously, many stations and independent producers cannot afford to do this and must reuse tape from outtakes or recorded programs. There are several pitfalls to this practice:

- *Improper splices.* They will cause **dropouts** (lost instants of sound) when recorded over.

- *Sticky splices.* With time, the "stickum" from most splicing tape will bleed onto one layer above, causing the tape to stick to a capstan or guide, or to the next layer of tape on the reel. The listener will hear an objectionable low "wow" in the speech or music.

- *Hidden internal leader.* Although you're likely to spot long lengths of leader tape on a reel, you may miss short ones buried within a reel of used tape. If you do, nothing will be recorded on them as they pass the record head, and you may lose crucial information.

- *Bent or cracked reels.* Metal reels can be bent out of "true"; plastic reels often crack. Don't use an imperfect reel—you may lose an entire reel of tape in rewind or fast-forward mode. Tape may also get momentarily stuck in a crack in a reel and distort during playback.

Storage of Tape

Completed programs designated for medium- to long-term retention should always be stored "tails out," uniformly wound onto reels or hubs (see below), and stored under controlled conditions of temperature and humidity. Most machines cannot produce uniform winds at fast-wind speeds. See tape manufacturers' literature for further information.

Hubs

Some facilities handle tape without a feed or take-up reel, or both. Rather, they wind the tape tightly onto a small piece of plastic that goes around the hub, usually with one side of a metal reel (called a platen) underneath to guide the wind. Tapes wound onto hubs are sometimes called **pancakes**. *Never* rewind or fast-forward *onto* a hub—your tape will likely end up all over the room.

Added Considerations of Editing Tape

Once the mechanical skills of editing tape become second nature to you, editorial concerns will blend in with the technical process. Some people assume a preference for smooth editing is a preference for style, or form, over content. It is not. At the editing level, the two are the same. When making editing decisions, you are the sole arbiter of how someone's comments are going to be presented. Editing balances style and content. It is not an either/or question.

By editing tape, you can control a person's ability to express himself to others. This is a heady responsibility. Within the constraints of working with what's given to you, there is still a lot of leeway for determining what somebody means to say, what needs to be said, and what remains to be said. I believe editors must be certain that their work does not distort the intended thought of a speaker. *Don't* edit a tape to turn it into something you think the speaker *should* have said. You should aim to make it into something he or she *would* have said. The highest compliment a tape editor can receive is to have someone hear himself on a highly edited tape, and turn to the editor and say, "I thought you were going to edit this."

Jonathan "Smokey" Baer first learned to edit tape in 1968. He was working at WBFO in Buffalo, N.Y., when someone came up to him, pointed at a tape on a machine, handed him a razor blade, and said, "Here, kid, put leader on that." He's been editing tape ever since, primarily for ALL THINGS CONSIDERED. *Smokey also served as NPR's associate producer in Chicago from 1979 to 1983. He describes his work by borrowing from A.J. Liebling: "I edit tape better than anyone who can edit tape faster, and edit faster than anyone who can edit better."*

14

Studio Production

Skip Pizzi

A good radio producer must be a good radio listener. The primary purpose of producing for the radio is communicating with listeners, and the production techniques we will talk about here are merely tools to that end. In many ways, radio production is an art, and although we can discuss artistic techniques here, this book cannot teach you "radiophonic art." That must come from within you, the producer, as you develop and hone the techniques of making good radio.

As you do so, you should remember that journalistic responsibility must always take precedence over imaginative production when you're doing radio news and features. That thunderstorm sound effect on your CD may be the perfect thing for a drama or music production, but sounds in a journalistic piece must be recorded on location for that piece.

Most importantly, always remember that radio production is a means to an end. Even the most experienced radio producer can fall prey to the temptation to let production form overwhelm content. This only defeats the purpose of production: enhancing the presentation of information and entertainment to listeners.

The Elements of Radio Production

There are four basic elements of radio production—the tools that will help your radio production affect listeners the way you want.

1. Level (or "Loudness") Control
2. Mixing

3. Transition
4. Timing

Level (or "Loudness") Control

Perceptions of loudness. The ear is a complicated and amazing instrument. It senses sound in a way that is far more advanced than our best sound recording and reproduction equipment. As radio journalists, we are constantly challenged to fulfill this hungry sense with interesting sounds.

Handicapping us right from the start is the fact that although we may begin with real, live sounds, the listener finally hears approximations of those sounds. Most sounds go through a number of replications before they finally reach the listener's ear, and each replication degrades the sound. The process includes recording, playback, re-recording (sometimes several times), broadcast, and reception by the listener (see Figure 14.1). The highest quality equipment will minimize sound degradation (we will discuss ways to reduce the number of steps later in the chapter), but with any equipment, the better the sound going in, the better the sound coming out. With this in mind, let's go back to the ear, and the way it determines loudness.

There are several factors involved. First, look at an oscillograph (see Figure 14.2 A). This is a graphic representation of the electrical impulses produced by a microphone responding to sound waves. Note in this example that the peaks, or highest electrical values, occur at the oscillograph line marked +10. Figure 14.2B is an oscillograph of another sound; the maximum values also reach +10, but note that more of the other (non-maximum) electrical impulses' peaks come closer to +10 than those in Figure A. This means the *average* level of Figure B is higher than Figure A, because higher valued peaks occur *more often* in B. To the ear, the sound in Figure B sounds louder than the sound in Figure A, even though their maximum electrical values are equal. This is the heart of the concept of *"subjective loudness,"* or the ear's qualitative judgment of sound intensity.

Spectral density. Another important factor in loudness is the **spectral density** of sound. Sounds as they occur in nature are combinations of **fundamentals** and **harmonics**. In other words, most sounds are a composite of several different frequencies. The fundamental is the lowest and loudest frequency component of a sound; it determines a sound's **pitch**. Harmonics are multiples of the fundamental frequency and occur at lower amplitude levels than the fundamental. For example, a given piano note has a fundamental frequency of 440 **Hertz (Hz)**, or cycles per second, meaning that the piano strings for that note vibrate 440 times each second. Secondary vibrations—harmonics—occur on those strings at 880 Hz (440 x 2), 1320 Hz (440 x 3), 1760 Hz (440 x 4), 2200 Hz (440 x 5), and so on. The number of harmonics that occur, and their respective intensities, determine the **timbre** or tonality of the sound.

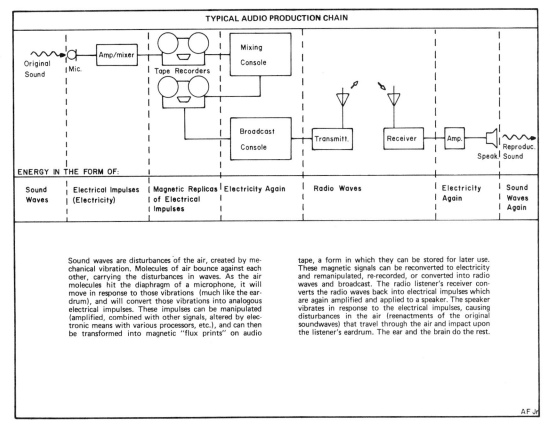

Figure 14.1. Audio Path.

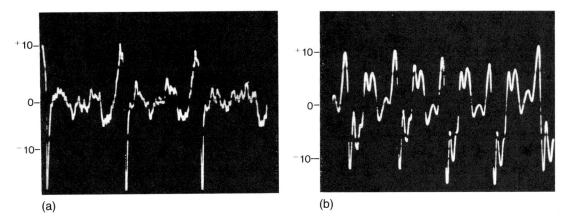

Figure 14.2. Oscillographs. (A) Osciilograph of a sound whose maximum peak energy reaches the value arbitrarily called +10. (B) Oscillograph of another sound whose maximum peak energy also reaches +10, but whose average intensity is higher than that of the sound represented in A. To most people, the sound depicted by oscillograph B will seem louder. (Photos by Skip Pizzi.)

The spectral density of the sound is the amount of harmonic energy it contains. Loudness is also affected by spectral density. *The higher the spectral density* (i.e., the more harmonics in the sound), *the louder the sound will seem to the ear.* Meters or other level-sensing devices are not sensitive to this effect. A flute (which has relatively few harmonics) and a violin (which has many) recorded at the same "level" on a tape recorder's meters will have different loudnesses. The violin will sound significantly louder, due to its higher spectral density.

The only way to determine how loud the listener will think a sound is, is to listen to the sound yourself. We will encounter various meters and other level-sensing devices, but none of them can judge subjective loudness as accurately or as simply as the ear. One of the cardinal rules of radio production, then, is *to accustom your ear to a particular volume in your monitor speakers or headphones, and leave the volume there for the duration of your production session.* The listener will not want to make frequent adjustments to the radio volume, so the producer should listen at one constant and comfortable level and adjust the production's contents to that level. This will ensure that the program has a consistent overall listening level. When a voice is followed by music, or even by another voice, be careful to match the subjective loudness of the two elements, avoiding a sudden jump or drop in the apparent level. Abrupt changes in loudness can cause the listener's attention to wander. If sound level variations require listeners to adjust their volume controls, they may adjust their tuning knobs to other stations instead.

Volume. Not only is it important to keep the monitoring level constant, but the absolute volume at which the producer listens is critical. Another phenomenon of human hearing is at work here. Studies have shown that the ear's sensitivity to sound varies with the sound's frequency. In other words, at a comfortable volume for "mid-range" (voice range) sounds, the ear usually cannot hear bass or high treble sounds as well. In addition, frequency sensitivity changes with the volume of the sound; the louder a sound is, the better the ear hears the low (or bass) frequencies of that sound, and vice versa. For example, if you are listening at a very loud level when producing a radio piece, you may think it has too much bass, but, to the audience, listening at a moderate level, the bass content will be normal.

The loudness button on some stereo equipment is designed to compensate for this effect. When it is turned on, more bass is automatically applied as the volume knob is turned down.

Loudness as a production tool. There are situations where you may want a change of loudness to achieve a certain effect. For example, we have all heard the musical portion of a radio, TV, or film soundtrack swell suddenly to heighten the emotional impact of a scene. The same scene might fall flat without it. Creating an element of surprise is another example. Here, an abrupt loudness change can provide an attention-riveting shock. But these are special cases; unless you are trying to achieve such an effect, keep the program's loudness comfortable and consistent.

Mixing

Radio production is a *dynamic art form*, meaning that it exists not as an object in space (like sculpture), but as an event in time. In this respect it is akin to music, and mixing radio elements, like creating a musical composition, involves controlling and blending volumes and placement of several different audio sources.

Mixing as a production tool. The power of sound mixing in radio production is enormous. It can present listeners with two or more events recorded at separate times and/or separate places as if they had been simultaneous. Things that happened independently can be tied together; ideas can be emphasized or paraphrased; vast distances or time gaps between two events can magically disappear. The possibilities for manipulating and juxtaposing time are endless.*

In addition, you can vary the relative loudness or levels of the sounds being mixed so that one is louder than the others. This emphasizes the louder sound, of course, but you can continually adjust sound levels to shift the listener's primary focus from one element to another, while keeping the other sounds in close aural proximity. Moreover, you can do this discreetly so the listener is not distracted by the mixing effect, but is engaged by the content.

Mixing is also used to add music and sound effects to the spoken word for dramatic or comedic effect. These effects, usually mixed below the voice level, can enhance otherwise dry readings. The so-called "Golden Age of Radio" owes much of its success to the early mastery of this technique, and to the stimulation of listeners' imaginations. Even a minimal use of these effects can evoke suspense, humor, pathos, and other emotions, along with a great deal of believability. In some sophisticated productions, dozens of *effects tracks* will be mixed in at different levels in a layering technique to create surreal or convincing radio tableaux. And in nondramatic productions, effects can add to the listener's understanding or involvement.

Transition

The popularity of amusement parks and their thrill rides attests to the fact that people enjoy being transported in exciting and surprising ways. Successful

---

*A producer of radio journalism can put all these techniques to good use, but must strive to make sure that the manipulations and juxtapositions don't result in misrepresentation of the ideas and opinions gathered in the reporting phase of the project. Mixing, like editing, requires that content of the story be the determining factor in style.

radio production takes this into account when it moves the listener from place to place or idea to idea with transitions in sound.

On a more basic level, transitions are instrumental in presenting complex ideas on the radio. An orderly sequence of voices can improve the listener's comprehension and increase his attention span. A transition from one sound to a reinforcing sound, avoiding repetition, can stress the importance of an idea. News reporters often will follow a description of an event with an eyewitness account—a simple and quick transition that works. In a more involved production, transitions may be slower or more complex.

Timing

Timing is closely related to transition. Timing is to radio production what tempo is to music. The overall length of a radio production should be appropriate to the subject. A good rule of thumb: *When in doubt, make it shorter or faster.*

Usually, listeners are only subconsciously aware that timing is influencing their interest in a program. This is as it should be; if the listener notices technique, form has overtaken content. In longer or highly produced programs, an effect can be introduced gently, then subtly intensified or enhanced as the program continues. The first use of the effect should not shock, but entice, the listener. Subsequent occurrences can employ more radical treatments and build a climax, as a good work of fiction does.

Finally, the overall pacing of a radio production must be consistent with, as well as appropriate to, the subject matter. Strike a balance between boredom and sensory overload. Let ideas flow at a rate the listener finds comfortable; don't disturb the rate once you establish it.

Preparing for Production

The real workplace for radio production is the production studio. The specific equipment and functions of a studio are not standardized. In fact, there are probably no two production studios exactly alike. But to a good producer, changing from one properly equipped studio to another is no more difficult than changing from one car to another.

One significant variable is who actually operates the equipment. In many studios, the producer does everything—both the mental and the manual work. This is usually referred to as a **combo** operation. In some studios, an engineer operates the equipment according to the producer's instructions. In either case, the producer must understand the basic workings of the studio so he can perform or explain the procedures necessary to accomplish the production.

The first step in radio production is preparing to use the studio. Studio time is extremely valuable; preparation can save more studio time than any other production technique or shortcut. Before entering the studio, you should know the exact nature and order of the work to be done and, especially in the combo situation, exactly *how* to do it. You should have a prepared script, and your tape should be edited (and leadered, if on open-reel tape), put in the proper order, and, if necessary, timed. Plan the production in the simplest possible way, not just for efficiency in the studio, but because planning usually results in the most effective production. Some production sessions are complicated, so it's often worthwhile to work out a plan on paper. Take the final work plan or **production script** with you into the studio. (See Appendix G, "Sample Production Plan.")

One decision you need to make before entering the studio is whether the piece will be *mixed* or *cut-together*. Cutting-together requires less time and equipment than mixing. It is a quick and simple method of putting uncomplicated radio pieces together by splicing. If you use this technique, the subjective loudness of all the elements must be nearly equal to avoid objectionable level jumps. If you are going to **mix** the piece, all the elements will go through the console and be re-recorded, so matching their *original* levels is not as critical.

The decision to mix or cut-together is usually determined by the complexity of the production and the time available to do it. If you are doing a simple news spot, you probably will read your script, play a recording (an **actuality**), and then read a conclusion. This piece could be cut together if the actuality has been properly recorded. If, however, you want a **sound bed** underneath the entire spot, using sound recorded at the scene, you will need to mix the spot.

It is important to assess the capabilities of your particular studio and what is feasible in it before planning a production. The number of sound sources (playback machines) available at any one time is one important consideration. (See Appendix B, "Assessing the Studio.")

Setting Up the Studio

Assuming you have made proper preparations, the first step upon entering the studio is to set up the equipment. First, clean all tape recorder heads, capstans, pinch rollers, tape guides, and other parts of the tape path (see Figure 13.2). Next, **line up** all the tape machines to the console. This means adjusting all the tape machines' meters so that a "0 VU" (volume unit, pronounced "zero V-U") reading shows up on them whenever that same reading appears on the console meter (see Figure 14.3). Adjust digital recorders' inputs so their input meters read "-15." On digital machines "0" is the maximum recordable level, so a meter setting of "-15" gives plenty of **headroom**. On analog recorders, "0 VU" is a nominal recording level allowing about 10 dB (decibels) headroom above "0 VU" for occasional louder sounds (see Figure 14.6).

Lining up tape machines requires an **oscillator**. The oscillator produces an electrical signal at a steady frequency (or pitch) and at a constant level. It creates a pure *sine wave* with no overtones at a given frequency. The studio operator can control both of these parameters. Select a frequency somewhere in the center of the audio range, usually **1 kilohertz (1 kHz,** also known as **1000 Hertz),** although you can use anywhere from 400 to 2000 Hz. Send the output of the oscillator into the console (on some consoles it is a built-in feature), and adjust it to make the console meter(s) read "0 VU." Then, set each tape machine's monitor switch (see Fig. 14.4) to *SOURCE, INPUT* or *RECORD* (the name used for this setting varies from one brand of tape recorder to another). Adjust the *input level*, or *record level*, or *gain* (all names for the same thing) so the tape machine's meter reads "0 VU." (If the tape machine is two-track or multi-track, follow these procedures for each channel.) The tape machine is now lined up to the console.

Perform this process on all tape machines that are hooked up to record from the console. Now, as you observe good levels on the console VU meter, you can be sure the tape machines recording audio from the console have the same level.

Achieving Unity Gain

Next, set the output of each open reel tape machine in the calibrate position (*CAL* or *SRL*). (For machines without a calibrate function, see the set-up procedures

Figure 14.3. 0 VU Meter Reading. A "0 VU" reading on the standard VU (volume unit) meter. Note that the scale above the line is calibrated in dB (decibels) relative to "0" or "reference level," and the scale below the line is calibrated in percentage of modulation for broadcast transmitters. "0 VU" equals 100% modulation. (Photo by Skip Pizzi.)

at the end of this section.) With the oscillator still sending a "0 VU" level, record a minute or so of the 0 VU tone from the oscillator onto a blank tape *of the type for which the machine is set.** Record the tone at the tape speed that will be used in the production. Professional broadcasters in the United States use 7½ inches per second (ips) or 19 centimeters per second (cm/s) for most voice recording and 15 ips (38 cm/s) for music. As the tone is being recorded, change the monitor switch to respond to signals coming from the tape (*TAPE, REPRO* or *PB*). This does not affect the recording; it only changes the point to which the meter and output are connected. When the switch is made, the meter should remain at "0 VU," or at least stay between -1 VU and +1 VU. If the meter moves by more than this when you switch from *SOURCE* to *TAPE*, or *INPUT* to *PB*, etc., and the output is in the calibrate position while recording a mid-frequency (1 kHz) tone, then the tape machine is improperly set up or malfunctioning. If the meter stays at approximately 0 VU after switching to *PB* or *TAPE*, adjust the *RECORD GAIN* or *INPUT LEVEL* as needed to return the meter to exactly "0 VU." An adjustment of the knob will take a half-second or so to show up on the meter, because the knob you are adjusting is changing the level going *onto* the tape via the record head, but what you are watching on the meter is coming *off* the tape from the playback head (see Figure 14.4). The delayed reaction results from the time it takes for any point on the tape to travel from the record head to the playback head. (This phenomenon also provides for some interesting special effects—see Appendix E.)

Now you have recorded a bit of *0 level tone* on the recording machine. You will use this tape to align the output of all playback machines. Rewind the tone tape and turn off the oscillator. Next, play back the tone tape on the machine it was recorded on. Adjust the tape machine's *OUTPUT*, if necessary, so the meters read "0 VU." Adjust the console **fader** (also known as a **pot**, short for potentiometer) that the tape machine is playing back through until the console meter reads "0 VU." Mark the position of the fader at this point.

Then, rewind the tone tape, and use it to repeat this process on each playback machine. Don't forget to check the *OUTPUT* of each playback machine before moving to the console. Again, mark each console fader at the point at which "0 VU" tone on tape makes the console meter also read "0 VU." Marking the console (using a wax pencil, magic marker on masking tape, colored adhesive tape or any other non-defacing technique) allows you to reset the fader to the same point at any time. When the fader is set to this mark, **unity gain** is

---

*To "set up" a tape machine, a technician adjusts its *playback* electronics to an industry-standardized test tape. Once adjusted, any tape will play back properly on this machine. The technician also records tones from an oscillator onto blank tape, and adjusts the *recording* functions of the machine to adhere to the same standard. These adjustments will differ from one type of tape stock to another. Therefore, the type of tape used to adjust the machine is the *only* kind of tape that should be used for *recording* on that machine, but any kind of tape can be played back with proper fidelity.

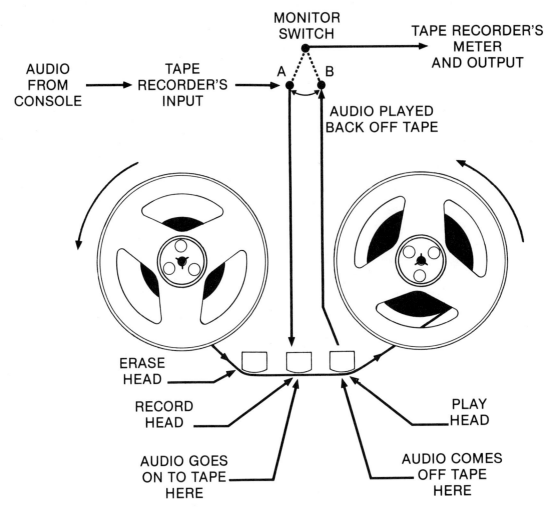

MONITOR
SWITCH

TAPE RECORDER'S
METER
AND OUTPUT

AUDIO
FROM
CONSOLE

TAPE
RECORDER'S
INPUT

A   B

AUDIO PLAYED
BACK OFF TAPE

ERASE
HEAD

RECORD
HEAD

PLAY
HEAD

AUDIO GOES
ON TO TAPE
HERE

AUDIO COMES
OFF TAPE
HERE

Figure 14.4.   Tape Monitor Switch Position. The monitor switch selects the point at which audio is sampled and sent to the meter and output. In position A, the meter and output get audio as it comes into the recorder from a mixer or microphone. In position B, meter and output get audio as it comes off the tape. For playing back a tape, the monitor must be in position B. For recording, the switch can be in either position. Position A is called *SOURCE, INPUT,* or *RECORD* depending on your tape machine; Position B is called *TAPE, REPRO* or *PB.*

achieved. (It is called "unity" because nothing is added or subtracted from the level of the signal as it travels from one tape machine to another through the console; in mathematical terminology, unity means multiplied by a factor of one, i.e., equivalence.) By the way, the unity gain point should fall between 12 o'clock and three o'clock on rotary faders, and around the -10 to -15 mark on linear faders

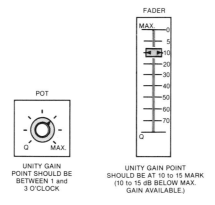

Figure 14.5. Unity Gain Point on Pots or Faders. The unity gain points are shown in their appropriate positions for rotary pots or linear faders.

(see Figure 14.5). If this is not the case, the console is not set up properly and needs adjustment by electronics maintenance personnel.

The preceding set-up procedures may seem rather complex, but after you perform them a few times, they will become routine. Until they do, you may want to refer to this abbreviated review of set-up procedures:

1. Use an oscillator to set console meter to "0 VU" with approximately 1 kHz tone.
2. Set tape monitor switches to *SOURCE* or *INPUT*, and adjust record levels (inputs) to "0 VU" on tape machines' meters.
3. Place tape machines' outputs in *CAL* or *SRL* position.
4. Change monitor switches to *TAPE* or *PB*, and readjust record gain to "0 VU" on meters if necessary.
5. Record about 60 seconds of tone onto blank tape of proper type.
6. Turn off oscillator, and rewind tapes.
7. Play back tone tape on each tape machine, setting each console fader for "0 VU" on console meter.
8. Mark console at each fader where "0 VU" point occurs.

Preparing To Mix

Once the set-up is complete, the next step is to dub any music or other material on vinyl records onto tape. This not only saves time during retakes but saves records as well. Repeatedly playing the same section of a record in a short

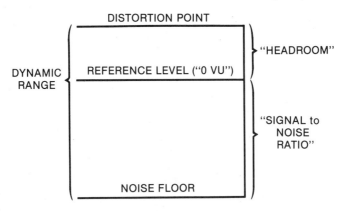

Figure 14.6. Dynamic Range Chart. This is a conceptual diagram of the limitations in volume extremes inherent in all audio systems. Too high a level causes distortion; too low a level causes the audio to be masked by system noise. A happy medium, or "reference level," has both sufficient headroom (15 to 20 dB) between reference level and distortion and sufficient signal-to-noise ratio (60 dB or more) between reference level and the system noise level, or "noise floor."

period of time causes serious, irreparable damage to the record surface. This is especially disturbing when the dramatic impact of a sound effect is accompanied by the easily recognizable clicks and pops of record-surface noise. Clean records thoroughly before dubbing them. (Repeated playings of compact discs will not damage them, but you may obtain more precise control over any music and effects by transferring them to tape first.)

When dubbing the LP or CD, make sure the level going to the tape is optimum, peaking the VU meters between -3 and 0 VU. (If your console is equipped with peak reading or other meters instead of or in addition to VU meters, see Appendix C.)

Now place the various elements on the tape machines or cart machines in accordance with your production plan. A **cart**, or cartridge machine, is a tape deck that uses tape contained in a plastic cartridge. The tape is wound in a continuous loop inside the cartridge. The major advantage of the cart is its ability to "re-cue" itself, by means of an inaudible tone put on the cart when it is recorded. If any carts need to be recorded, they should be done at this time. Carts are especially useful for inserting sound effects. A wide assortment of them can be kept on hand and dropped into a mix quickly and conveniently, because they don't require cueing or threading and have a fast start-up.

There are disadvantages to carts, however. Their wow and flutter (speed variations) can be audible, especially in music. Their noise and distortion performance is usually inferior to reel-to-reel recording, and their high-frequency response is often deficient as well. (In stereo work, tape skewing, an up-and-down motion of the tape as it passes the heads, can cause an even greater problem—**phase cancellation** of the high frequencies for the mono listener. Phase cancellation occurs when the time relationship between two signals is not synchronous. When the two signals are combined [summed], some frequencies are lost.)

Recording Voices

For complex productions, make sure the voice tracks are precisely recorded, edited, and leadered. For simple sessions, you may be able to record voice tracks live as you produce your piece. If you have an engineer in the control room, give him the tape elements with a script, then go into the studio to read the voice tracks.*

When **tracking** (recording voice), the voice level and loudness must match the level and loudness of other principal elements. If the piece you're producing is going to be cut together (as opposed to mixed), play the actuality cut(s) at unity gain (adjust the tape playback fader on the console to the mark you made during set-up), and match your voice level (by ear) to the tape level by adjusting the microphone fader.

Watch the meter to ensure you are not exceeding any electronic parameters, but perform the **level matching** process by listening. This may be difficult in a combo studio, when you have to listen live to your own voice on headphones. Do a little trial and error. Play the first sentence of a sample voice track recording back at unity gain and check its loudness against the first actuality at unity gain. Once the levels are balanced, record your voice tracks onto blank tape, and assemble the piece by intercutting them with your previously recorded actuality. (There is no need to rerecord the actuality, unless it is a complicated production or the tape is not in suitable condition and needs fixing.) For mixing, especially if the work is to be done combo, it is usually best to prerecord your voice tracks.

Beware of **plosives,** also known as P-pops. You can avoid these by positioning the microphone off to one side of your mouth rather than dead center in front of you. You can feel the ''plosive region'' by placing your open palm two or three inches in front of your mouth as you say the letter *p*. You will feel the sudden burst of air hitting your palm, but if you continue to make that sound and move your hand gradually to one side, you will find that the width of the wind-burst is limited and is barely noticeable at the corners of your mouth. This

---

*The term ''studio'' is often used here to denote both the control room and the studio per se. The control room is where the console and tape machines are located; the studio is the adjacent room used only for microphone pickup of acoustically produced sound—voices, instruments, etc. In the combo situation, the control room also serves as a studio.

is where you should place the microphone.** (See Chapter 12, "Field Recording: Techniques," for illustrations of mike placement techniques.)

Sibilance is a related problem. It is the excessively sharp whistling sound associated with the letters *c*, *f*, and *s*. When you say words containing these sounds, you force air through very narrow mouth spaces. Close miking accentuates this sound, but to eliminate it you would have to move too far away from the microphone for acceptable voice tracking. However, an electronic device called a **dynamic sibilance controller,** more commonly known as a **de-esser,** can help. (See Appendix E.)

Mixing Techniques

Once you are ready to mix, just follow your plan, remembering to set a comfortable monitoring level and leave it there for the entire session. When fading sounds down, take them down smoothly and decisively, and leave them at a level that doesn't fight with the new sound introduced over them, but not so low that they are indistinguishable.

Get into the habit of using the *RECORD SAFETY* or *SAFE* switches when loading tapes onto decks for playback. These switches ensure that the record functions, which would erase the tape, cannot be accidentally engaged. In fact, it's best to keep your tape decks in the *SAFE* mode, and only place a machine into the *READY* mode when you are preparing to record.

A/B Reels

If you have five elements to be placed consecutively with a bit of overlapping of each, they can be set up on **A/B reels,** where elements #1, #3, and #5 are on one reel (the A reel), and elements #2 and #4 are on a second reel (the B reel). Separate all elements by two or three seconds of leader tape. Put each reel onto a different tape machine, and alternate the cuts. As cut #1 ends on the A reel, start cut #2 (the first cut on the B reel) on the other machine. Meanwhile, stop the first machine and cue up cut #3 in the cue or audition channel of the console. As cut #2 runs out, start the first machine again with cut #3. Now cue cut #4 on machine two, and so on (see Figure 14.7).

**Other consonants are plosives as well. The letter *b* makes a plosive burst in the same area as the p, but it is usually much less severe. The *t* and the *k* can be a problem, but their plosive region is located below that of the *p*. Using the open palm again, the rush of air from *t* or *k* can be felt out in front of the chin, as it proceeds at a downward angle from the mouth. This is another reason to select the corner of the mouth as the "plosive-free" area for mike placement.

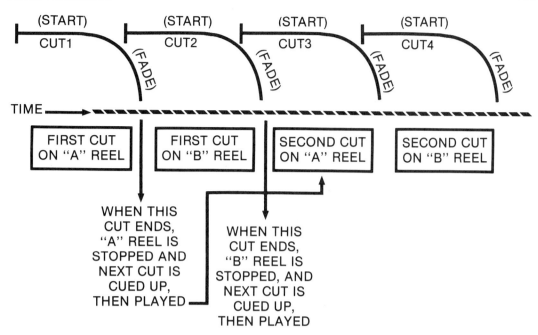

Figure 14.7. A/B Reels. As shown, odd-numbered cuts are assembled onto the A reel, and even-numbered cuts go onto the B reel. When played back from two tape decks through a mixing console, the cuts alternate between reels for the proper sequencing, with short mixes between them.

Pickup Edits

In long or complex mixes, it is often impossible to perform all the required operations in one take. At these times, the **pickup edit** becomes invaluable. Instead of attempting to mix a long section in one take, do it in several shorter sections, which you can edit together later. To do this, you must select **pickup points** in the mix—the places where the short sections can be edited together.

For example, if a piece begins with a mix of several elements, followed by a voice track (on tape), followed by more mixed elements, the voice track can serve as your pickup point. This means that you can record the first mix through the voice track and stop. Then note the position of the fader on which the voice track was just played, and prepare for the second section. Now begin to record the second section, rerecording the *same* voice track that ended the first section, played at the same level as the first section. After the second mix, rewind the recording just made and find a suitable edit point, like a hard consonant, in the voice track section of both mixes. Then just splice the two mixes together at the edit point (see Figure 14.8).

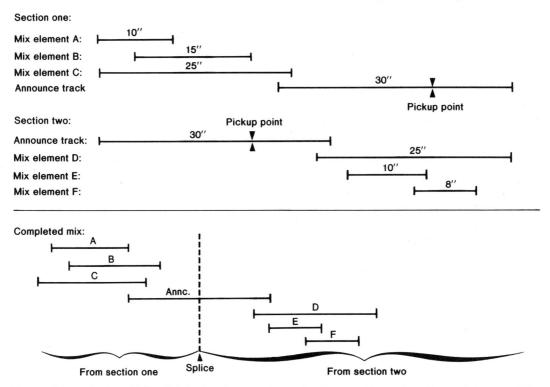

Figure 14.8. Pickup Edits. This is the timing plan of a two-section mix with a pickup edit in the announcer bridge between them. Mix elements C and D are ambience tracks or sound beds for each section. C fades out under the beginning of the announcer bridge, and D fades up under the end of the announcer bridge. The pickup point is any loud consonant in the announcer track where the announcer's voice is "in the clear," i.e., without any other elements mixed under it. The producer/engineer was careful to have the announcer's voice level exactly the same during the recording of both mix sections to avoid any level jump at the pickup edit.

Overlapping

A related technique is called **overlapping.** Consider a situation where you must repair or replace a 30-second section in the middle of a long program. You can't just cut out the old section and replace it because of an extended mixed passage surrounding it.

Begin the overlapping procedure by playing the master tape and rerecording it onto blank tape about 15 seconds ahead of the problem area, with the playback machine's console fader at the unity gain mark. At this point, you are really just dubbing. When you reach the problem, roll in whatever changes or additions are required to improve the problematic section. For example, you might mix in another sound effect as the master rolls by, or you might stop the master, roll in another element, and then restart the master. You also could fade down the master

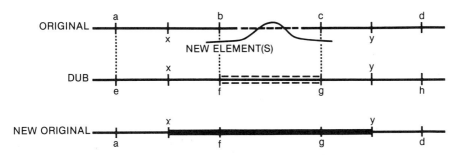

Figure 14.9. Overlapping. Original has problem between points B and C. Dub is made at unity gain starting at point a and running through point D on original, but with original levels changed and/or new elements mixed in between points B and C on original. Dub is virtually identical to original between points E and F and between points G and H. Between F and G is a new, fixed section. Points X and Y are found (easy edit points in the unchanged section) on both the original and the dub, and the section between X and Y on the original is removed and replaced by the same section from the dub. New original is one generation down between X and Y but is also repaired between F and G.

momentarily under an added new element. Or you might just make a simple level correction to the original mix.

In any case, after you pass the problem area and are back into the good territory of the original mix, bring the master tape's playback fader *back* to unity gain (if it was moved during the fix), and roll for about 15 more seconds, making sure that all other input channels are closed. Then stop both the record and the playback machines. Those last 15 seconds were also just dubbing. Now find an easy edit point on the original master and the same point in the new recording, during those 15-second-long sections before and after the "fix." Cut out the flawed original section and cut in the new, fixed recording. There should be no noticeable change at the splices, because both versions are essentially identical at the splice points (see Figure 14.9).

When picking edit points for overlaps, select a good, loud, transient or percussive sound. The change of tape generation at the splices will change the hiss level, making the splice noticeable or even objectionable if it occurred during a soft passage. If a splice takes place at a loud event or word, the sound will mask any hiss change.

The Art of Mixing

Mixing makes it possible for radio production to ascend to true art: You can discreetly introduce and remove subtle effects, add layers of ambience for realism, and inject music for emotional impact. Enter and exit elements slowly and carefully, without abruptness. An operator must become familiar with the *taper* of

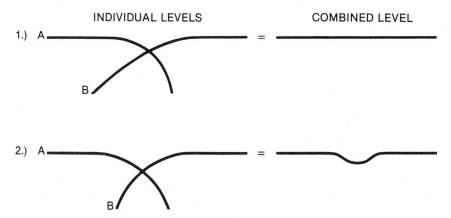

INDIVIDUAL LEVELS   COMBINED LEVEL

1.) A

B

2.) A

B

Figure 14.10. Crossfading. Item 1 above shows how to do a true crossfade of two voices or sound elements. Notice that the second element, B, is introduced and faded up partially before element A has begun to fade out. Usually A is completely gone as (or just after) B reaches full level. This creates a stable overall sound level, as shown in the combined level diagram. A good rule is not to begin fading A until you can *hear* B.

the console faders, which determines how much volume change occurs with a given movement of the fader. Developing a feel for this is the essence of mixing ability.

Even in a simple news piece, with studio voice tracks alternating with location actualities, a quick fade up and out of an actuality's background ambience, as opposed to an abrupt transition in and out, adds listenability to the piece.

The Montage

Another mixing technique is the **montage.** Here, several short sound elements are played one after another, with the first fading into the second, the second into the third, etc. The transition between elements can either be a true **crossfade,** where the first element fades out as the second fades up (see Figure 14.10), or the second can start at full level as the first fades out (see Figure 14.7). The latter—something called a "waterfall" mix—is especially effective with voice montages or **vox pop.** Subjective loudness matching of the different voices is important here.

Yet another technique is to use ambient sound mixed under a voice montage to mask noticeable edits or ambience changes in the voice recordings. This is called **edit covering.** It also can be used in live music productions to mask edits between songs, where significant ambience changes are created by the editing.

Entrance/Exit-Covering

A more subtle technique called *entrance-* or *exit-covering* can be used to conceal the final fadeout exit or initial fade-in entrance of a sound mixed under voice. To do this, time the exit or entrance to occur under a group of closely spaced words, rather than "in the clear," that is, in a pause in the speech.

Multiple Elements

When mixing many sounds together, it is advisable to mix all the desired elements at once, rather than mixing two elements, then playing back the mixed recording, adding two more elements, rerecording, and so on. Each generation you take the tape down will lower the sound fidelity. It's better—if you have the machines—to mix all the elements simultaneously. You'll get better quality, and you will have total control of all the relative levels in the mix; you won't be stuck with premixed balances.

Multitrack Recording

If the number of elements starts to make the project intimidatingly complex, and if the equipment is available, you may want to try multitrack production. Multitrack recorders can record several audio elements—all at once, or by "laying up" one track at a time—keeping them magnetically separate, but locked to each other in time. You can then mix down the separate signals without having to stop, start, and recue individual tape machines for each element.

Take another look at the top of Figure 14.8. You could mix the announcer tracks and elements A through F by first transferring each element onto a track of a 4-track recorder, taking care to transfer each element at the proper cue point relative to previous elements. It helps to lay up the main voices (both your narrator tracks and the actualities) in sequence first; this is the "backbone" of the piece. Then add sound beds and music on the other tracks at the appropriate points.

Once all the elements are transferred onto the multitrack, it's time to mix them down to make a mixed master. Bring the audio outputs of the various tracks of the multitrack into the mixing board in such a way that each track can be treated as a separate sound source, just as in multimachine mixing. The big advantage of multitrack is that the timing of each element is locked in place; all you have to worry about is adjusting the loudness of each track during the mix.

But be careful. In other circumstances, this advantage can become an albatross. Because the timing is locked in place, you can't change it if you decide it doesn't work. Also, keep in mind that you are adding another tape generation to the process by first dubbing to the multitrack and then mixing from there.

With multitrack, just as with multimachine mixing, you can use the technique of pickup editing to break the mixing process into manageable sections. In fact, with multitrack you don't have to find places in the piece where there's only one sound source to do a pickup. All you have to do is remember the relative volume settings of all tracks that are in the mix at your pickup point, and set the mixing console appropriately.

Multitrack recorders come in 4, 8, 16, 24, 32, and even 48 tracks, in analog or digital recording formats. Some use open-reel tape; some are cassette-based; some use a variety of proprietary tape formats. There are even "virtual multitracks" where the audio is stored on hard disk or other computer storage format, but treated like a multitrack tape recorder. Some of these "virtual multitracks" allow you to adjust the relative timing of individual elements after you've assembled the backbone. This can give you the assembling ease of a multitrack coupled with the timing flexibility of multimachine production.

Sound Effects

When using sound effects in a production, you often will get significantly better results if you record the sound effects yourself on location (although many are available commercially on CD, LP, or tape). "Rolling your own" is almost always worth the extra effort required, and in journalistic pieces the sound *must* be real, not generic.

In dramatic productions, sound effects are crucial to the credibility of the program. Some studios specializing in sound effects use something known as **"Foley-work" equipment.** Named after a well-known sound-effects man from the "Golden Age" of radio, it usually is set up in the form of a multiple-sectioned sandbox on the studio floor. Each section contains a different walking surface (flagstone, dried leaves, grass, twigs and branches, gravel, sand, etc.). Someone walks in place in the appropriate box to create the effect of movement of the characters within their aural environment.* Another typical accoutrement of such a studio is a small portable door and frame (about 2' x 4'), which is used to denote the entrances and exits of characters. Portability is important, because placement in the studio and proximity to the microphone(s) affect the aural *perspective* of the sound effects.

It is critical that effects appear to be in the same "space" as the characters, and in the correct proximity. "Off-stage" sounds should not be miked as closely as the "on-stage" actors' voices, for example. This is another problem with prerecorded sound effects, since their acoustical space is predetermined. If you must use "canned" effects, however, you can sometimes place them in the

---

*In addition to footsteps, today the term "Foley" generally is applied to any live sound effect performed in studio by a "Foley actor."

proper perspective. If, as is often the case, the sound effect on the record is close-miked and "dry" sounding, and you need a more distant sound, you can rere-cord the effect by playing it through a speaker in the studio and picking it up through a mike (or mikes) arranged to place the sound in the proper space. The acoustics of the studio are thus added to the sound. Artificial reverberation can occasionally help, too. (See Appendix E.)

Using Music

Music plays an important role in radio production, of course. As with any effect, it should always be appropriately styled and not used gratuitously or just for the sake of the effect. A proper level ratio between the music and other elements is critical. A speaking voice over a singing voice (voice-over-vocal) should usually be avoided, because the two voices will compete for the listener's attention.

Backtiming. Voice-over-music often works well when the voice is placed over an instrumental section and ends just before the vocals in the music start. This is a traditional and effective timing technique, and can easily be achieved by a process called **backtiming.** This is the basic technique behind most timing effects in radio production, and it is simpler to perform than to read about.

Essentially, backtiming is deciding at which point in time two events must occur simultaneously, and then measuring back in time so you know when each element must start to reach that magic point. If you are using tape machines with built-in time counters, backtiming is a pretty straightforward calculation. But, if your tape machine doesn't have this feature, you may be able to use a mechanical technique called **reverse threading.** You can do this on most tape machines, as long as the capstan and pinch roller are exposed and not enclosed within the head assembly housing (see Figure 14.11).

Instead of threading the tape to pass straight through the capstan and pinch roller in the normal way, you reroute it as shown in Figure 14.11. When you press *PLAY*, the tape is pulled in the opposite direction from its normal, forward movement, but at the same approximate speed. Tape-to-head contact is often radically impaired in this mode, so don't attempt critical playback or dubbing in this mode; it is purely a timing technique.

Only use this process with professional standard thickness (1.5 mil) tape. The extremely sharp turns of reverse threading place unusual stress on the tape, and can stretch thinner tapes. However, if you must perform backtiming on 1.0 mil or thinner tape, or if your tape machine does not have an exposed capstan and pinch roller, you can exchange the supply and take-up reels and use the normal play function to roll the tape. The machine will be rolling forward, but the recorded sound will be moving in reverse. After the *backroll,* exchange the reels again, resetting the tape in the forward direction.

Figure 14.11. Reverse Threading. This shows one method of reverse threading a tape for backwards playback, used in the backtiming process. Arrows show the direction of motion when the *PLAY* function is engaged if the tape is threaded around the capstan and pinch roller in the fashion shown. To accomplish this alternate threading, pull a little tape slack off the take-up reel, make an S-loop out of the slack, and slip it around in front of the capstan and behind the pinch roller, instead of the usual threading straight through between the capstan and roller.

For example, assume you have a piece of music with a 15-second instrumental introduction followed by vocals. You also have a voice track (more than 15 seconds long) that you want to mix over that introduction, and have the music's vocals start just after the voice track ends. Cue the voice track tape up on the end of the last word, set up the tape for reverse threading, push *PLAY*, let it roll 15 seconds, and stop it. The point on the tape at the play head of the machine is now 15 seconds *before* the end of the voice tape. Mark the voice tape carefully with a wax pencil against the playback head. Undo the reverse threading, and add a horizontal wax stripe mark just ahead of this point on the voice track tape (see Figure 14.12). Recue both elements to their beginnings. Start the music when you see the wax stripe pass the play head of the voice tape's machine, and the music's vocals will begin at the end of the voice track.

Figure 14.12. Wax-Striping a Tape. To draw a wax stripe on a tape, line the wax-marked cue point up to a tape guide, head-lifter, or roller (*not* a tape head), then press the wax pencil, holding it as shown in a sort of sideways method, onto the mark. With the other hand, slowly turn the feed reel clockwise, while pressing the pencil against the tape. (It is advisable to scrape any excess wax off the tape with the thumbnail after drawing the line.) When playing this tape back, the line serves as a visual warning to prepare for the passing of the cue point, which follows at the end of the line. A six-inch line usually is adequate for 7½ ips; double this for 15 ips. (Photo by Phoebe Chase Ferguson.)

Better still, instead of timing the intro of the music with a stopwatch, then backrolling the voice track by so many seconds, combine the processes into a quick and easy single step. Perform the cueing and reverse threading process described, but, instead of backrolling and watching 15-seconds tick off, *play* the music (forward on another tape machine or turntable) simultaneously. As the music starts, hit *PLAY* on the reverse-threaded voice track machine; when the *vocals* start, stop the voice track. Now, carefully mark the voice tape with a wax pencil at the playback head, and undo the reverse threading around the capstan and roller. Add a wax stripe on the tape, just ahead of the wax mark. Recue and set up both machines for mixing, and proceed as above.

Sometimes the pacing isn't quite right, and a bit more or a bit less space is required between the end of the voice track and the beginning of the vocal. You

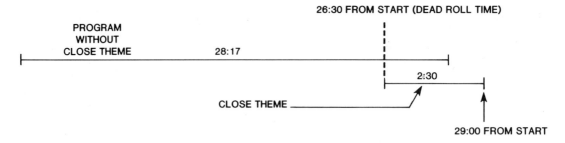

Figure 14.13. Deadrolling. Assume that a program must be produced to a 29:00 length. The program without closing music is 28:17. The theme is 2:30 long. Start a clock when the program begins (or the tape timer available on some machines can be used), and, when that clock reads 26:30, start the closing theme, but keep the fader down. As the program body ends, fade in the already rolling music. Since it is 2:30 long, and was started at 26:30, it will end at 29:00 on the clock.

can redo the mix, this time starting the music tape a bit *after* the end of the stripe passes the play head (if more space or a looser cue is desired), or starting the music tape while the stripe is still passing over the head (for a "tighter cue" or less space). After a few attempts, you'll become comfortable with it, and develop variations as necessary. (Don't forget to clean the playback head of accidentally applied wax—*before* you begin your mix.)

Deadrolling. Let's say you are producing a 29-minute program, and you want it to end with a piece of theme music or sound. You have 28 minutes, 17 seconds of program material, plus a 2½-minute closing theme. As the clock you are running on the body of the program (or timer for a prerecorded program) reaches 26:30 (29:30 minus 2:30), you **deadroll** the closing theme—that is, you start it but do not open its fader, so it is not heard at first. Then, about 15 or 20 seconds later, as the program begins to wrap up, you fade up the closing theme and bring it up full as the program ends. As the clock reaches the required 29:00 endpoint, the music will end exactly on time (see Figure 14.13). **Deadpot** is a synonym for deadroll.

Tape Loops

The **loop** is used to extend the useful length of a short bit of ambience, or to repeat a sound effect or section of music to create a rhythmic, repetitive, or hypnotic effect.

An electronic device called a **sampler** is the best way to loop a short section of audio. The audio is recorded from whatever source is available into the digital memory of the sampler and stored. The start and end points of the sampled audio can be edited, and the sampler can be set to play that segment over and over again.

Most samplers have only enough memory to record a maximum of a few seconds of audio. For longer looping needs, splice an actual loop of tape and play it back over and over for the desired running time.

It is not difficult to make a loop, but select the sound carefully. For an ambience loop, it must be free from noticeable sounds, such as coughs, shouts, clatters, etc. And the level or tonal quality of the ambience must not change from the beginning to the end of the section. For music loops, observe proper timing so the beat or *meter* of the music is not disturbed. When playing back a loop, since the tape is not on a reel, you must provide tape tension creatively, depending on how long the loop is, and how much slack needs to be taken up. You can double (or halve) the tape length of a given loop by dubbing to the next higher (or lower) tape speed.

The loop has to be at least long enough to make it around the head assembly. You can take up slack with a pencil held vertically or with a soda can (see Figures 14.14 A and B). If the loop is long enough, you can place it around a reel hub on the take-up spindle. It is usually advisable to keep the take-up reel stationary either by holding it or by using the *EDIT* function of the tape machine (if the machine has one) instead of the *PLAY* function. For longer loops, you can use a plastic five or seven inch reel to take up slack, and hang it over the edge of the tape deck (see Figure 14.14 C). Or, you can use a stationary reel on another adjacent machine or a reel on a pencil in mid-air. You must supply enough tension to provide good tape-to-head contact, but not too much, or the tape speed will slow, and the tape may stretch. Music loops are particularly sensitive to speed changes because they affect the pitch of the sound, and pitch changes are quite noticeable to the ear. It is best to set up a music loop without any sharp turns (soda can or reel hub rather than a pencil), with a very short piece of splicing tape on the splice, and with fixed tension corners (i.e., don't use hand-held devices to provide tension). If you use a reel hung over the side of the tape machine, it is best to attach the reel to the side of the machine with a piece of adhesive tape to keep the reel from turning or bouncing.

Working with an Engineer

If you're working with an engineer rather than in a combo situation, the key to success is teamwork. A lot depends on the people involved and their attitudes; without a good working relationship, the production session can be inefficient and frustrating.

The producer can help things get off to a good start by being completely prepared with materials, a production plan, and all tapes properly leadered, labeled, and heads out. Clearly establish the sequence of work. Don't confuse the engineer by overwhelming him with excessive detail all at once, or with unnecessary

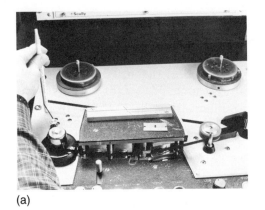

(a)

(b)

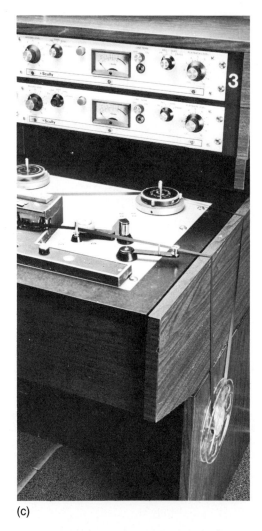

(c)

Figure 14.14. Tape Loops. (A) Tape loop held with pencil. (B) Tape loop held with a soda can and reel. (C) Longer tape loops can be handled by using a five or seven inch reel hung over the edge of the tape deck. (Photos by Phoebe Chase Ferguson.)

information. Show engineers that you are conversant with the production process, but don't try to impress them with your knowledge of the studio. Maintain a professional attitude at all times, even if things aren't going well.

If you're stuck, ask the engineer for a suggestion or feedback on the content, not just on technical matters. The engineer may hear something that you don't, or he may have the objectivity you lack after spending three weeks in an edit booth with your material. But the responsibility to make the final decisions is the producer's. The pacing and flow of a production is an important aspect of the art of radio production. Getting the right "feel" is essential. But remember that the most important criterion for including any production idea or sound element is its *meaning*. Do not include anything that doesn't have a purpose or doesn't fit.

Skip Pizzi is the technical editor for Broadcast Engineering *magazine, published by Intertec Publishing Corporation in Overland Park, Kansas. Skip spent 13 years at National Public Radio headquarters in Washington, D.C., serving in various technical production and technical training positions. Programs that he engineered or directed during his tenure there have won numerous national and international broadcast awards. His recording work is still heard daily on NPR newsmagazines' themes and music bridges. Skip has developed training programs for producers, managers, and engineers at NPR and its member stations. A member of the Society of Broadcast Engineers and the Audio Engineering Society (AES), Skip has presented papers at both of those societies' conferences and at the National Association of Broadcasters convention. He is a contributing author to the* NAB Engineering Handbook, *and has written articles for* db, Mix, Journal of the AES, Radio World, Billboard, *and* BME. *Skip has also been a guest lecturer at universities and chair of the Committee for Digital Radio Broadcasting (CDRB), an industry group formed to foster education and discussion about digital radio broadcasting technology.*

15

Emerging Technologies and Techniques

Flawn Williams

Advances in the field of computers have brought the dream of combined audio, video, and text information closer to reality. Faster operating speeds, cheaper memory, and increased data storage capacity mean that computers are now more ready to handle the mountains of data that it takes to store and manipulate sound and pictures.

In fact, both audio and video production are benefiting from the computer industry's research and development work. Computers are a far larger industry, and more research and development dollars are being invested there. Development of audio and video tools is becoming a story of building peripherals for computers, and finding better ways to turn sound and pictures into the digital data that computers love to crunch.

More and more audio equipment is being designed to work alongside video gear. Witness the emergence of audio recorders and **MIDI (musical instrument digital interface)** control devices designed to synchronize sound with film or video images via "time code." And some audio products engage in wholesale borrowing of video technology. A case in point is **digital audio tape (DAT),** an audio recorder whose rotary-head helical-scan recording system comes right out of home camcorders.

This headlong rush into development of "multimedia producing platforms" is fraught with headaches, though. Innovation is placed ahead of standardization, and the result can be a Tower of Babel. We're faced with clusters of miracle boxes, each of which can work wonders with audio within its own "environment." But try to get information out of one box and into the next, or get one box to talk to another, and the headaches begin!

Amid all the hoopla about multimedia and hypermedia, there is a place for radio. Listening to something *without* a visual accompaniment can still stimulate the imagination best. And our listeners tell us they can absorb information by ear while doing other things like driving, throwing clay pots, jogging, or washing the dog. In fact, they say, the combination of listening and doing is more satisfying than either activity alone.

Still, as you continue to produce audio programs for radio or other distribution in the future, you may find that you'll be doing it on equipment that is built for video and text as well.

The Switch to Digital

What has made all this integration possible is a stream of advances in transforming sound and pictures into digital data. This isn't easy. After all, sound exists as a continuous series of pressure ridges and troughs in the molecules of air between the sound's source and your ears. How can you turn that into packets of ones and zeros, and then be able to change it back into sound for your listeners?

The first order of business is to change the sound to **analog audio.** This is done with a microphone, which responds to the continuous stream of pressure ridges in the air by producing a continuous electrical signal that varies in the same way the sound waves did. The microphone, if you will, is making an electrical *analogy* of the sound.

Next we can take this analog audio signal and make periodic electrical measurements of it. In practice, to get high-quality audio through this process, this measuring needs to take place more than 40,000 times per second!

The value we've measured at each point in time could still fall on an infinite number of positions between the upper and lower limits. Each value needs to be quantified as a discrete number, which requires rounding off. This rounding off process is called **quantizing.** That is, we can set up a stepladder of discrete positions, and then round off each measured value to the nearest step. (For "CD-quality" digital sound, there are 65,536 steps—2 to the 16th power—on the stepladder from the minimum to the maximum limit. This is what is called "16-bit resolution.")

At this point, we've succeeded in converting our continuous audio signal into numerical data: a string of discrete values. If we identify each of the steps on the stepladder of values with a binary number—a string of ones and zeros—then all of our data will be in **digital** form.

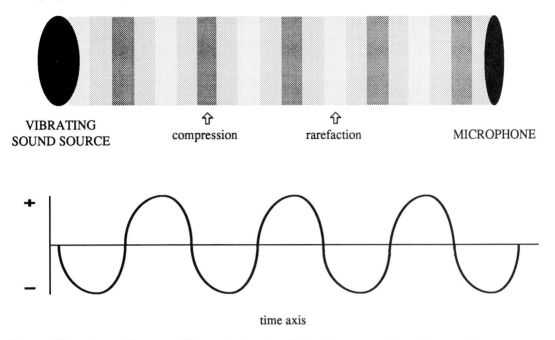

Figure 15.1. Sound Pressure Waves. In the top illustration, sound travels away from a vibrating surface as pressure ridges (alternating areas of compression and rarefaction). A microphone senses these changes in air pressure and produces an electrical signal that fluctuates in a similar fashion.

Once the information has been translated into these binary numbers, the awesome power of modern computers can be tapped to store or manipulate the data. To change the data back into sound, the computer chip in your CD player or other digital source plays a very fast game of connect-the-dots, and reconstructs an analog audio signal. From there, the audio can be amplified and sent to loudspeakers, where it is changed back into sound pressure waves by the pushing and pulling of the cones (woofers and tweeters) in the speakers. Computers need to do all this data manipulation very quickly, of course: The digital audio from a stereo 16-bit compact disc spits out data at a rate of about one and a half *million* bits per second!

Why Bother With Digital Audio?

At first glance, digitizing sound may seem like more trouble than it's worth. It requires huge quantities of memory to store, large chunks of radio **spectrum** to broadcast, and lots of computer power to accomplish such a seemingly simple task as changing the volume setting. Also, while analog audio quality deterio-

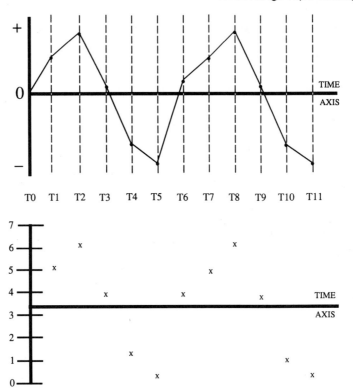

Figure 15.2. Sampling an Audio Signal. The top graph shows an audio signal being sampled at intervals of time. The bottom graph shows the results of that sampling plotted along the same axis, where the actual samples can be compared to a stepladder of discrete values (in this case, between 0 and 7). For each point in time, the position of the ``x'' can be rounded off to the nearest step on the ladder. Doing this produces a string of numbers: 5,6,4,1,0,4,5,6,4,1,0. There are eight steps on this stepladder. Eight is the same as 2 to the third power, so this graph shows ``three-bit resolution'' encoding. Using binary numbers instead of base-10, the string of numbers is 101,110,100,001,000,100,101,110,100,001,000. That's digital!

rates gradually as you raise the recording level beyond the capabilities of the system, digital audio quality stays pristine right up to its ceiling, and then suddenly degenerates into noise and static when its limits are exceeded. Digital audio is like the nursery-rhyme girl: "When she was good, she was very, very good, and when she was bad, she was *horrid!*"

BASE TEN NUMBERS	DIGITAL NUMBERS (16 BIT RESOLUTION)
0	0000000000000000
1	0000000000000001
2	0000000000000010
3	0000000000000011
4	0000000000000100
5	0000000000000101
6	0000000000000110
7	0000000000000111
8	0000000000001000
9	0000000000001001
10	0000000000001010
65,536	1111111111111111

Figure 15.3. Digital Numbers and Their Base-10 Equivalents. The numbers we use in everyday life are base-10. That is, we start with zero, count up through nine, then add a place and start over. In digital (binary) counting, only ones and zeros are used, so places are added much more often. For 16-bit resolution, binary numbers are carried out 16 places.

But in the long run, digital's advantages probably outweigh its disadvantages. First, digital gets away from analog audio's shortcomings. From the point where sound is changed to audio by the microphone, until it's changed back to sound for your listeners, it may go through dozens of conversions: through amplifiers and equalizers, changes from electronic signal to magnetic pattern (on tape) or mechanical pattern (the surface of a vinyl LP), back to electronic, then into a radio wave, then back to an electronic signal. In each of those conversions, tape hiss, LP surface noise, speed variations, and other distortions are unavoidable, and they add up through each generation of change the audio goes through. Digital storage media—digital audio tape (DAT), **compact discs (CDs)**, computer hard discs, and the various newer formats of recordable disc and tape—avoid this degeneration. Variations in speed, momentary losses of data, and other potential corruptions of the audio can be corrected electronically, so the data coming out can be identical to the data going in.

Once sound is converted into digital data, it's also possible to perform various transformations, some of which are difficult or impossible to do using analog equipment. Using **digital signal processing (DSP)**, you can adjust volume levels; change the tonal character of the sound, using equalization; add reverberation, echo, or other sense of acoustic space to the sound; shift pitch without changing timing; remove most pre-existing noise and hum from audio; and more. DSP

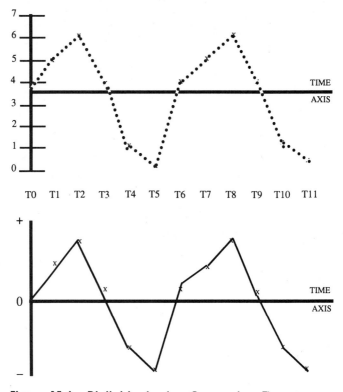

Figure 15.4. Digital to Analog Conversion. The digital-to-analog converter takes the sampled values from the digital information and uses it to create a new analog audio signal. In order to avoid audible errors in the decoding process, the data must be encoded with high resolution and sampled at a very fast rate.

even allows you to compress or expand the running time of audio without changing its pitch, making it possible to shorten or lengthen a segment slightly without editing out or adding material.

Data Compression and Psychoacoustic Coding

Digital audio, however, can strain the ability of computers and digital recorders to store and transmit all the data it generates. It is possible to reduce the amount of room this digital audio takes up, either by lowering the **sampling rate** (the number of times each second that the analog-to-digital converter takes a measurement), or by reducing the **resolution** of the encoding (fewer steps on the

Figure 15.5. Compact Disc Player. (Photo by Anthony Buttitta.)

stepladder of values, see Figure 15.2). But each of those changes carries a stiff penalty of reduced quality. Lowering the sampling rate cuts down on the frequency response of the sound, removing its crispness and clarity; lowering the resolution makes the digitized version of the sound less smooth to the ear.

But using DSP, there are other ways to cut back on the data without as much audible penalty. These are a variety of techniques under the heading of **psychoacoustic coding.** These methods grow out of research on the nature of human hearing.* The research shows that humans don't hear all pitches equally well. According to the "Equal Loudness Principle," in the low bass range or in the high treble area, we hear only very strong sounds, but in the midrange our hearing is more acute (see Figure 15.6).

The same research indicated that our ears' ability to hear a particular sound may be **masked** by a louder sound close to the same pitch at the same time, or by an even louder sound of different pitch happening shortly before or after that particular sound. These phenomena are known as **frequency masking** and **temporal masking.**

---

*Harvey Fletcher, *Speech and Hearing,* (Van Nostrand Co., 1929). This includes published results of psychoacoustic studies done at Bell Labs.

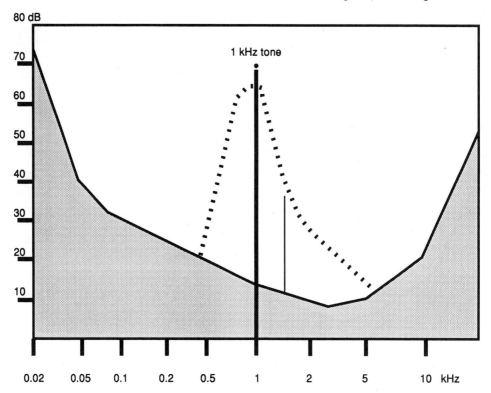

Figure 15.6. Frequency Masking. Human hearing responds differently to sounds depending on the frequency (heard as pitch) of the sound. Sounds in the low bass range must be 60 dB more powerful than sounds around the midrange (2–5 kHz) to be heard with equal loudness. A similar fall-off in sensitivity occurs as the pitch rises above 10 kHz. The solid dark line denotes the threshold of audibility; sounds that fall in the shaded area are inaudible.

Psychoacoustic coders, using DSP, can take a full 16-bit, 44.1 kHz sampling-rate digital signal (like that used for CDs) and examine the data in little packets (1000 or so per second). The coder applies psychoacoustic rules to analyze which sounds in each packet will be audible and which will not. It then removes the inaudible sounds from the data. This coding can reduce the amount of data by a factor of five or six, with little audible impact on the quality of the sound.

Data compression using applied psychoacoustics is enabling the development of several new technologies, including Philips' Digital Compact Cassette (DCC), Sony's Mini Disc recordable magnetic-optical disc, and various proposals for over-the-air digital audio broadcasting. In all these cases, the smaller quantities of data made possible by psychoacoustic coding make it feasible to deliver high-quality stereo sound using constricted storage space or broadcast spectrum.

But coding is not without its problems. As a final delivery mechanism for broadcast, tape, or disc, it accomplishes its purpose handily. But audible noise may show up in the sound if it is run through several cycles of encoding and decoding, or if equalization and other processing is applied to the sound after psychoacoustic coding. This may limit its usefulness in field recording or studio production.

Also, the number-crunching required to do the coding takes a small fraction of a second to accomplish. It's amazing how much is being done in that short interval. But if you're a radio announcer, speaking into a mike that's being broadcast "live" through a coder and a digital radio system, what would that small delay mean to you? If you're monitoring the off-air signal of your station with headphones, you'll hear your own voice delayed by that fraction of a second. Just try talking normally while hearing a delayed version of yourself!

Changing Techniques of Radio Journalism

These changes in technology aren't altering many of the fundamental processes involved in making good information radio. But over the next few years you'll probably need some new skills to do your work.

Just as the computer has virtually replaced the typewriter for text work, audio and video editing and production capabilities will shift to the computer, too. There will still be production studios for more complex work, but much of the editing and simpler production that's been done in studios and edit booths will move to the desk top.

As field recorders using discs become available, it may become practical to do all your production without transferring audio from one medium to another. Currently, reporters gather material in the field on analog cassettes, then transfer actualities to open-reel tape for editing or to carts for convenient playback. But by making original recordings on a random-access disc—or transferring them to such a disc—you could turn the editing process into just the preparation of an *edit list* of playback instructions for the disc player. There would never be any destructive cutting of the original material. Digital editing machines that do this already are being manufactured. The best of them sound and feel like tape editing machines: They have a wheel of some sort that allows you to "rock" the "tape," "mark" it, and "cut" it—all actions that are really taking place only in a computer's memory.

Even the filing of news reports from the field to the station is changing. The quality of phone-fed material has been improving as phone systems are upgraded with digital switches and transmission systems. Now people in Tokyo can sound to your listeners as if they're on a phone in the next room, if they can place a call "on the fiber" (digital transmission over fiber optic cable).

And thanks to all those other computer users out there who are demanding telephone links that carry more data than their current modems, telephone companies around the world are installing dial-up lines that can carry data at 56,000, or even more, bits per second. Using psychoacoustic coding equipment with these *Switched 56k* or *Integrated Service Digital Network (ISDN)* lines, it's already possible to send a mono signal that is almost equal to FM sound quality over one of these dial-up data lines. Gradually, live reports from the field will lose the stigma of "phoner quality"!

Field Recording: Digital Options

Most sound and radio interviews recorded outside the studio are recorded on analog cassettes or open-reel tape. But that's changing, due to the availability of several formats for making portable digital recordings. In general, these offer better sound quality than analog cassettes, and the new machines rival analog cassettes in size and weight.

One major drawback of these digital formats, at least in their infancy, is that they need more power to operate than their analog counterparts. For long recording stints using batteries, you may find that you must change a battery each time you change a tape or disc.

Among the digital formats vying for favor are:

- *Digital Audio Tape (DAT).* This tape format uses a rotary-head recording system, similar to that found in video recorders, to record up to two hours of CD-quality stereo sound on a DAT cassette, *without* using data-compression techniques. It also offers four hours of recording at FM-radio sound quality, using a lower sampling rate to cut down on data.

  DAT is a proverbial ugly duckling: Planned and introduced as a consumer format, it was stymied by the threat of litigation from music copyright holders concerned about DAT's ability to make "digital clone" copies with no loss of quality. An agreement with the music industry concerning copyright infringement in home DAT recordings was reached in 1991. Its mechanical complexity also has kept its price on the high end of the consumer market's audio products. But radio professionals and recording studios have embraced it as a less-expensive alternative to other professional digital formats, and the computer industry has adapted DAT for use as a data-storage tape.

- *Digital Compact Cassette (DCC).* Developed by Philips, the same European company that brought out the analog cassette in the 1960s, DCC is a stationary-head digital recorder. It uses psychoacoustic coding to reduce data to fit 90 minutes on a tape. DCC machines can play regular analog cassettes, as well as record and play digital tapes, giving some added playback life to old analog cassettes. The digital cassette is auto-reverse, but there *is* a break in the sound while the tape is reversing.

- *Mini Disc.* Developed by Sony, it, too, uses psychoacoustic coding to help fit up to 74 minutes of stereo sound on a 2½-inch disc. The disc format can actually transfer data to and from the disc much more quickly than the data-compressed audio signal requires. This leaves time to check each burst of data, and rerecord it if necessary, if jostling caused the first recording attempt to go awry. During playback, data are read from the disc into a small memory buffer at high speed, then drawn out of memory at the steady rate needed to recreate the audio. If the disc player is bumped during playback, the sound will continue uninterrupted as long as the laser inside can find its way back to the right spot on the disc within three seconds. These error-correction techniques make this a much more dependable disc format than the early portable CD players.

- *Other Optical Disc Formats.* At this writing, recordable CD technology is being slowly introduced into the high-priced studio equipment market, but no battery-operated portable recorders other than Sony's Mini Disc have been shown. The advantages of getting the original recording onto a random-access disc, though, will make development in this area inevitable.

Editing and Mixing

The ability to edit quickly and simply with a razor blade is one of the strengths that will keep open-reel analog tape a major player in broadcast production for some time to come. Electronic editing is on the rise, though, and many of the recording and production formats being introduced will handle *only* electronic editing.

It is possible to do some kinds of editing electronically on an open-reel recorder. You do this by transferring the desired bits of audio one after another onto the open-reel tape in sequence, in what is called **assembly editing**. Or some new audio can be rerecorded over an existing section using **insert editing** (sometimes called a **punch-in**).

Most video editing also uses these techniques. For assembling programs where all the elements are already known, this is a very efficient system. But what happens when you find, at the last minute, that you need to *remove* a second or two of material from the middle of a tape, to shorten its running time? With electronic editing, you would have to redub all the material after the edit onto the produced tape; with razor editing, you just cue up to the desired cut points, make two cuts and a splice, and you're done!

Figure 15.7. New England Digital's **PostPro** is an 8-track, direct-to-disk multitrack recorder used for post-production applications such as dialog and sound effects editing.

The Computer Editor

When your audio information exists as digital data, the editing possibilities broaden considerably. If you can load that data into a form of storage where a computer can have random access to it, then a variety of manipulations are possible. That's a big *if*, though.

Early versions of digital editors required that the audio data be loaded into either **random-access memory (RAM)** chips, or onto a **hard disk**. This meant that, although the actual edits could be done very quickly, additional time would be needed to transfer the audio data *into* the computer, and then transfer the finished edited material back out of the computer. It also was expensive.

Later models of these systems are being designed to work directly with digital audio recorded on optical discs. This greatly speeds the process of getting projects into and out of the computer: Pop in the disc at the beginning of an editing session, and pop it out at the end! The optical disk drive costs more than a hard disk of equal capacity, but the ability to store audio on many easily removable optical disks makes this a cheaper and more efficient system to operate.

There are several different modes of editing within a computer editor. First is a **basic removal** of designated chunks of audio data. This is akin to the process of cutting a piece out of an open-reel tape and then splicing the remaining sections together. Unfortunately, this editing technique in some computers is *destructive*—the

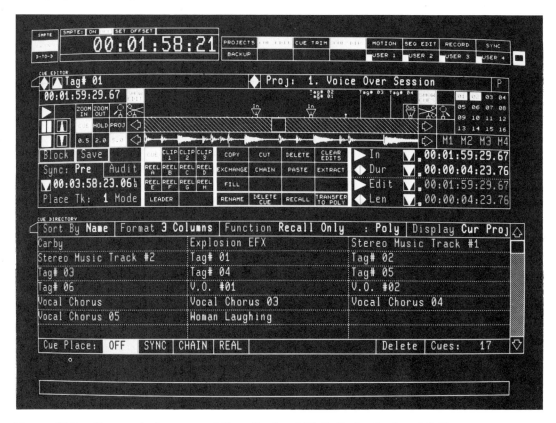

Figure 15.8. The control screen of New England Digital's Audio Event Editor.

edit can't be undone afterwards if you change your mind, since the data have been removed from the file.

A more common technique is sometimes called **playlist editing.** This doesn't physically alter the data; you simply place electronic markers at the beginning and end of section after section of audio, and then make a computer list of which sections to play and in what order. This playlist information can then be stored with the original audio data file.

A third option, in some more recent editing systems, combines the best attributes of the first two. It allows you to pick and choose sections in an assembly or play list manner, but also lets you do **subtractive editing**—akin to quick razor-blade style removals—in a manner that is not destructive to the original data.

Computer editing offers several advantages over razor-blade and video-style electronic editing:

- *Accuracy:* Computer editors can zoom in to choose an edit point to the nearest 44,000th of a second. To get that accuracy with a razor blade, on tape recorded at 15 inches per second, your mark would have to be within 1/6000th of an inch! And video editors are typically able to edit with only video-frame accuracy, about 1/30th of a second.

- *Crossfade Edits.* When a video-style editor or electronically edited open-reel recorder makes an edit, generally there's an abrupt transition from the old material to the new. A razor-blade splice is a little easier on the ears: it's actually a quick mechanical 20-millisecond crossfade from the old material to the new, as the diagonal cut gradually reduces the tape ahead of the splice and widens the tape after the cut. But a computer editor allows you to choose either an immediate cut or a variety of styles of crossfades, and choose how long you'd like the crossfade to last. This can make edits far smoother to the ears, and more difficult for a listener to spot in your final program.

- *Easy Repetition of Material.* The laborious process of making tape loops to lengthen sound or music beds (detailed in Chapter 14, "Studio Production") can be replaced with easy computer commands. You can mark a section of audio data and have the computer repeat it as many times as you need, with a seamless crossfade from repeat to repeat.

Mixing

Digital technology's first inroads into the broadcast audio production room have come in those areas where it offered the most improvement: in *recording* and *storage*, and in *signal processing functions*, such as adding reverberation and echo. But there are still some areas where analog offers better quality and/or cheaper, easier design. The most noticeable instance is in basic volume control and mixing of audio signals. So, for some time to come, you'll be dealing with "islands" of digital audio in an analog "sea."

Another factor slowing the arrival of the all-digital production system is the difficulty of connecting several pieces of digital audio equipment with direct digital links. In an era of rapid technological development, manufacturers place more importance on new features than on standards. So the optical disk you've recorded on one brand of digital recorder probably won't play back properly on another brand of machine. And the computer editor on which you've assembled your report may not be able to feed its data directly into a DAT recorder, even though both pieces of gear may profess to implement the same digital interconnection "standard."

The interim solution, until these headaches are resolved, is to keep doing the mixing and interconnecting in analog audio form, letting each piece of digital gear encode the analog audio into its own particular digital code and then decode back to analog on the way back out of that digital box.

As the number-crunching power of computers gets faster and cheaper, though, it will gradually become practical to create a computer "workstation" that will perform the duties of *all* the equipment in a traditional radio studio: recorders, mixing console, editing station, carts, and all. This kind of integrated mixing and production environment will be best suited to high-quality production of complex programs, but with some design ingenuity it will be possible to make these things as simple to operate as the analog gear they replace.

The "mixing," or relative volume control of several audio sources, can be automated in various ways within these workstations. The simplest control selects a fade-in ramp for each element, then a steady volume setting for the duration of that segment, then a fade-out ramp. This rudimentary level control is not nearly as precise or intuitive as what can be done by hand with an analog mixer.

A better form of level control is accomplished through **snapshot automation**. Once you have all the audio elements in the computer and arrange them in a time line, you choose a series of points in time. For each point, you specify a volume control setting for each audio element in the mix. Then, as the computer "mixes" the final version, it gradually adjusts the level of each audio source from its setting at one "snapshot" to its setting at the next.

The most elegant form of automated mixing is **dynamic automation**. This mimics the functions of a mixing board, and lets you make continuously varying adjustments of the volume of one or more elements in a mix. The computer then remembers what your hands did on the volume controls, and plays it back for you. You can update settings for one source or for various sources to fine-tune the mix without having to perform the whole mix from scratch each time.

An important part of this work is the *interface* provided by the computer. Simple, snapshot automation is often done using a computer *mouse* or *keyboard commands* to mark the desired fade points and levels, or to control the faders on a *virtual mixer* displayed on the computer screen. A mouse may be a wonderful controller for some kinds of computer work, but sound mixing can be done much more intuitively with faders you can actually put your hands on. The best digital workstations will provide a control surface that looks a lot like a traditional audio mixing console.

Multisource Production

A computer workstation has the potential to give you the advantages of a multitrack recorder (see Chapter 14) and eliminate the biggest disadvantages. Some workstations let you bring in many elements and arrange them in time relative to the other elements, just as you would do in the process of **laying up** elements onto a multitrack tape. This saves the quality that would be lost by going down another generation of analog tape.

Another disadvantage of multitrack tape production, as opposed to multi-source techniques, is that once the various elements are laid up on the multitrack tape, it's very hard to move one element earlier or later in the piece without affecting the timing of other elements. Some computer workstations mimic multitrack tape techniques so closely that they share this limitation. But the better ones let you change elements and give you the choice of keeping all the following elements in their original places or adjusting them to follow the changed element. This makes for a flexible production environment, and, when combined with dynamic automation of volume settings, makes for the best of both worlds.

Getting It To Your Audience: Digital Audio Broadcasting

When the day arrives that all of your field recording, editing, and mixing of sound is being done with digital equipment, and even the link from your studio up to the station's transmitter is digital, the audio still must be changed back to analog in order to be broadcast. FM and AM radio are analog transmission systems, and all the AM/FM radios your listeners use are essentially analog receivers, even if they sport "digital tuning" or other control features.

There are already audio distribution channels on many cable-TV systems, though, that can deliver digital audio directly to the home. The next challenge is to find ways to let AM and FM broadcasters send digital signals directly to their listeners. This has many potential benefits. First, the sound will have "CD quality," with its wider frequency response and dynamic range. All schemes for digital broadcasting proposed as of this writing use some sort of psychoacoustic coding and data compression, so they're not precisely CD quality, but they definitely offer better sound than analog FM or AM.

Also, digital error-correction techniques can eliminate most of the reception problems encountered in FM or AM radios. When you pull up to a stoplight in a crowded city, your FM radio may fade into static, but clear up when you move the car a few inches. This is caused by **multipath interference**: Your antenna picks up the direct signal from the radio station, and also the same signal reflected off nearby buildings or hills. These delayed reflections interfere with the main signal. But digital receivers can actually put these delayed reflections to use to make reception better, not worse. Digital broadcast coding techniques also can reduce the lightning-induced crackles, fade-outs under bridges, and generally noisy sound common to AM radio.

Even in data-compressed form, though, digital radio takes a large chunk of valuable space in the electromagnetic spectrum. It has to compete with other new demands, everything from garage-door openers to high-definition TV, for a new band in the broadcast spectrum. Or methods must be developed to allow the broadcast of digital signals alongside the analog signals on the same frequencies currently used by FM and AM stations.

Most other countries that have started or are considering digital broadcasting are using satellites to broadcast directly to homes and cars, using small terrestrial transmitters to fill in where the satellite's signal is blocked by buildings or terrain. But in the United States, both economic pressures and the tradition of broadcasting strongly favor having digital radio be a locally broadcast service, rather than a national satellite service. Perhaps some hybrid system will emerge that will allow both techniques to be used. This should also make it easier to build radios that will work in many different countries, which in turn will make manufacture of those radios cheaper.

The More Things Change . . .

All these new technologies have altered broadcast production, and the pace of change is likely to accelerate. But the basic techniques of producing radio journalism will remain the same, even as some new techniques and work patterns emerge:

- *Interviewing.* Newer recorders will make it easier to get clear recordings, and there will be fewer interruptions to change tapes, or discs, or memory chips, or whatever recording medium wins out. But the speaking, research, and listening skills that make you a good interviewer will continue to be your strongest allies. The best interview on radio will continue to be a person speaking to a person.

- *Editing.* The computer workstation will make the technical process of condensing and rearranging sounds and words far less difficult. But in doing that, it will increase your ethical responsibility to your "editees" and your listeners. You'll need to be more careful to ensure that your edits don't cause a misrepresentation of opinions, syntax, or speech patterns.

- *Being a Sound Reporter.* The ability to listen for good environments to record interviews will still make for compelling radio reports free from acoustic distractions. Better microphones and recorders will let you record interesting sounds, even those that are so quiet that they'd be buried in tape hiss if recorded on a typical cassette recorder. But you'll still need the "awareness of ears," an ability to listen and *find* those sounds, and the know-how to use them to enhance the production of engaging radio reports.

THE
NPR
STYLEBOOK

Part I
Usage, Grammar, Pronunciation

compiled by
Marcus D. Rosenbaum and John Dinges

"What's the big deal with grammar?" we often hear. "I mean, like, people know what I'm saying anyway!"

Maybe yes, maybe no. The simple fact is that people *don't* always know what you are saying. Proper English is the way we communicate clearly, avoid ambiguity, and know that others will understand us.

At NPR, our desire to use proper English goes even deeper than that. For one thing, bad English cheapens our work. When we use bad grammar or use words incorrectly, our listeners hear our mistakes—and, often, *only* our mistakes. They may miss altogether the important things we are saying. And even if they do understand what we are trying to say, they are likely to think, "If they're wrong about the little things, how can I trust them on the big stuff?"

There's also another reason to use proper English at NPR: Radio, where the spoken word is the only word, is the single best medium to preserve the language and to guide its growth. At NPR, all of us should see ourselves as guardians of the language, keeping it alive and vibrant. After all, if *we* don't protect it, who will?

A stylebook must do more than merely point out the incorrect. It also must set standards for consistency's sake. It is sloppy, for instance, for one person on a radio program to pronounce a word one way, and for another to pronounce it another way—even though both usages technically may be correct. When a host introduces a piece from Port-oh-PRINS, and the reporter calls his location Port-oh-PRANZ, it sounds as if the reporter hadn't heard the host, or vice versa.

Thus, in addition to listing items that are commonly misused or misunderstood, this stylebook serves to arbitrate competing "correct" usages. To be consistent, once NPR style is determined, we all should follow it.

Although we recognize there are acceptable regional variations in American English, it is important to be consistent. For further details, see the "American English" and "foreign words, foreign pronunciations" entries below.

Certain reference books are considered standard for NPR usage. They are the *Associated Press Stylebook*, the *NBC Handbook of Pronunciation* (Fourth Edition), Theodore M. Bernstein's *The Careful Writer: A Modern Guide to English Usage,* or a good dictionary, such as *Webster's New World* (Third College Edition).

-A-

a, an—Use *a* as the indefinite article before consonants, including aspirated *h*'s (*house, historic,* etc.) and before *u*'s pronounced *yew.* Use *an* before vowels (except *u*'s pronounced *yew*) and before consonants that are not aspirated (*hour, honor,* etc.). Examples: *In an hour, we will hear about a historic event from a U.S. senator with an unusual perspective.* See **historic, historical.**

abbreviations, acronyms, and initialisms—Except for a few very well-known examples (e.g., CIA), make sure you give the entire name of an organization before you use its initials or acronym. And don't use too many initialisms or acronyms in any one story; it too easily can end up sounding like gobbledygook.

ABC—Acceptable in all references for the television network that is part of Capital Cities/ABC Inc.

abortion—No one set of terms is acceptable to all sides of this controversy, so avoid labeling as much as possible. When you must, use the term *anti-abortion* to refer to people who are opposed to abortion, and use *abortion-rights* for people who are in favor of legalized abortion. *Pro-life* and *pro-choice* may be used as part of an organization's proper name.

accused—Someone is *accused of* a crime, not *accused with* a crime.

active voice, passive voice—Generally, use the active voice rather than the passive voice. Preferred (active voice): *The dog bit the man.* Not preferred (passive voice): *The man was bitten by the dog.* Too often, sloppy writing leads to writing in the passive voice because it seems to be more formal or more official. Avoid these tendencies. As Bernstein puts it: "[T]he active voice . . . conveys greater force, greater speed, greater vigor. . . . The passive voice, used without cause, tends to weaken writing. It also usually requires the use of more words. Which may be another way of saying the same thing. Compare . . . *Our seas have been plundered by him* with *He has plundered our seas.*" Nevertheless, Bernstein offers four situations in which he says the passive voice is desirable: "(1) When the agent performing the action is thought of as too unimportant or too obvious to mention and is less significant than the object of the action. *The mail was delivered at 11 o'clock this morning. Jones was indicted for the kidnapping.* (2) When the agent performing the action is indefinite or unknown. *Silk hats are not worn these days.* (3) When the intention is to emphasize the doer or the thing done by placing that element at the end of the sentence, which is an emphatic position. *The play was written by Eugene O'Neill. We can't drive because our car is being repaired.* (4) When the intention is deliberately to avoid strong language, to play it pianissimo. Science and diplomacy, two fields in which equanimity is the advisable attitude, particularly favor the restrained statement. *It has been sug-*

oh **boat,** oi **boy,** oo **noon,** oor **poor,** or **for,** ow **now,** sh **sheep,** th **thank,** th/**that,** u **under,** uh **ago,** ur **burr,** uu **hook,** zh **azure**

gested that 0.06 gr. of mercury sali-
cylate can be given three days before
each dose of the Tryparsamide. The Russian delegation is of the opinion that
certain positive work has been done."

adverse, averse—*Adverse* means unfavorable: *There were adverse weather conditions. Averse* means opposed to
something or reluctant. *He was averse
to speaking frankly.*

African-American—Interchangeable with
black when referring to Americans of
African descent.

ages—Avoid using before a person's last
name, although it is acceptable to
use an age before a person's full
name or occupation. Wrong: *The 42-
year-old Smith is a good ballplayer.*
Right: *Smith, who is 42 years old, is a
good ballplayer.* Right: *Forty-two-year-
old Bill Smith is a good ballplayer.*
Right: *The 42-year-old ballplayer has a
good throwing arm.*

AIDS—Acceptable in all references for
acquired immune deficiency syndrome. AIDS is a disease that weak-
ens the body's immune system. The
disease is caused by the human im-
munodeficiency virus, or HIV. Do
not say *HIV virus*, because this is redundant; say *HIV, the virus that
causes AIDS.* Most "AIDS tests" are
really tests for antibodies that the
body has developed to fight HIV; a
positive test does not mean that the
person has AIDS, but is only evidence of infection with the AIDS
virus.

alcoholic—Alcoholics who have stopped
drinking are *recovering*, not *reformed*,
alcoholics.

allege—Use the word carefully. You must
not indicate that you are making the
allegation, but you should be sure to
say who is. You *should* use the word
to indicate that something is not a
proven fact (*the alleged theft took place
on Wednesday*). But beware of redun-
dancies. You can say: *The prosecutor
charged him with murder.* Or: *The
prosecutor alleged that he committed the
murder.* But not: *The prosecutor
charged him with allegedly committing
the murder.* Also, don't overuse *allege*; use synonyms.

alumnus, alumni, alumna, alumnae—
Alumnus (uh-LUM-nuhs): A man
who has attended a school. *Alumni*
(uh-LUM-niy): Men, or a group of
men and women, who have attended a school. *Alumna* (uh-LUM-
nuh): A woman who has attended
a school. *Alumnae* (uh-LUM-nee):
Women who have attended a school.

American English—Because NPR is an
American radio network, we use
standard, American (i.e., U.S.) English. This does not mean that all
voices on NPR should sound the
same. Far from it. We've always had
regional accents on the air, and such
diversity is one of the many things
that distinguishes NPR from the rest
of the electronic media.
   NEE-th/er and *NIY-th/er, AWNT*
and *ANT, ROOF* and *RUUF* are regional pronunciation differences that

a **bat,** ah **farm,** ahr **bard,** air **fair,** aw **saw,** ay **ray,** ch birch, e **net,** ee **beet,** eer **near,** g **good,** hw
when, ih **is,** iy **fry,** j **job,** o **on**

are a matter of reporter preference. Likewise, a reporter from New York might prefer to say *standing on line*, where other reporters would say *standing in line*. The principle is that regional language variations are acceptable as long as they do not make the piece unintelligible to listeners elsewhere in the country.

Non-American reporters and commentators are not expected to lose their accents, but their editors should take care that departures from basic American pronunciation and usage are minimal. Examples: It's *SKEJ-ool*, not *SHEJ-ool*. It's *They were taken to the hospital*, not *They were taken to hospital*. Collective nouns take singular, not plural verbs.

amicable—AM-ih-kuh-buhl, not uh-MIK-uh-buhl.

among, between—Generally, use *between* for two items. *Among* is used for more than two.

anxious, eager—Both terms mean desirous, but *anxious* connotes a sense of apprehension or anxiety. Right: *I am anxious to get the exam behind me.* Wrong: *I am anxious to go swimming.* Right: *I am eager to go swimming.*

apartheid—uh-PAHR-tayt.

arbitrate, mediate—The terms are not interchangeable. An *arbitrator* hears both sides and hands down a decision. A *mediator* hears both sides and tries to bring them to an agreement acceptable to both.

Arctic, Antarctic—AHRK-tihk, ant-AHRK-tihk. Pronounce the *k*.

Argentine—AHR-juhn-teen. A native of Argentina, or an adjective referring to Argentina.

as . . . as—This is correct. *As . . . than* is incorrect. Wrong: *Four times as much is spent on Florida than on Texas.* Right: *Four times as much is spent on Florida as on Texas.*

astonished, surprised—This story tells the difference: A man comes home to find his wife with another man. "Matilda," he says, "I'm surprised!" "No, dear," she replies, "I'm surprised. You're astonished."

attorney general, attorneys general

-B-

backward—Not *backwards*.

bad, badly—*Bad* is an adjective; *badly* an adverb. However, it is *He feels bad* (not *badly*) because it is idiomatic usage for *He is in bad health. He feels badly* would mean that he has a bad sense of touch.

because, since—When there is a cause-effect relationship, use *because. Because he stepped off the curb into traffic, he was run over by the oncoming car. Since* is acceptable when one event led to another but was not its direct cause: *Since he was going to the store anyway, he bought a watermelon.*

Beijing—bay-JEENG, not bay-ZHEENG.

bemuse—Do not confuse with amuse. Bemused means muddled, plunged in thought, bewildered.

---

oh **boat**, oi **boy**, oo **noon**, oor **poor**, or **for**, ow **now**, sh **sheep**, th **thank**, th/**that**, u **under**, uh **ago**, ur **burr**, uu **hook**, zh **azure**

between—See **among, between.**

biweekly—Every other week. Twice a week is *semiweekly.*

British Broadcasting Corp.—*BBC* is acceptable in all references.

brutalize—It means to make brute-like, as in *Alcohol brutalizes families.* It is wrong to say, *Saddam brutalizes his people,* if you mean that he is brutal to his people.

burglary, larceny, robbery, theft—Legal definitions vary, but generally *burglary* means entering a building (not necessarily breaking in) with the intention of committing a crime. *Larceny* means unlawfully taking property; the non-legal terms are *stealing* and *theft. Robbery* is larceny with violence; *theft* is larceny without violence or threat. USAGE NOTE: You *rob* a person, bank, house, etc., but you *steal* the money or jewels.

but despite—Don't use *but* before the word *despite.* It is superfluous.

-C-

Canadian Broadcasting Corp.—*CBC* is acceptable on second reference.

CBS—Acceptable in all references for CBS, Inc., the broadcasting network.

Ceaucescu—chow-SHES-koo.

celebrant, celebrator—A *celebrant* is someone who conducts a religious rite. A *celebrator* is someone having a good time.

Centers for Disease Control—With headquarters in Atlanta, the centers (note plural) are run by the U.S. Public Health Service. They take a plural verb. But its abbreviation, CDC, can be followed by a singular verb.

character, reputation—People's *character* refers to their moral qualities. Their *reputation* is how they are regarded by others.

chauvinism, chauvinist—The words refer to having an unreasonable devotion to one's race, sex, country, etc., with contempt for others'. When referring to men who have an unreasonable devotion to their sex and contempt for women, the words must be preceded by *male.* The words, by the way, are a reference to Nicholas Chauvin, a soldier of Napoleon I who became famous for his devotion to lost causes.

chief justice—William H. Rehnquist's title is *chief justice of the United States,* not *chief justice of the Supreme Court.*

clichés—It is a truism to say that a cliché is a usage that should be avoided. But watch out. Clichés can creep up on you unexpectedly, especially in two-ways and other conversations. *It brought tears to my eyes. It blew my mind.* The list, unfortunately, seems endless. Avoid them like the plague.

climax—The word comes from the Greek word for ladder, so, strictly speaking, it means a series of words or phrases arranged in order of ascending forcefulness. Of course, in modern usage, the word also has come

---

a **bat,** ah **farm,** ahr **bard,** air **fair,** aw **saw,** ay **ray,** ch **birch,** e **net,** ee **beet,** eer **near,** g **good,** hw **when,** ih **is,** iy **fry,** j **job,** o **on**

to mean the highest point. However, it should never be used to mean the lowest point. Wrong: *The decline in the president's popularity climaxed when he announced yet another trip abroad.*

CNN—Acceptable in all references for Cable News Network.

collective nouns—In American English, collective nouns—*class, company, family, group,* etc.—take a singular verb.

collide, collision—A *collision* takes place only when both objects are moving. *The car collided with the truck.* A car cannot *collide* with a telephone pole.

colloquialisms—Generally, colloquialisms—words like *yeah, gads, done in,* and *gab*—are best avoided. Do not use them merely as shortcuts for proper usage, but they can be used deliberately in certain circumstances. Just be sure their use fits their context.

colored—In some societies, including the United States, the word is considered derogatory and should not be used. In some places, particularly in South Africa, the term denotes someone of mixed racial ancestry. When used in this context, be sure to define it.

Common Market—Use *European Community* instead. (Second reference: *E.C.,* not *E.E.C.*)

compared to, compared with—This is a complicated concept, but generally, use *compared with*, not *compared to*. *Compared to* illustrates only similarities (not differences), and is always used without elaboration: *Mr. Bush compared himself to George Washington. Compared with* can illustrate similarities *or* differences. *Compared with the stairs, the elevator was much faster. The Kenyan's time in the marathon compared favorably with the Swede's.*

compose, comprise—*Compose* means to put together or to create, and it may be used in the active or the passive voices. *He composed the tune. Iowa is composed of 99 counties. Comprise* means to embrace, to contain. It takes a direct object; it is not followed by *of*. Use it only in the active voice: *Iowa comprises 99 counties.* Tip: This sentence provides an easy way to remember the difference: *The whole comprises the parts.*

contagious, infectious—A *contagious* disease is communicated by touching; an *infectious* disease is communicated by air or water, and it may or may not be *contagious.*

contrasted to, contrasted with—The use is similar to *compared to* and *compared with.* Use *contrasted to* only for items that have opposite characteristics; there should be no elaboration. *He contrasted her appearance this year to her disheveled look last year.* Use *contrasted with* for similarities or differences. As with *compared, contrasted with* is usually the better choice of words.

Copenhagen—KOH-puhn-hay-guhn.

copyright—(n., v., and adj.) *Copyrighted* is the past tense of the verb; it is not

oh **boat,** oi **boy,** oo **noon,** oor **poor,** or **for,** ow **now,** sh **sheep,** th **thank,** th/**that,** u **under,** uh **ago,** ur **burr,** uu **hook,** zh **azure**

the adjective. *It was a copyright story. He copyrighted the story.*

court-martial, court-martialed, courts-martial

courtesy titles—Generally, courtesy titles (Mr., Mrs., Miss, Ms.) are not used in news stories, and the last name only is used in second references. However, in features—as well as some softer news stories—courtesy titles may be appropriate. But be sure to be consistent: Don't call one person *Mr. Jones* and the next person *Smith*. (Exception: For the president of the United States, first reference is *President Bush*; subsequent references are *the president* or *Mr. Bush*. Be careful in stories involving politics or other heads of state that the use of a courtesy title for the president does not denigrate the status of others in the story. For instance, if the story is about a debate between President Bush and Senator X, do not say *Mr. Bush and X answered questions.* Rather, say *Mr. Bush and Mr. X answered questions.* Likewise, do not say *Mr. Bush and Yeltsin spoke for four hours.* Say *Mr. Bush and Mr. Yeltsin spoke for four hours.* Remember: Courtesy titles always can be used.)

credit, responsibility—Terrorists are said to *take responsibility*, not *credit*, for dastardly acts.

criterion, criteria—*Criterion* is singular and takes the singular verb; *criteria* is plural and takes the plural verb.

Croat, Croatian—Croatian is preferred, but Croat is acceptable. It is pronounced KROH-aht, not KROHT or KROH-at.

-D-

damage, damages—*Damage* is destruction: *The damage from the earthquake was enormous and could total billions of dollars. Damages* are awarded by a court: *The jury awarded her one million dollars in damages.*

data—A plural noun, *data* normally takes the plural verb. DAYT-uh is the preferred pronunciation.

datelines—Generally, say where you are in your outcue. For more details, see the **datelines** and **identification** sections in Part II of this Stylebook.

daylight-saving time—Not *savings.*

decimate—Literally, it means to take one-tenth of. It can be extended to mean to do away with a large part of. It does not mean to destroy, or to do away with completely.

demolish, destroy—The words mean to do away with something completely. Something cannot be *partially demolished* or *partially destroyed.* And it is redundant to say *totally demolished* or *totally destroyed.*

demonstration, protest—A *demonstration* is a public display of feeling or opinion, so *public demonstration* is redundant. A *protest*, however, may be either public or private.

---

a **bat**, ah **farm**, ahr **bard**, air **fair**, aw **saw**, ay **ray**, ch **birch**, e **net**, ee **beet**, eer **near**, g **good**, hw **when**, ih **is**, iy **fry**, j **job**, o **on**

different—It never takes the preposition *than.* The proper preposition to follow *different* is *from.*

discomfit, discomfort—*Discomfit* and *discomfort* have nothing in common, except a similarity in spelling. *Discomfit* means to rout or to overwhelm; it also means to thwart or frustrate the plans of. *Discomfort* means to make someone uncomfortable, or uneasy; in its noun form, it means being in an uncomfortable state. To quote Bernstein, "If you suffer *discomfiture,* you suffer *discomfort,* too, but the reverse is not necessarily (or even usually) true."

disinterested, uninterested—Use *disinterested* to mean impartial; *uninterested* lacking interest.

dissociate—Not *disassociate.*

dive, dived, diving—The past tense is not *dove.*

drunk, drunken—Use *drunk* after the verb to be, when it's not followed by a noun. Use *drunken* before a noun. *He was drunk. He was a drunken driver.*

-E-

eager—See **anxious, eager.**

either—It means one or the other, not both. Right: *She said either road would get us there.* Wrong: *There were trees on either side of the yard.* Right: *There were trees on each side of the lawn. There were trees on both sides of the lawn.*

either . . . or, neither . . . nor—The verb must agree with the noun that is nearer the verb. *Either the girls or Bob is going. Neither Bob nor the girls are going.*

elderly—Listen to the AP's advice: "Use this word carefully and sparingly. It is appropriate in generic phrases that do not refer to specific individuals: *concern for the elderly, a home for the elderly, etc.* If the intent is to show that an individual's physical or mental capabilities have deteriorated as a direct result of age, cite a graphic example and give attribution for it. Apply the same principle to terms such as *senior citizen.*"

entitled—Books are *titled,* not *entitled.* Right: *The book was titled War and Peace. She was entitled to a promotion.*

essential clauses, non-essential clauses— These terms are used instead of *restrictive clause* and *non-restrictive clause* to convey the distinction between the two in a more easily remembered manner. Both types of clauses provide additional information about a word or phrase in the sentence. But an *essential clause* cannot be eliminated without substantially changing the meaning of the sentence. The *non-essential clause,* however, can be eliminated without altering the basic meaning of the sentence.

PUNCTUATION, VOICING: In the written language, an essential clause must not be set off from the rest of a sentence by commas; a non-essential clause must be set off by commas. The commas that set off a non-essential clause in a radio story should be *heard* to avoid the kind of confusion that is described in these examples:

oh **boat,** oi **boy,** oo **noon,** oor **poor,** or **for,** ow **now,** sh **sheep,** th **thank,** th/**that,** u **under,** uh **ago,** ur **burr,** uu **hook,** zh **azure**

—*Reporters who have not read the stylebook should not criticize their editors.* (The writer is saying that only one class of reporters, those who do not read the stylebook, should not criticize their editors. If the *who . . . stylebook* phrase were deleted, the meaning of the sentence would be changed substantially.)

—*Reporters, who have not read the stylebook, should not criticize their editors.* (The writer is saying that all reporters should not criticize their editors. If the *who . . . stylebook* phrase were deleted, this meaning would not be changed.)

USE OF THAT, WHICH: In general, for inanimate objects, use *that* to introduce essential clauses. Use *which* to introduce non-essential clauses, separating the clause from the rest of the sentence with commas/pauses.

USE OF WHO, WHOM: Use *who* or *whom* for people; do not use *that.* Wrong: *He's the kind of guy that likes to hang out in bars.* Right: *He's the kind of guy who likes to hang out in bars.*

experts, sources—See **sources, experts.**

-F-

fallout—If you insist on using this as a daily metaphor for consequences, then what do you do when Chernobyl comes along? Use *fallout* as a nuclear term. Substitute *aftermath* or similar word in other uses.

farther, further—*Farther* refers to physical distance; *further* refers to time or degree. *He ran farther than his opponent. She took the idea one step further.*

fewer, less—Use *fewer* for individual items, *less* for bulk or quantity. *The farmer harvested fewer bushels this year than last* year. The farmer harvested less corn this year than last year.

filibuster—*To filibuster* is to make long speeches in an attempt to block legislation. A legislator who *filibusters* also is a *filibuster*, not a *filibusterer.*

first, firstly—In a list or series, use *first, second, third,* etc., not *firstly, secondly, thirdly.*

flaunt, flout—*To flaunt* is to make an ostentatious or defiant display. *To flout* is to show contempt for. *He flaunted his knowledge of the language. She flouted the law.*

flounder, founder—A *flounder* is a fish; *to flounder* is to flop around like a fish. *To founder* is to sink or to become disabled. *For hours the ship floundered in rough seas before it foundered.*

flush—To become red in the face. See **livid.**

flutist—Not *flautist.*

following—The word usually is a noun (*he has a large following*), verb (*the water skier was following the boat*), or adjective (*the following ideas are good ones*). To avoid potential confusion for the listener, it is best to use *after* for the preposition. *After the dinner he went to sleep.* Not: *Following the dinner he went to sleep.*

forbid—Past tense is *forbade* (pronounced fuhr-BAD).

---

a **bat,** ah **farm,** ahr **bard,** air **fair,** aw **saw,** ay **ray,** ch **birch,** e **net,** ee **beet,** eer **near,** g **good,** hw **when,** ih **is,** iy **fry,** j **job,** o **on**

foreign words, foreign pronunciations— The general principle is to sound as much like American English as possible without compromising too much. Therefore: Use Anglicized pronunciation for well-known places and those that have an established English pronunciation: *PAR-uhs,* not *pah-REE; nik-uh-RAH-gwuh,* not *nee-ka-RAAH-wah.* Do not attempt sounds that do not exist in English: umlaut-O's, trilled r's, etc. But do determine the accurate pronunciation of names that may not be pronounced the way they are spelled: *va-WEN-sah* for Walesa. However, without neglecting these principles, pronounce peoples' names as nearly as possible to the way they do themselves: *DAN-yel* Zwerdling, but *dan-YEL* Ortega. It is important for the network to be consistent. When in doubt, ask for guidance.

formidable—FOR-muh-duh-buhl.

formula, formulas

forte—As a noun, meaning something that someone does well, it is pronounced FORT. As an adjective or adverb, it is a musical term for loud and is pronounced FOR-tay.

fortuitous—Strictly speaking, it only means that something happened by chance. It is not a synonym for lucky or fortunate.

forward—Not *forwards.*

founder—See **flounder, founder.**

fulsome—It means excessive to a disgusting degree. It does not mean lavish or profuse.

-G-

gender—*Gender* is a grammatical term, denoting whether a word is classified as masculine, feminine, or neuter. This is only occasionally important in English. *Gender* is not a substitute for *sex*—but, as Bernstein says, "What is?"

gibe, jibe, jive—*Gibe* means taunt, sneer, or scoff at: *They gibed her about her grades. Jibe* means to shift direction; colloquially, it means to agree: *His story didn't jibe with hers. Jive* means hip language: *He told her he couldn't understand her jive.*

good, well—Use in accordance with **bad, badly** entry.

gourmand, gourmet—A *gourmand* likes food and eats too much; a glutton. A *gourmet* likes fine food and is an excellent judge of culinary matters.

government, junta, regime—These words may not be synonymous. Here is AP's explanation: "A *government* is an established system of political administration: *The U.S. government.* A *junta* (HUUN-tuh) is a group or council that often rules after a coup: *A military junta controls the nation.* A junta becomes a government after it establishes a system of political administration. The word *regime* is a synonym for *political system*: *a democratic regime, an authoritarian regime.* Do not use *regime* to mean government or junta. For example, use *the Franco government* in referring to the government of Spain under Francisco Franco, not *Franco regime.* But: *The Franco government was an authoritarian*

oh **boat**, oi **boy**, oo **noon**, oor **poor**, or **for**, ow **now**, sh **sheep**, th **thank**, th/**that**, u **under**, uh **ago**, ur **burr**, uu **hook**, zh **azure**

regime. An *administration* consists of officials who make up the executive branch of a government: *the Reagan administration."*

governor general, governors general

-H-

half-mast, half-staff—Ashore, except at naval installations, flags are flown at *half-staff* for mourning. On ships and at naval stations ashore, flags are flown at *half-mast.*

handicapped, disabled, impaired—Describe someone as *disabled* or *handicapped* only if it clearly is relevant to the story; and be sure to state clearly what the handicap is and how much it affects the person's physical or mental performance. Some terms are offensive per se to some people with disabilities. Here are the AP's suggestions for usage: *"Disabled* (a general term used for a condition that interferes with an individual's ability to do something independently). *Handicap* (a term that should be avoided in describing a disability). *Blind* (describes a person with complete loss of sight; for others use terms such as *partially blind). Deaf* (describes a person with total hearing loss; for others use *partial hearing loss* or *partially deaf). Mute* (describes a person who physically cannot speak; others with speaking difficulty are *speech impaired). Wheelchair-bound* (do not use this or variations; a person may use a wheelchair occasionally or may have to use it for mobility; if it is needed, say why)."

hang, hanged, hung—Whether talking about a picture, a criminal, or oneself, the present tense is *hang.* The past tense and passive is *hanged* for executions or suicides, *hung* for everything else.

harass, harassment—huh-RASS, huh-RASS-muhnt. The controversy surrounds not only the act, but the word itself. Here's how William Safire explains it: HAR-ass-ment "is no longer in the mainstream of pronunciation preference. The increased preference for ha-RASS-ment is unmistakable, and has been reflected in the change in most leading dictionaries. . . . Today, the original HAR-ass remains British English; the newer ha-RASS is preferred in American English."

his, her—Don't presume maleness in a sentence, but don't use constructions like *his or her,* either. Try, first, to revise the sentence; if you cannot, use the pronoun *his* when it refers to an antecedent that may be male or female. Wrong: *An editor must be kind to his or her reporters.* Right (but use this construction only when necessary): *An editor must be kind to his reporters.* Preferred: *Editors must be kind to their reporters.*

historic, historical—A *historic* event is an important one that stands out in history. Anything that occurs in the past is a *historical* event. Note that the indefinite article preceding either word is *a,* not *an.* Just as you would not say *an history book,* don't say *an historic document.*

---

a **bat,** ah **farm,** ahr **bard,** air **fair,** aw **saw,** ay **ray,** ch birch, e **net,** ee **beet,** eer **near,** g **good,** hw **when,** ih **is,** iy **fry,** j **job,** o **on**

hone, home—*Hone* means sharpen, as in *to hone one's skills*. *Home,* usually followed by *in,* means zero in, as in *to home in on the target.*

hopefully—It means in a hopeful manner, not it is hoped or we hope. Right: *We hope it won't rain.* Wrong: *Hopefully, it won't rain.* Right: *He spoke hopefully about his pay raise.*

hurricane—Use the pronoun *it,* not *he* or *she* for hurricanes. *Hurricane Bob is 50 miles from shore. It is expected to reach land tonight.*

-I-

impact—Do not use as a verb (intransitive or transitive), except when referring to teeth. Wrong: *Let's see how the bad decision impacts on him.* Wrong: *Let's see how the bad decision impacts him.* Right: *He has an impacted wisdom tooth.* Right: *Let's see whether the bad decision has an impact on him.* Right: *Let's see how the bad decision affects him.*

impeachment—The constitutional process by which an elected official is accused of a crime as part of an attempt to remove the official from office. It is not a synonym for convicted or removed from office. In the federal government, the House of Representatives impeaches an official, and the Senate tries the official. When the president is impeached, the chief justice presides in the Senate trial, and conviction requires a two-thirds vote.

imply, infer—Speakers *imply* something by what they say; listeners *infer* it from what is said.

index, indexes—The plural *indexes* is preferred to indices.

innocent victim—Be careful of the term when it could imply that other victims somehow can be blamed for their calamity, as in distinguishing among AIDS victims.

interpreter, translator. See **translator, interpreter.**

in the wake of—This has become a cliché, so use it only in its literal sense. *The water skier followed in the wake of the speedboat.*

ironically—This is a word that seldom should find its way onto the air. Irony should be perceived on its own, without a signboard.

irregardless—A double negative. *Regardless* is correct.

it—Use *it,* rather than *she,* in references to nations, ships, and hurricanes.

-J-

jail—Not the same as *prison.* See the **prison, jail** entry.

jibe—See **gibe, jibe, jive.**

junta—(HUUN-tuh) See **government, junta, regime.**

-K-

kilometer—kuh-LOM-uh-tuhr.

kudos—(KYOO-dahs, not KOO-doz) The word is singular. It takes a singular verb. It means praise.

---

oh **boat,** oi **boy,** oo **noon,** oor **poor,** or **for,** ow **now,** sh **sheep,** th **thank,** th/that, u **under,** uh **ago,** ur **burr,** uu **hook,** zh **azure**

Ku Klux Klan—KOO-KLUX-KLAN, not KLOO-KLUX-KLAN.

-L-

lady—Do not use as a synonym for *woman*.

last—Be careful if you use it as a synonym for latest, because it might imply finality. It's probably okay to say, *It rained the last time I went to the store.* But *The last show was a good one* could leave the listener wondering whether you meant, *The final show was a good one.* As for days or months, go for clarity. In December 1991 your listeners probably would know that *last February* meant February 1991. But in March 1991, they might think that *last* February meant February 1990.

late—Do not use it to describe something someone did when he was alive. Wrong: *The late CIA director may have lied to Congress* because he was not dead when he did so.

latter—*Latter* refers to the second of two things. It does not mean the last of more than two. Right: *Both Bill and Bob are cowboys, but only the latter can rope a steer.* Wrong: *Bill, Ted, and Bob are all cowboys, but only the latter can rope a steer.* Right: *Bill, Ted, and Bob are all cowboys, but only Bob can rope a steer.*

lay, lie—Here's how AP sorts this out: "The action word is *lay*. It takes a direct object. *Laid* is the form for its past tense and its past participle. Its present participle is *laying*. *Lie* indicates a state of reclining along a horizontal plane. It does not take a direct object. Its past tense is *lay*. Its past participle is *lain*. Its present participle is *lying*. When *lie* means to make an untrue statement, the verb forms are *lie, lied, lying*." For good examples, see the AP Stylebook.

lend, loan—*Lend* is the preferred verb.

lie—See **lay, lie**.

lie in state—Only people entitled to a state funeral may lie in state. In this country, it occurs in the Capitol Rotunda.

like, as—*Like* is a preposition, which requires an object: *He writes like an amateur.* Use the conjunction *as* to introduce clauses: *He writes as an amateur would.*

lists, series—In a list or series, use *first, second, third*, etc., not *firstly, secondly, thirdly*.

lingerie—LAWN-zhuh-RAY (by popular demand).

literally—An often-misused word. Listen to Bernstein: "Picture this in your mind, if you can: *The job of selecting the jury was carried out in a courtroom that literally bulged.* And this: *But yesterday the United States Court of Appeals literally put the money in his pocket.* What the writers of those sentences were afraid of was that we would take them *literally*, but instead of escaping from the danger they plunged more deeply into it. *Literally* means true to the exact meaning of the words. What most writers (and speakers) mean when they use *literally* is *figuratively*, which is just about its opposite. When they do not intend to warn us against taking what they say *literally*, they use the word as a mere means of underlining a thought; usually the thought needs no underlining."

livid–A person who turns *livid* with rage turns white or gray, not red or green.

long-lived—LAWNG-LIYVD, not LAWNG-LIVD.

-M-

major—The word is a *comparative* adjective that means greater in importance (or size, value, etc.) than other similar things. Because it is comparative and not superlative in degree, *major* should not be preceded by the word *the*. One may speak of *a major artistic achievement*, but not *the major artistic achievement*. In addition, the word is overused. Use *important* instead.

majority, plurality—*Majority* is more than half; *plurality* is more than the next highest number. For details on computing majority and plurality, see the AP Stylebook.

media—A plural noun that takes a plural verb.

metaphors—Be careful that a metaphor's literal meaning does not interfere with its metaphorical one. It would be inappropriate, for example, to say in a story about how Congress had appropriated money for AIDS research that *the fight against AIDS got a much needed shot in the arm*.

midnight—It stands alone; never say *12 midnight*. It is part of the day that is ending, not the day coming up.

minuscule—Often misspelled and mispronounced. It's not *miniscule*. (It's MIHN-uh-skyool, not MIHN-ih-skyool.)

modifiers—Adjectives and adverbs can bring a story alive, but make sure the words say something. Don't fudge reality with *cheap* modifiers. Examples: *Skydiving is a solo sport. Even if you leave the plane as part of a group, you're ultimately on your own as soon as you pull the rip cord.* Why *ultimately*? It added nothing to the sentence. Here's another: *Despite the inherent danger, he still jumped on the tracks.* Why *inherent*? Or: *His last film was so outrageous it forced Hollywood to create an entirely new ratings category.* Does the sentence really need *entirely*? Robert Siegel, who brought the Creeping Cheap Modifiers Syndrome (CCMS) to our attention, added the following: "This may be the general stylistic tick that I had previously noticed only in one variety. I used to tell reporters to insist on the right word, rather than split the difference between a powerful word and a weak modifier. This happens when a reporter or newscaster is about to call Adolph Hitler 'the worst mass murderer in history.' Overcome with doubt about this assertion, the writer changes it to, 'Probably the worst mass murderer in history.' Perhaps we devote so little effort to choosing the right noun or the right adjective that we

---

oh **boat**, oi **boy**, oo **noon**, oor **poor**, or **for**, ow **now**, sh **sheep**, th **thank**, th/**that**, u **under**, uh **ago**, ur **burr**, uu **hook**, zh **azure**

have taken to overseasoning the bad cut of meat with cheap modifiers."

more than—Preferred to "over."

Moscow—MOS-koh, not MOS-kow. (This is an exception to NBC.)

Mulroney—Brian Mulroney (Mul-ROO-nee), the prime minister of Canada.

Muslim(s)—The preferred term for adherents to Islam. Not *Moslem.* (This is an exception to AP.)

-N-

National Association for the Advancement of Colored People—*NAACP* (N-double-A-C-P) is acceptable on second reference.

National Institutes of Health—This agency is part of the Department of Health and Human Services. It is the government's biomedical research agency. It consists of the National Library of Medicine and 12 separate institutes: National Cancer Institute; National Eye Institute; National Heart, Lung, and Blood Institute; National Institute of Allergy and Infectious Diseases; National Institute of Arthritis, Metabolism, and Digestive Diseases; National Institute of Child Health and Human Development; National Institute of Dental Research; National Institute of Diabetes and Digestive and Kidney Diseases; National Institute of Environmental Health Sciences; National Institute of General Medical Sciences; National Institute of Neurological and Communicative Disorders and Stroke; National Institute on Aging.

National Organization for Women—Not *of.* NOW is acceptable on second reference.

NBC—Acceptable in all references for the *National Broadcasting Co., Inc.,* a subsidiary of General Electric Co. Divisions are NBC News and NBC-TV. *NBC Radio Network* is now a subsidiary of Westwood One Inc. and is not affiliated with NBC. Mutual Broadcasting System also is a subsidiary of Westwood One.

Nevada—The state is pronounced Nuh-VAD-uh, not Nuh-VAHD-uh.

no one—It is followed by the singular pronoun. If the sex of the people in question is not known, or if it refers to men and women, the proper pronoun is *his,* not *their: No one gets what he wants.* If this construction sounds strange because of the mixed nature of the group, change the sentence around. Try using plurals: *They cannot get what they want.*

non-controversial—All issues are controversial. There is no such thing as a *non-controversial issue;* it is redundant to talk about a *controversial issue.*

non-restrictive clauses—See **essential, non-essential clauses.**

none—It usually means no single one and takes singular verbs and pronouns.

noon—It stands alone; don't say *12 noon.*

notorious—Well-known, usually in an unfavorable sense. Do not use as a synonym for famous.

a **bat,** ah **farm,** ahr **bard,** air **fair,** aw **saw,** ay **ray,** ch **birch,** e **net,** ee **beet,** eer **near,** g **good,** hw **when,** ih **is,** iy **fry,** j **job,** o **on**

nuclear—NOO-klee-uhr, not NOO-kyoo-luhr.

-O-

oasis, oases

obscenities, profanities, vulgarities—See the **objectionable language** entry in Part II of this Stylebook.

observance, observation—An *observance* is an act in accordance with a tradition, custom, or duty. An *observation* is a perceiving of something. Bernstein offers this example to make the distinction clear: *A little boy finds a vantage point for observation of a parade in observance of the Fourth of July.*

off of—The *of* is unnecessary. *He fell off the couch.* Not: *He fell off of the couch.*

often—AWF'n is preferred to AWF-ten.

on the heels of—This has become a cliché, so use it only in its literal sense. *The puppy dog left the barn on the heels of its mother.*

Oregon—OR-uh-guhn, not AHR-uh-guhn or OR-uh-gawn.

outcues—For descriptions of standardized outcues, see the **identification** section of Part II of this Stylebook.

-P-

panacea—The word means a cure-all, or remedy for all ills. It does not mean a remedy for specific ills, so it generally shouldn't be followed by a phrase beginning with *for.* Wrong: *This tiny pill is a panacea for headaches.*

passer-by, passers-by

PBS—Acceptable on second reference for the Public Broadcasting Service (not System).

Peking—See **Beijing.**

penitentiary—See **prison, jail.**

people, persons—Use *person* for the singular, *people* in all plural forms. (This conforms with AP, but is an exception to Bernstein.)

personal pronouns—Do not use them when discussing U.S. foreign policy. You should ask the secretary of State, *What should the United States do next?* not *What should we do next?*

phenomenon, phenomena—*Phenomenon* is singular, *phenomena* plural. Make sure verbs agree.

pianist—pee-AN-uhst is the preferred pronunciation.

picket—Verb and noun. Do not use *picketer.*

plead, pleaded—*Pled* is colloquial for the past tense.

plurality—See **majority, plurality.**

politics—Usually it takes a plural verb: *His politics are liberal.* When it is used as a study or science, it takes a singular verb: *Politics is hard to teach.*

practicable, practical—*Practicable* means capable of being done; *practical* means capable of being done in a way that is useful or valuable.

predominant, predominantly—Not *predominate, predominately.* The verb, however, is *predominate.*

---

oh **boat,** oi **boy,** oo **noon,** oor **poor,** or **for,** ow **now,** sh **sheep,** th **thank,** th/that, u **under,** uh **ago,** ur **burr,** uu **hook,** zh **azure**

premier, prime minister—The titles are used interchangeably for the first minister of a national government that has a council of ministers. *Prime minister* is correct throughout the Commonwealth, and it usually is the best term for other countries as well. However, for France it is *premier*, in parts of Asia it is *premier*, and in Austria and Germany it is *chancellor*. Canadian and Australian provinces use *premier*, but the national governments are headed by a *prime minister*.

presently—It means *in a little while*, not *now*.

press conference—Use *news conference* instead.

prime minister—See **premier, prime minister**.

prior to—*Before* usually is the better choice of words.

prison, jail—Do not use the two words interchangeably. Here is AP's excellent description of the difference: "*Prison* is a generic term that may be applied to the maximum security institutions often known as *penitentiaries* and to the medium security facilities often called *correctional institutions* or *reformatories*. All such facilities confine people serving sentences for felonies. A *jail* is a facility normally used to confine people serving sentences for misdemeanors, people awaiting trial or sentencing on either felony or misdemeanor charges, and people confined for civil matters such as failure to pay alimony and other types of contempt of court."

profanity—See the **objectionable language** entry in Part II of this Stylebook.

protest, demonstration—See **demonstration, protest**.

prove, proved, proving—The past tense of *prove* is *proved*. Use *proven* only as an adjective: *a proven cure*.

Public Broadcasting Service—Not *System*.

Pulitzer—PUUL-uht-suhr, not PYOO-liht-zuhr.

-Q-

quote—A verb. The noun is *quotation*.

"quote"—Under most circumstances, use your voice to indicate quotation in script. In some rare cases, for precision, use the formulation, *The attorney general said, quote, We will not let up until we get a conviction*. Do not close with *unquote* unless it is absolutely necessary for clarity.

-R-

raised, reared—Only humans may be *reared*. Any living thing, including humans, may be *raised*.

random sample—This is a scientific term having to do with a sample in which every member has an equal chance of occurring or occurs with a particular frequency. Thus, when we gather vox pop, we are not taking a *random sample*. Call it an *unscientific survey* instead.

---

a **bat**, ah **farm**, ahr **bard**, air **fair**, aw **saw**, ay **ray**, ch **birch**, e **net**, ee **beet**, eer **near**, g **good**, hw **when**, ih **is**, iy **fry**, j **job**, o **on**

ravage, ravish—*To ravage* is to devastate: *The troops ravaged the city. The city was ravaged by the storm.* To *ravish* is to abduct, to rape, or to carry away with emotion: *The Nazi troops ravished the young girls.* The words are not interchangeable; inanimate objects like buildings and towns cannot be *ravished*.

Realtor—A *Realtor* is a member of the National Association of Realtors. The preferred generic term is *real estate agent*.

reared—See **raised, reared.**

rebut, refute—The words are not interchangeable. *Rebut* means to argue in opposition: *He rebutted the candidate's argument. Refute* connotes winning an argument; it almost always requires an editorial judgment on the part of the reporter, so use *deny, dispute, rebut,* or *respond to* instead.

recently—It's usually just a way to conceal the fact that we're late in reporting a story. Avoid it.

recur—Not *reoccur.*

referendum, referendums

reformatory—See **prison, jail.**

refused, declined—When someone won't agree to an interview or to allow his name to be used, that is his right. Say, politely, that he *declined*, not *refused* to be interviewed or allow his name to be used.

refute—See **rebut, refute.**

regime—See **government, junta, regime.**

reluctant, reticent—*Reluctant* means unwilling to act. *Reticent* means unwilling to speak.

responsibility, credit—See **credit, responsibility.**

restaurateur—Not *restauranteur.*

restrictive clauses—See **essential clauses, non-essential clauses.**

Reuters—A private British news agency. When used as an adjective, drop the s: *A Reuter correspondent.*

right of way, rights of way

Roh-Tae-Woo—The Korean leader's name is pronounced NOH-TIY-OO, not NO-TIY-WOO.

Romania—Not *Rumania.*

-S-

sanitarium, sanitariums

schism—SIHZ-uhm.

schizophrenia, schizophrenic—The words refer to a serious personality disorder involving the distortion of reality. They do not mean split personality.

sculptor—Use for both men and women.

sewage, sewerage—*Sewage* is waste matter. *Sewerage* is the drainage system for the waste matter.

she—Do not use this pronoun in relation to ships, nations, or hurricanes. Use *it* instead.

short-lived—SHORT-LIYV'D.

should, would—*Should* expresses an obligation: *We should always use good*

oh **boat,** oi **boy,** oo **noon,** oor **poor,** or **for,** ow **now,** sh **sheep,** th **thank,** th/that, u **under,** uh **ago,** ur **burr,** uu **hook,** zh **azure**

grammar. Would expresses a customary action: *We would use good grammar at work.*

Smithsonian Institution—Not *Smithsonian Institute.*

sound-bites—We call them *cuts* or *actualities* because we want to avoid emulating the nine-second TV soundbite. In news reporting, actualities should express full and interesting thoughts. Avoid the quick inanity—unless, of course, your purpose is to show the speaker is being inane.

sources, experts—There is a temptation to use these words to cover a reporter's own opinions or even legitimate analytical points. This is a temptation to avoid. There are two things to keep in mind if these words are used: First, the words are plural and mean that the reporter is quoting more than one expert or more than one source. Second, when reporters use these words, they should describe the experts' expertise or the sources' reliability, even if the experts and sources cannot be named.

spokesman, spokeswoman—Not *spokesperson.* Use another word (*official, representative*) if you don't know the sex of the person.

stadium, stadiums

subjunctive mood—AP has a good explanation of when to use the subjunctive: "Use the subjunctive mood of a verb for contrary-to-fact conditions, and expressions of doubts, wishes, or regrets. *If I were a rich man, I wouldn't have to work hard. I doubt*

that more money would be the answer. I wish it were possible to take back my words. Sentences that express a contingency or hypothesis may use either the subjunctive or the indicative mood depending on the context. In general, use the subjunctive if there is little likelihood that a contingency might come true: *If I were to marry a millionaire, I wouldn't have to worry about money.* But: *If the bill passes as expected, it will provide an immediate tax cut.*"

Supreme Court of the United States—It is *chief justice of the United States,* not *chief justice of the Supreme Court.* Other justices are *associate justices.* Before the name: *Chief Justice* and *Justice.*

surprised, astonished—See astonished, surprised.

-T-

tablespoonful, tablespoonfuls, teaspoonful, teaspoonfuls—not *-spoonsful* for the plurals.

Taiwan—Use *Taiwan,* not *Formosa.*

temblor—Not *tremblor* for earthquake.

terrorism, terrorist—*Terrorism* is the act of causing terror, usually for political purposes, and it connotes that the terror is perpetrated on innocents. Thus, the bombing of a civilian airliner clearly is a terrorist act, but an attack on an army convoy, even if away from the battlefield, is not. Do not ape government usage. The Israeli government, for instance, routinely refers to PLO actions as

---

a **bat**, ah **farm**, ahr **bard**, air **fair**, aw **saw**, ay **ray**, ch **birch**, e **net**, ee **beet**, eer **near**, g **good**, hw **when**, ih **is**, iy **fry**, j **job**, o **on**

terrorist. A journalist should use independent criteria to judge whether the term is accurate.

that—Use it to introduce a dependent clause if the sentence sounds clumsy without it. When in doubt, use it.

that, which—See **essential clauses, nonessential clauses.**

theft—See **burglary, larceny, robbery, theft.**

think—Reporters are paid to think, but hearing them speculate and express opinions on the air not tied to the facts they are conveying is a dangerous departure from the journalist's role. In interviews with reporters avoid the "What do you think?" questions when they elicit opinion going beyond journalistic analysis. Leave the opinion-making to the pundits and the newsmakers.

Third World—Refers to the developing nations of Asia, Africa, and South America. Don't substitute *nonaligned*, which is a political term.

tonight—You can say *8 o'clock tonight* or *8 p.m. today*, but *8 p.m. tonight* is redundant.

toward—Not *towards*.

translator, interpreter—A *translator* renders written words into another language. An *interpreter* does the same for spoken words. Thus, in explaining actualities, it is almost always *He spoke through an interpreter.* Note: Remember that our listeners may understand the foreign language that is being heard in an actu-

ality before the English voiceover. Make sure what is heard in the foreign language is heard in English.

trustee, trusty—A trustee (trus-TEE) is a member of a board of trustees. A trusty (TRUS-tee) is a person who can be relied upon, especially in a prison.

-U-

Ukraine—yoo-KRAYN, not YOO-krayn. It is not preceded by *the*.

United Nations—Generally, use the full name as a noun, *U.N.* as an adjective only.

United States—Generally, use the full name as a noun, *U.S.* as an adjective only.

-V-

volatile—It refers to something that evaporates rapidly; it is not necessarily explosive.

vulgarities—See the **objectionable language** entry in Part II of this Stylebook.

-W-

weapons—See the AP Stylebook for good descriptions of different kinds of weapons.

weather terms—See the AP Stylebook for detailed descriptions of various weather terms.

whence—It's an old-fashioned word that should be avoided, except for effect. If you do use it, remember that it means from which place or from

---

oh **boat**, oi **boy**, oo **noon**, oor **poor**, or **for**, ow **now**, sh **sheep**, th **thank**, th/**that**, u **under**, uh **ago**, ur **burr**, uu **hook**, zh **azure**

which position. Thus, *from whence* is redundant.

whether or not—Usually, the *or not* is superfluous.

which—See **essential clauses, non-essential clauses.**

who, whom—*Whom* is the word for someone who is the object of a verb or preposition: *Whom do you want to go?* Be careful with *whomever*: *Give it to whomever.* (*Whomever* is the object of the preposition *to.*) But: *Give it to whoever wants it.* (*Whoever* is the subject of the clause *whoever wants it.*)

-X-Y-Z-

zoom Here's one you probably didn't know, courtesy of Bernstein: "Aside from its meanings connected with sound and camera, *zoom,* originally an aviation term, denotes rapid upward motion. Both the following sentences are therefore incorrect: *Melville zoomed down the incline in 2:15.2, a full second ahead of Tommy Burns of Middlebury. At least 12 large hawks are making their homes atop city skyscrapers and zooming down to snatch pigeons.* Both writers may have had in mind the word *swoop. Swoop* is usually down; zoom is always up."

---

a **bat,** ah **farm,** ahr **bard,** air **fair,** aw **saw,** ay **ray,** ch **birch,** e **net,** ee **beet,** eer **near,** g **good,** hw **when,** ih **is,** iy **fry,** j **job,** o **on**

Part II

NPR Editorial and Production Guidelines

compiled by Marcus D. Rosenbaum and John Dinges

Datelines Do not say you are somewhere you are not, but use a location in your outcue unless you have a good reason not to do so. The most common good reason not to use a location is that you have gone to City A to report a story, but returned to City B to produce it. If you are close enough to report on a story in a nearby city, use the location where you are. When in doubt, use a location in your outcue. Examples: Natalie Nipper, a staff reporter who is based in Washington, goes to Kalamazoo to report on an exciting city council race. She returns to Washington to produce the story. Her outcue is, *I'm Natalie Nipper,* or, *I'm Natalie Nipper, reporting.* Joe Nipper (no relation) is a staff reporter based in Denver. He reports on a plane crash in Aspen by contacting his sources by telephone. His outcue is, *I'm Joe Nipper in Denver.* Joe Nipper does a national survey story about horse racing from his home base in Denver. He collects some tape on his own, does some telephone interviews, and has some station reporters send him tape they have gathered. His outcue? *I'm Joe Nipper in Denver.*

Election coverage It goes without saying that NPR's coverage of politics should always be balanced and fair. Nothing should give even the impression of bias, and reporters and editors must take great care that they do not unwittingly give one candidate—or one side on an issue—an unfair advantage.

The trickiest time is Election Day and the day before Election Day, when extra-special care must be taken. There are two principles at play: (1) Balanced coverage requires that potential voters have the opportunity to hear all the coverage, and (2) Candidates (and advocates of issues) must always have the opportunity to answer all charges. For these reasons, most substantive election reports should not be carried on Election Day. News spots or short reports about turnout, for instance, would be acceptable. But on Election Day, an eleventh-hour charge by one candidate against another would not (the other candidate would not have the opportunity to respond). Nor would the last in a series of in-depth reports on the race be suitable; the series might be balanced overall, but many voters might not hear the last report before they voted, so they would not be able to hear the full balanced coverage.

Election-eve coverage that goes beyond a horse-race status report carries similar dangers and should be approached with extreme caution.

Identification   The designation *NPR's* is reserved for on-air identification of NPR staff reporters and, in some cases, for reporters working on a contract (rather than free-lance) basis with NPR. Examples: (1) Joe Nipper is the NPR defense correspondent. He should be identified as *NPR's Joe Nipper*. When it is relevant, he also can be identified as *NPR Defense Correspondent Joe Nipper*; this would be particularly appropriate if his report is analyzing defense topics. (2) Karen Contract is working in a foreign country on an NPR contract. She should be identified as *NPR's Karen Contract*. (3) Randy Retainer is based in the United States and working for NPR on a retainer contract. He should be identified as *Randy Retainer*. (4) Susie Stringer is a free-lance reporter. Wherever she is based, foreign or domestic, she should be identified only as *Susie Stringer*. Free-lance reporters should not be identified according to other news organizations they string for, unless there is a special reason; for instance, if Susie Stringer wrote an exclusive report for the *Washington Post* and we did a two-way with her, we would mention the *Post*. (5) Sam Station is a reporter for KQED in San Francisco. He should be identified as *Sam Station of Member Station KQED*.

In **outcues**, the rule is: A reporter not identified as *NPR's* in the intro should SOC* out, *For National Public Radio, I'm* (or *this is*) *Susie Stringer, Randy Retainer, or Sam Station [in Somewheresville]*. Reporters who are identified as *NPR's* should *not* say *for National Public Radio* in their SOCs. See **datelines** for a discussion of when a reporter's location should be included in the SOC.

BBC's: Only BBC staff reporters receive the designation *BBC's* on our air. Do not assume that a report taken off the BBC feed is by a BBC staffer. The reporter may be a stringer who also strings for NPR. If he is a stringer—or if you're in doubt—say *So-and-So filed this report for the BBC*.

---

*SOC is an abbreviation for standard outcue.

When interviewing staff reporters from other news organizations, identify them with the name of that organization.

Internal editing of tape At NPR we take care that whenever we cut a piece of tape, we maintain the integrity of its meaning. There are times, however, when we should not make internal edits at all. Generally, these occur when our listeners are likely to hear the same actuality from other sources—television, newspapers, etc. If they hear the actuality one way on NPR and a different way elsewhere, they will realize that NPR has cut it. And even though we know we have not changed the speaker's meaning, our listeners may suspect otherwise, and we may lose their trust. This is particularly true in dealing with tape of the president of the United States. The NPR rule, therefore, is that there should be no internal editing of the president.

Objectionable language NPR's policy is to avoid offending our listeners. We are, in a genuine sense, a family network. Under normal circumstances, we do not allow offensive language to be broadcast without a specific and strong justification. Our policy is to avoid any gratuitous or unnecessary use of such language. In cases when offensive language is contained in actualities, and cannot be edited out, it should be electronically blocked ("bleeped"). In the rare instances in which the reporter, the editor, and the producer all agree that certain offensive language is vital to the meaning and journalistic integrity of a report, NPR mandates certain procedures, including advance notice to stations, before the language may be broadcast (see below). Again, the use of such language on the air will be approved in only the rarest of cases.

Definition: It is difficult to provide a precise definition of obscene or offensive language and impossible to provide one agreeable to everyone. Language that is objectionable to some people is considered by others to be within acceptable norms. Therefore, the criterion an NPR editor, producer, or reporter uses in this regard is not personal attitudes and sensibilities, but rather a considered, journalistic judgment about what may be offensive to others. *Webster's New World Dictionary*, in attempting to define "obscene," calls it something that is "offensive to one's feelings, or to prevailing notions, of modesty or decency." (For a discussion of the legal aspects of this issue, see p. 271.)

In general, what is offensive under "prevailing notions" includes graphic language about sexual activity and excretory functions; curses and expletives; epithets derogatory to racial, ethnic, or religious groups, or to women or men; and vivid descriptions of violence and gore. In many cases it is not the words themselves that are offensive but their use in a way that is sensational or appeals to prurient interest—i.e., intended to be sexually provocative or exciting.

The so-called "seven dirty words" listed by the FCC are always considered offensive in the context of broadcasting. For your information, if not enlightenment, they are *shit, piss, fuck, cunt, cocksucker, motherfucker,* and *tits.* Their use is always subject to NPR approval and notification procedures. Other words are also obviously in the category of offensive language, slurs like *nigger*, *kike*, *bitch*, and *faggot*.

On the other hand, most Americans would not be offended by hearing relatively mild expletives like *hell* or *damn*. Of course, a reporter or commentator should not use these words in a script without a special reason, but when they occur in an actuality, they would not need to be bleeped. Nor would they trigger NPR approval and notification procedures.

For the myriad of words and expressions in between, it is a matter of taste and judgment. You may wish to ask yourself whether your parents or your grandparents would object, and, if they would, think twice about how vital the words are to the story. Can another word be substituted without loss of meaning—for example, using a Latin derivative instead of its Anglo-Saxon equivalent? Remember, though, that while clinical descriptions generally are less offensive than graphic ones, even clinical descriptions may offend some.

We can be careful without being prudish. For a description of a sex act, you may wish to ask yourself what you would do if your 10-year-old child heard it. Would you be embarrassed? Would you have to explain it to the child? Would that be easy or difficult? For descriptions of gore and bodily functions, you may want to ask whether it would affect your digestion if you heard it during a meal.

A general rule: Err on the side of caution. Taste and sound judgment are a better guide than rigid application of a set of rules. When in doubt, don't trust the decision to yourself alone. Ask your colleagues for their comments.

Procedures: When the reporter, the editor, and the producer all agree that offensive (or potentially offensive) language cannot be edited out or electronically blocked and that its inclusion in a report is vital to the meaning and integrity of that report, the following procedures *must* be followed, even though these steps require extra time and work:

1. The vice president of news or, in his absence, the managing editor must give prior approval. Each request should include a considered explanation of why the offensive language must be used and a copy of the tape. No report containing offensive language may be broadcast without this approval.
2. If the vice president or managing editor gives approval, the stations must be notified via DACS message.

How to DACS the stations: A separate early DACS (12–24 hours before broadcast, not just part of a show rundown) must be sent to stations explaining what the offensive language is, and how it appears in context. The DACS should say precisely where the wording is in the report (how many minutes and seconds from the start) and give the complete paragraph, with sentences before and after, as it is actually used. This extra wording is essential to allow stations to cut away from the program if they so choose.

In addition to the early DACS, the show rundown should provide a warning about the offensive language. It may also be appropriate in many cases to advise listeners on the air (in the introduction to the piece, for example) that the upcoming report contains potentially offensive language or descriptions parents may not deem appropriate for their children.

". . . prepared this report" Avoid starting a report with tape. For the most part, such construction is only a poor substitute for good writing. You also will have to make sure that the listener does not think that the first voice after the intro is the reporter's. The intro cannot say *NPR's Joe Nipper reports* if the first voice the listener hears is Senator George Mitchell. The easiest way around this problem has been to write, *NPR's Joe Nipper prepared this report*. But over the years that construction has become hackneyed. Use your imagination. Often a way can be found to take into account the beginning of the report: *NPR's Natalie Nipper reports on an unusual Sunday session of the Senate, which opened with a statement from Senator George Mitchell*. Corollary: If a piece opens with natural sound, it is *not* necessary to use the words *prepared this report*.

Tape use in newscasts and shows The relationship between newscasts and the shows in which they appear is a tricky one, especially when it involves the use of tape (actualities and reports). The principle to follow is this: Listeners should not hear the same material repeated within only a few moments of the first time they hear it. You don't want an ALL THINGS CONSIDERED half-hour to start with a billboard containing a tease cut of tape, followed by a newscast with the same actuality, followed by the lead story with the same tape. For the same reason, a reporter's news spot should not appear within close range of the reporter's piece in a show. But just as reporters' spots and pieces can appear in the same program if they are separated by enough air time, so, too, can those good cuts of tape.

". . . told NPR" This construction should not be used to enhance otherwise routine reporting, as in *The ambassador told NPR that 4,000 people had died*. Its purpose is to point out not just that someone talked with us, but that the discussion was exclusive and that NPR is breaking the news and advancing the story.

Part III

A Legal Guide for the Radio Journalist

William E. Kennard and Jacqueline R. Kinney

National Public Radio is committed to providing comprehensive, accurate, and thoughtful news coverage. Fulfilling this commitment requires that NPR reporters and editors—as well as radio station managers—fully exercise the rights guaranteed under the First Amendment. NPR not only uses free press and free speech guarantees to defend its news coverage and practices when problems arise, but also considers the active assertion of those rights a part of every reporter's and editor's daily job. The surest way to lose one's freedom is to take it for granted.

Journalists must recognize, however, that the First Amendment does not sanction all behavior merely because it occurs while you are covering the news. Certain fundamental rights of individuals are balanced against the right to freedom of the press. These include individuals' rights to privacy, not to have false statements made about them, not to have their reputations unjustly destroyed, and not to have their solitude disturbed on their private property. Generally, you will avoid infringing these rights simply by practicing good journalism—by checking all facts carefully, writing fair and balanced stories, and using good judgment. But familiarity with basic legal principles will go a long way toward minimizing the chance of being sued. You should be able to recognize potential legal problems. The ultimate goal, of course, is to ensure that you spend your time on the news, rather than in court.

A general knowledge of the law also is necessary to produce the kind of stories that meet NPR's standards. You must be able to use state and federal laws granting access to government information, records and meetings. You must know how the law protects you against being forced to identify your sources and other news-gathering information. You should know how far the First Amendment lets you go in seeking to give listeners the best and most accurate information.

Finally, you must be sensitive to the fact that aggressive exercise of the First Amendment can be an expensive proposition. Given the high cost of defending against legal claims, even a victory can take a huge financial toll. Plaintiffs sue news organizations for a variety of reasons, often the least of which is a meritorious claim. They sue to intimidate, to create the appearance that they have been wronged, or to generate publicity for themselves or for a cause. For anyone covering the news, there is no foolproof method to avoid being sued. But there are steps you can and should take to lessen the likelihood of a lawsuit, and to minimize the inconvenience and expense of one should it arise.

Defamation: Libel and Slander

Inaccurate, sloppy reporting accounts for a high percentage of libel suits against media organizations. The pressure to be first on the air with a breaking story can result in broadcasting statements before they can be verified. And if false statements also defame and harm someone, a libel suit is likely to follow.*

The rules governing libel claims—what a libel plaintiff must prove and what defenses are available to the accused—are generally a matter of state law, although because of the First Amendment, all libel plaintiffs must provide fault in order to collect damages. Thus, while basic principles are generally uniform throughout the states, the case law and libel statutes of the relevant state should be consulted when problems arise.

Elements of Libel

To collect damages, a libel plaintiff must prove that the defendant broadcast a *false* statement that defamed the plaintiff's reputation or good name, causing injury. The defamatory statement need not have been made by an employee of the defendant. A free-lance reporter, a commentator—even a call-in listener—can libel someone. And every time a libelous statement is rebroadcast, a new claim

---

*Technically, "libel" refers to a written defamation and "slander" refers to an oral defamation, but the legal standards governing both are similar.

may arise. So check and doublecheck your facts, particularly if your story could cast someone in a negative light.

Some statements are defamatory per se—those, for instance, that accuse someone of criminal action, morally reprehensible behavior, business impropriety, bad business practice, mental illness, or a disreputable disease. A plaintiff who can prove that such a statement is *false* can collect damages without having to prove any actual injury to reputation.

Other false statements can be libelous even though their defamatory nature is not readily apparent. Extrinsic facts about someone or the context of a particular statement in a story can make it defamatory. For instance, a false statement that a businessman had flown to Paris on a certain weekend would not be libelous in and of itself. But it might be if the statement were part of a story about a bank fraud in which a key meeting was held in Paris on that same weekend.

Because a libel plaintiff must be identified by name or by reference, the manner in which a person or group is accused of wrongdoing is also significant. When a statement refers to a group, no single member of the group is libeled unless there is enough detail to identify the individuals in the group. For example, if a story about a big city police force falsely stated that "some members of the police department are crooks," it would be difficult for any one officer to sue. Of course, if the details of the story more clearly indicated specific individuals, the identifiable persons would have a better case.

Public figures vs. private individual. The required proof of fault for broadcasting a libelous statement depends on whether the plaintiff is a public official/public figure or a private person. A public official/public figure must show that the defendant acted with "actual malice." "Actual malice" is a legal term that has little to do with the common usage of the word "malice." Instead, it means that the reporter or the news organization had actual knowledge that the published statement was false, or had a reckless disregard for the truth or falsity of the statement. A private person need only show that the reporter was negligent in publishing a false statement.

To illustrate the difference, assume a reporter's story falsely states that a local politician and a school bus driver were both leaders of an organized crime ring. The politician would have a more difficult time collecting damages in a libel action. As a public official, he would have to show that the reporter either knew or should have known that the statement was false *or* that the reporter did not really care whether it was true and broadcast it anyway. The school bus driver, on the other hand, is not a public figure or public official, and therefore merely has to show that the reporter failed to take reasonable steps to determine the truth of the statement—such as asking the bus driver whether the statement was true to attempting to verify the statement independently.

Sometimes an otherwise private person may be deemed a "limited purpose" public figure if he voluntarily involved himself in the controversy that gave rise to the libel claim. In such cases, the plaintiff must meet the actual malice, not the negligence, standard.

Defenses Against Libel Claims

A general awareness of the defenses available to a libel claim can help you minimize the basis for a libel suit. Keep in mind, however, that these defenses, particularly the scope of the testimonial and public-record defenses, vary from state to state.

Truth. Truth is an absolute defense to claims of libel. But truth is rarely a simple matter. Thus, reporters should keep notes of all information that will help demonstrate the steps taken to verify the facts in a story.

Testimony taken during court and legislative hearings. Statements made in official judicial and legislative proceeding are immune from libel claims. Be sure to attribute those statements to the official proceeding; if you were not there to hear them yourself, be sure the transcript is official or from a reputable source.

Fair and accurate reports of public records. Reports based on the contents of public records typically are immune from libel claims as long as the reports are fair and accurate. Carefully attribute all such statements to the precise public record in which they appear, describing the nature of the document if necessary. Check state open-records laws to determine which records are public.

Consent. If the plaintiff made statements to you knowing that you are a reporter and that the statements would be broadcast, you may reasonably infer consent. If in doubt, ask for written consent, because consent is a defense to a libel claim. Be aware, however, that the defense is limited by the scope of the consent. If consent is conditioned upon review of the story by the subject, then only those statements that have been reviewed by the speaker or his agent may be broadcast. *NPR policy is not to allow such conditional consent agreements.* Do not agree to let anyone you interview hear your report before it is broadcast.

Opinion. Stations that editorialize or air editorials or commentaries should be aware that a statement of opinion is not necessarily immune from a libel claim. The U.S. Supreme Court has ruled that opinion can be libelous if assertions of facts underlying the opinion are defamatory. Thus, like any other broadcast, an editorial or commentary can be libelous if it contains false assertions of fact.

Corrections and retractions. NPR policy is to correct errors. More to the point of this chapter, a carefully worded correction or retraction may let you avoid a suit, or at least mitigate damages. Retraction statutes vary from state to state, and you should be extremely careful not to admit fault or otherwise preclude defenses in case a claim is filed later. Always have legal counsel review any such correction or retraction before it is broadcast.

Invasion of Privacy

Claims of invasion of privacy can arise not only from stories broadcast but from reporting practices as well. NPR reporters must be sensitive to the fact that the immediacy of radio and the necessity to record sound make them especially vulnerable to violating someone's personal privacy. Like libel, privacy is a matter of state law.

Invasion of privacy is divided into the following principal areas:

Intrusions. This branch of privacy is aimed at protecting a person's private space or solitude. Regardless of the story that is broadcast, the act of reporting may be an invasion of privacy if it involves trespassing or otherwise intruding into a plaintiff's reasonable realm of privacy. To avoid an intrusion claim, always try to obtain consent before entering private property for news-gathering purposes.

Public disclosure of private facts. A story that reports private, intimate, embarrassing facts about a person—such as details about personal hygiene or sexual conduct—is likely to cause legal problems if those facts are highly offensive to a reasonable person. Truth is *not* a defense, but "newsworthiness" is. Thus, as long as the information is lawfully obtained, stories may lawfully disclose such facts if they are of legitimate public concern. The public has a legitimate interest in information about the public lives of public figures and even some aspects of public figures' private lives, for instance. But the newsworthiness defense is generally much more difficult to use successfully in claims brought by private individuals. Private individuals must be directly involved in a *newsworthy event* before such a defense is available.

False light invasion of privacy. Stories involving a plaintiff's private life that cast the plaintiff in a false light also may cause legal problems. Although the false light cause of action technically is an invasion of privacy, it includes elements of defamation (libel). If the story involves a public figure, for instance, the plaintiff must show that the statement was broadcast with knowledge of, or in reckless disregard for, its false nature. And the statement's truth *is* a defense in this area of privacy law.

Misappropriation. The tort of misappropriation is rare, and it does not apply to satire or political commentary. But it is an area of concern. Misappropriation typically occurs when a well-known person's name is used to endorse a product without obtaining the person's permission. Avoid including segments in stories that may create a seeming endorsement of a product or service.

Impersonations of famous persons are also troublesome and may give rise for misappropriation in some states if the impersonations are used to promote products or services.

Consent as a Defense

Consent is always a defense to a claim of invasion of privacy. You cannot invade someone's privacy if he or she allows you access knowing that you will broadcast the information. If questionable statements concern a minor or incompetent person, however, be sure to get the consent of a parent or guardian.

Use of Recording Devices

In addition to providing a basis for a claim for invasion of privacy, certain uses of recording equipment may also violate federal or state wiretap statutes. The key to avoiding legal problems when taping a conversation is *consent*— knowing when it is needed and being sure to get it. Again, the law varies from state to state.

Generally, you can record speeches and conversations where the recording would be reasonably expected under the circumstances. Recording a face-to-face interview when the subject can see the recorder is permissible because consent can be presumed. If a recorder is not visible, or the conversation takes place over the telephone, consent of the other party may be required, depending on the state where the call or interview takes place and how the material will be used. When a conversation is being recorded for the purpose of a live or later broadcast, the FCC requires you to state your intent to broadcast the conversation, unless the other party is already aware the conversation will be broadcast.

Both federal and state laws apply to interstate telephone conversations. You must be familiar with the law of the state in which the call originates and the law of the state in which it is received. The federal government and most states allow the taping of a call when one party (i.e., the caller) consents. Eleven states, however, require the consent of *both* parties.* Even in the states where one-party consent generally is allowed, the laws vary greatly, so do not presume it is legal to use material from a call to which only one party has consented. When in doubt, consult an attorney.

Whatever the legal requirement, NPR policy is clear: The person being recorded is always told. There is no surreptitious recording.

---

*The 11 states that require both parties to consent before a telephone call can be taped legally are California, Delaware, Florida, Illinois, Louisiana, Maryland, Massachusetts, Montana, New Hampshire, Pennsylvania, and Washington.

The Reporter's Privilege

On the eve of the U.S. Senate's vote on the confirmation of Judge Clarence Thomas as a Supreme Court Justice in October 1991, NPR reporter Nina Totenberg and *Newsday* reporter Timothy M. Phelps reported allegations by Anita Hill that Thomas had sexually harassed her while she worked for him at the Equal Employment Opportunity Commission. As a result of the reports, the Senate Judiciary Committee delayed the confirmation vote and held many hours of additional hearings to investigate the allegations. Although Thomas ultimately was confirmed, the dramatic hearings riveted the nation and sparked national debate over sexual harassment and the process of selecting Supreme Court justices.

Totenberg and Phelps learned about Hill's allegations from a confidential source or sources. The committee, which was poised to vote on Thomas before the NPR and *Newsday* stories, apparently had planned *not* to disclose the allegations. Some senators, believing that the information had been "leaked" to the press to prevent Thomas' confirmation, called for an investigation and appointed a special independent counsel to investigate. The independent counsel issued subpoenas and demanded that the reporters identify who told them about Hill's allegations. Totenberg and Phelps refused to comply, claiming that the First Amendment protects against compelled disclosure of news-gathering information, particularly when the information is not essential to prosecution of criminal charges.

Ultimately, the Senate did not require the reporters to comply. But the story focused attention on a classic conflict between journalists and the legal process.

Promising a source confidentiality often is the only way to obtain information about such matters as government wrongdoing. If reporters are not able to keep names secret, some of their most valuable sources will dry up, and the public will be deprived of vital information about government and other institutions.

Because of high-profile cases like the Anita Hill-Clarence Thomas controversy, most reporters recognize the reporter's privilege issue in connection with a government demand to identify a confidential source. But reporters and news organizations frequently are served with subpoenas or other informal demands for a whole range of news-gathering information, including requests to turn over notes, tapes and outtakes, to testify at trials or depositions, and to reveal confidential background information not included in a story. Government prosecutors and law enforcement officers are a common source of such demands, but criminal defendants, civil litigants, and other private persons often ask reporters for information as well. Indeed, many view subpoenaing an enterprising investigative journalist as a quick and inexpensive alternative to a private investigation.

The U.S. Supreme Court has determined that the First Amendment does not afford journalists an absolute privilege against compelled disclosure in all circumstances. Countervailing interests, such as guaranteeing a criminal defendant access to all evidence that might exonerate him, may require you to identify a confidential source or turn over tapes from the scene of a crime—or face the possibility of being in contempt of court.

Whether you must endure the expense and hassle of compliance (or fighting compliance) with such requests depends on the jurisdiction. Many state courts have recognized a qualified privilege to refuse to disclose the sources for a story. Twenty-eight states have shield laws affording varying degrees of protection against subpoenas.* To overcome the privilege, the person seeking disclosure typically must show that the information sought is material and relevant to a probable violation of law, that the information is not available from alternative sources, and that there is a compelling, overriding interest in the information.

The privilege protecting news gathering is weakest when a criminal defendant seeks information that might prove his innocence, especially when that information is not available from any other source. In such cases, the defendant's constitutional right to a fair trial may outweigh the First Amendment right to protect news sources. You are less likely to have to comply when requests from civil litigants seeking information for private claims when alternative sources of the information have not been exhausted. No countervailing constitutional considerations are present in such cases.

It is essential that you consult your editors and your news organization's attorney before complying with any subpoena or demand for news-gathering information. Never simply ignore a subpoena, and never destroy tapes or other materials after they have been requested. Ultimately, the decision to comply or to suffer the consequences of protecting the source is yours. But your editors and attorneys can help you decide how and whether to comply with an official demand. If a subpoena requests only tapes of materials that already have been broadcast, there may be little reason not to turn them over. When unpublished or confidential information is sought, however, an attorney can determine whether it is appropriate to refuse to comply based on a state's shield law or common-law privilege. Note that partial compliance is problematic because it may be deemed a waiver and deny you the privilege against future disclosure of related material.

Access to Information and Places

All good journalists know the information that comes easily usually is not the basis of ground-breaking stories. Good stories, which provide listeners with

---

*The states are Alabama, Alaska, Arizona, Arkansas, California, Colorado, Delaware, Georgia, Illinois, Indiana, Kentucky, Louisiana, Maryland, Michigan, Minnesota, Montana, Nebraska, Nevada, New Jersey, New Mexico, New York, North Dakota, Ohio, Oklahoma, Oregon, Pennsylvania, Rhode Island, and Tennessee.

significant information, come from relentlessly pursuing leads, staying at "routine" government meetings until final adjournment, and pouring over government documents. But even the best, most hardworking reporters have trouble securing information from government officials or access to official proceedings. When polite requests are refused, you need to know how to use the law to gain access to information.

Become familiar with the federal and state statutes that guarantee public access to records, meetings, and judicial proceedings. Often government officials themselves will not know that they are compelled by law to provide access. In such cases, merely explaining the law may be all that is necessary. But when access is refused, you should know how to compel officials to let you in.

Access to Public Records

State public records laws and the federal Freedom Of Information Act (FOIA) guarantee public access to government records and are an indispensable tool of journalism. The public records laws vary from state to state, but, like FOIA, they generally make all government documents public unless they fall under specified exemptions. Documents typically exempt from access are those pertaining to national security, personal privacy, and law enforcement investigation. A government agency or office that refuses to release a document usually must specify the reason for the denial, so be persistent in making a request unless the information sought is clearly exempt from disclosure. If the reasons given to deny access to a significant document seem unjustified, appeal the decision to withhold the information.

Access to Meetings and Official Proceedings

Open meetings laws, or "sunshine" laws, guarantee the public—and, thus, journalists—the right to attend meetings of government officials. State law generally specifies which governmental bodies must comply and what procedures must be followed, such as giving advance notice, publishing agendas and maintaining transcripts.

Knowledge of the relevant open meetings law usually is most useful when a governmental body holds a closed meeting. Typically, the laws permit closed sessions but only to conduct certain business, such as personnel matters, and only if they comply with specified procedures for closing the meeting. Always demand an explicit reason for closing a meeting, and request a summary of action taken during the closed session.

Access to Courts

Criminal court proceedings generally are presumed to be open to the public, and reporters cannot lawfully be denied access.* Access to civil proceedings is more restricted, however, and varies from jurisdiction to jurisdiction. In any case, always demand an explanation when any court proceeding is closed. Judges are required to hold a hearing when deciding to close a proceeding, and news organizations can challenge a decision to close the proceeding. Ask the judge for an opportunity to object as soon as you learn that a proceeding may be closed. The closure may then be temporarily delayed, giving you time to consult with an attorney about how to object to the closing.

The Federal Communications Commission

Because radio stations are licensed by the Federal Communications Commission, radio journalists must concern themselves with compliance with FCC rules and regulations. Although prohibited by statute from censoring programming directly, the FCC administers several rules and policies that affect programming content.

The Political Broadcasting Rules

You should be particularly aware of FCC regulation in the political broadcasting area. The FCC administers a rather comprehensive system of rules and regulations designed to ensure that broadcasters do not use the public airwaves to favor one candidate over another during an election. The commission also has stated that one of its objectives in administering the rules is to encourage maximum coverage of political campaigns. As a general rule, these regulations do not come into play with regard to the kinds of news programming produced by NPR.

The equal opportunities provision. The "equal opportunities" provision of Section 315 of the Communications Act is commonly (and incorrectly) referred to as the "equal time" provision. If a broadcaster allows a legally qualified candidate for public office to "use" a station's facilities, the broadcaster is required to afford equal opportunities to all other opposing, legally qualified candidates for the same office, provided that another candidate requests the opportunity within seven days.

*Special rules may apply for juvenile courts.

A "use" of a broadcast station by a candidate is now defined as an appearance of a legally qualified candidate that is controlled, approved, or sponsored by the candidate or the candidate's authorized committee. Section 315 specifically exempts the following types of broadcasts from the equal opportunities provision:

- Bona fide newscasts;
- Regularly scheduled bona fide news interview programs, such as CBS's Face the Nation;
- Bona fide documentaries, if the appearance of the political candidate is incidental to the presentation of the subject of the documentary;
- Live coverage of bona fide news events.

In addition, the FCC has said that under certain conditions candidate debates and news conferences are bona fide news events and exempt from the provision. To be exempt, the broadcast of the debate or news conference must be intended to inform the public rather than to favor or disfavor any candidate. It also must be covered live or broadcast reasonably close to the time of the debate or news conference. If these provisions are met, a news organization may decide to include only major candidates in a debate. Debates may be sponsored by the broadcaster or by a neutral third party, e.g., the League of Women Voters.

If your broadcasts don't meet these conditions, you may be required to provide air time for *all* the other legally qualified candidates. This may cause you little consternation in a general election for city council with only a Republican and a Democrat on the ballot. But what about the gubernatorial election with a Republican, a Democrat, a Libertarian, a Socialist Worker, and 15 other "legally qualified" candidates?

What's more, when you provide the air time, you cannot edit or censor the candidate except for obscenity (although you *can* restrict the length of the broadcast if it unreasonably disrupts the station's daily programming). Thus, even if the proposed broadcast contains libelous statements, you cannot reject the broadcast, although you would be exempt from liability under state libel and slander laws.

The equal opportunities rule extends beyond the candidates themselves through something called the "Zapple Doctrine." It requires a broadcast station to extend equal opportunities to the supporters of political candidates. A station that affords air time to supporters or representatives of one candidate during a campaign period must afford comparable time to the supporters or representatives of opponents. Again, bona fide news programs are exempt.

The personal attack rule. A station is subject to this rule if, during a broadcast presentation of views on a controversial issue of public importance, someone attacks the "honesty, character, integrity, or similar personal qualities of an identified person or group." Station editorials are subject to this rule, but legitimate news broadcasts are exempt.* If an attack covered by the rule occurs, the station must take the following actions within one week:

• Notify the person or group attacked of the date, time, and title of the program on which the attack was made.

• Send the person "attacked" a script or tape of the attack, or an accurate summary if either is available.

• Offer a "reasonable opportunity" to answer the attack on the air. (The station does not have to allow the attacked individual on the air to respond as long as it reads his response.)

Station editorializing. The FCC defines an "editorial" as comments reflecting the viewpoints of the *licensee* of the station. A station editorial can be made by the station manager or any other employee permitted by the licensee to speak for the station. A statement may be an editorial even if it is not labeled as such. For example, if the station manager endorsed a referendum issue on the air, this would constitute a station editorial.

Public radio stations are prohibited by statute (47 U.S.C. 399) from supporting or opposing political candidates but are allowed to editorialize about issues. Commercial stations, which are allowed to support and oppose candidates, come under the FCC's political editorializing rule. Thus if a commercial station has endorsed a candidate in an editorial, the station is required to provide notification of date and time of the broadcast, provide a tape or transcript, and offer reply time to other legally qualified candidates.

To avoid triggering the equal opportunities rule, the commercial broadcaster may comply with the rule by offering either the candidate *or* the candidate's representative the opportunity to respond to the editorial. The station must notify the candidate within 24 hours of the editorial, unless the editorial is broadcast less than 72 hours before the election. In this case, the notification must be sent out sufficiently in advance of the broadcast of the editorial to allow the candidates or their representatives to respond before Election Day.

The Fairness Doctrine

Remember the fairness doctrine? The fairness doctrine required broadcasters to ensure the balanced presentation of opposing viewpoints on issues of public importance. In 1987, the FCC determined that the fairness doctrine could be unconstitutional and was contrary to the public interest, and abolished

---

*The personal attack rule also does not apply to attacks made by candidates or their campaign associates on other candidates, nor to attacks on anyone else made during a candidate's "use" of a station's facilities as part of the equal opportunities rule.

it. This controversial action was upheld in the courts, but Congress has considered legislation to resurrect the fairness doctrine each year since the FCC abolished it. None of these Congressional efforts has been successful thus far, but there is strong sentiment for the fairness doctrine from the Democratic leadership in Congress.

Obscenity and Indecency

Radio stations that broadcast obscene or indecent material are subject to fines and license revocation. In extreme cases, the FCC can refer the case to the Department of Justice for criminal prosecution. Obscenity and indecency are difficult areas because the stakes are high, but the standards for determining whether a broadcast is obscene or indecent are subjective and not altogether clear.

Material is obscene if a reasonable person applying contemporary community standards would find that the material appeals to "prurient interests" by describing sexual conduct in a "patently offensive manner," and if the material lacks any serious literary, artistic, political, or scientific value. At the risk of oversimplifying, obscenity is truly hardcore pornographic material without any redeeming social or scientific value. Material held to be obscene is prohibited from the airwaves altogether.

By contrast, it is legal to broadcast indecent material—but only during certain hours. The FCC defines indecency material as "language or material that describes, in terms patently offensive as measured by contemporary community standards for the medium, sexual or excretory functions." The determination of whether material is indecent depends upon the circumstances of each case. The FCC considers not only the material itself, but the context in which it is broadcast. The FCC would be unlikely to deem indecent a reading of some of James Joyce's more ribald passages during a radio program devoted to literary discussion. But it would be more likely to rule the other way about a morning talk show routine in which the announcers repeatedly use double entendre and innuendo to refer to various types of oral sex.

Most radio journalists have few occasions to be concerned about obscenity and indecency. News or documentary programming typically provides a sufficient context to eliminate concerns about running afoul of prohibitions against obscenity and indecency. But if you are in doubt, be sure to consult your editors, attorneys, and station manager. Obscenity and indecency are determined by reference to prevailing community standards, so it never hurts to get a number of people to assist you in dealing with a questionable story.

Also, note that in March 1992 the U.S. Supreme Court let stand a lower court ruling that the FCC's 24-hour ban on indecent programming was unconstitutional. As a result, the FCC plans to develop new standards for determining when children are not likely to be in the listening audience. During these "safe harbor" time periods, broadcasters will be able to air indecent programming legally. The current safe harbor period is 8 P.M. until 6 A.M., although most broadcasters delay questionable material until 10 P.M.

NPR's policy is to avoid gratuitous use of offensive language. When such language is used, it is to preserve the meaning and journalistic integrity of the report. This policy goes beyond the question of whether language is legally obscene or indecent. Policy and procedures regarding the journalistic decision to allow such offensive material on the air are set out in the section on objectionable language in Part II of this Stylebook.

William E. Kennard is a partner with the Washington, D.C., law firm of Verner, Liipfert, Bernhard, McPherson and Hand. He formerly served as assistant general counsel and First Amendment attorney for the National Association of Broadcasters. He is a graduate of Stanford University and Yale Law School.

Jacqueline R. Kinney is an associate with the Washington, D.C., law firm of Verner, Liipfert, Bernhard, McPherson and Hand. She formerly served as legal fellow for the Reporters Committee for Freedom of the Press. She is a graduate of the University of Wisconsin–Madison and the Columbus School of Law, Catholic University.

The authors acknowledge the contributions of Janice F. Hill, formerly Assistant General Counsel of National Public Radio, who prepared previous versions of this chapter.

APPENDIXES

Buying Equipment

There are many different sources for the equipment described in Chapter 11, "Field Recording: Equipment." Much of it is available through your local stereo shop or music-and-sound emporium. Prices range from list price down to 50 percent off list, depending on where you buy. Discount stores, however, are not necessarily the best places to shop. If you value good advice, the availability of a service department, or a better selection of equipment, consider spending a bit more money and getting a lot more in return.

Many mail-order establishments sell cassette and DAT recorders, microphones, accessories, and tapes at discount prices. Look for their ads in the classified sections of audio magazines.* With a bit of detective work and bargaining skill, though, you may be able to do as well in your local area.

Cassette Recorders

Top honors for portable cassette recorders go to Japanese manufacturers. Sony, Marantz, and Aiwa have the most popular models among reporters in the field. Sony's stalwarts are the TCD5 Pro II, a deluxe, stereo machine, and the TCD5M, a less expensive model with ¼-inch mike inputs instead of XLR jacks. Sony's WM-D6 "Pro Walkman" is a favorite of reporters who value light weight and small size.

Marantz's PMD-222 is, at this writing, the only mass-marketed mono cassette deck with an XLR input jack. It's more suitable for reporter uses—from phone feeding to tape logging—than the stereo Sony machines.

---

*It used to be that you could save the cost of sales tax when you ordered something from out of state by mail, but that's not always the case now. Many states are enforcing what are called "use taxes" on out-of-state purchases.

Cassette recorder models used in broadcast reporting aren't updated as often as other consumer electronics, but check with your dealer for the latest information on current models.

DAT Recorders

The turnover of models has been faster for DAT, befitting the latest technology. Panasonic's SV-255 and Sony's TCD-D10 Pro were the first stalwarts, but at this writing, smaller machines are coming into the market from Aiwa, Denon, and several other manufacturers, all of them potentially useful for field recording. *None* of these DAT decks does a very good job of feeding a phone line without an accessory amplifier, so if your work involves filing by phone, consider using analog cassette decks instead of DAT.

Microphones

Broadcasters' favorites in the microphone category have not changed much over the years. Omnidirectional mikes like Electro-Voice's 635A and RE50 and Shure's SM63 get a lot of use; the British Broadcasting Corporation (BBC) issues its reporters AKG D130 omnis. NPR reporters use Beyer's M58 at present.

One of the few recent advances in basic microphone technology is the use of neodymium magnets, which offer stronger electrical output than iron-core magnets. Shure's VP 64 is the first hand-held omni mike to take advantage of this.

Finding a cardioid mike that works well when hand-held is a tough job. Many popular broadcast studio mikes, such as the Sennheiser MD421, the Electro-Voice RE20, and the Shure SM7, are awkward for hand-held use; check out the Electro-Voice RE15, RE16, or RE18, or the Shure SM57 or SM58 instead.

Many manufacturers, lured by the market for highly directional mikes that can be attached to video cameras, have brought out "short shotgun" mikes that can be hand-held. Low-cut filtering in the mikes reduces handling noise, and you can cut it further by using a pistol-grip isolation mount to hold the mike.

Accessories

Most of the major items listed above are widely available. But some accessories are harder to locate: the special mike cables with XLR and phone or mini plugs, telephone interface boxes, and specialized clamps for attaching mikes to podiums or stands, to name a few. If you can't find a broadcast supply dealer in your area, try Audio Services Corporation (800–228–4429) on the West Coast, Full Compass Systems (800–356–5844) in the Midwest, or Bradley Broadcast Sales (800–732–7665) on the East Coast. You also can find suppliers by checking ads in *Broadcast Engineering*, *Radio World*, or *Broadcasting Magazine*.

Assessing the Studio:
A Checklist

1. *Number and Type of Sources Available:* Reel-to-reel tape machines, cart machines and erased carts, cassette machines, mike inputs, phone patches, turntables, compact disc players, DAT machines?
2. *Quality and Format of Mastering Recorders:* Full track, two-track, four-track, multi-track, DAT, other? Machines and heads clean and up to spec? Machines biased for your tape stock?
3. *Quality of Playback Sources:* Cart noise, turntable rumble, sampling rate match, wow and flutter, hiss, hum?
4. *Operation of Equipment:* Remote controls for tape and cart machines, turntables, CDs, DAT?
5. *Special Console Functions:* Auxiliary mix ability, mix-minus ability, equalization, "solo" function, patch points, pan pot, phantom power, metering, cue positions, talkback?
6. *Outboard Equipment Available:* Reverberation, delay units, compressors and limiters, filters, equalizers? Clocks, tape timers and counters?
7. *Unity Gain Set-Up:* Board master pot(s) and recorder input/output calibration (system design-centering)?
8. *Fader Action:* Taper-type? Smooth, noise-free operation? Track uniformity?
9. *"Hotpot" Ability on Playback Sources:* Can machines be started with the pot open without hearing "clicks" or "thumps"?
10. *Quality of Monitoring Sources:* Secondary monitors available? Mono-stereo switching?
11. *Quality of Studio and Control Room Acoustics?*

Appendix C
Meters

Audio equipment has a wide variety of meters. Some use a moving needle to show audio levels; others use light-emitting diodes (LEDs), liquid-crystal displays, or fluorescent-light segments in a bar graph. What do meters tell you? It depends on which type you're looking at, and the nature of the audio driving it.

"VU" Meters

The standard "VU" meter used by broadcasters to measure audio levels is actually a holdover from the past. In the early days of broadcasting, audio signals didn't extend into the high frequencies (not much beyond 5 kHz), and all equipment in the audio path used tubes. Today, we have wide-bandwidth audio systems (20 Hz to 20 kHz) and mostly solid-state or transistorized audio chains.

The slow "average-responding" VU meter was adequate in the past because the small audio bandwidth ignored any very fast, high-frequency "transient" sounds. Moreover, because the audio signal was passing through tubes, distortion increased gradually as the audio level increased, so the "averaging" VU meter display was accurate enough to avoid it. Transistors, on the other hand, keep distortion very low and *constant* as the level increases to a certain point. But when that level is exceeded, there is *extreme* and sudden distortion ("clipping") in most cases. So in today's wide-bandwidth, transistorized audio systems, a more accurate ("absolute" rather than "averaging") meter to display levels is better.

An additional concern is the difference between audio levels as displayed by a meter (*any* meter), and the audio's "perceived loudness"—that is, how loud it sounds to the human ear. Although the VU meter is designed to visually display audio levels in a way that is analogous to perceived loudness, it really doesn't do that; the meter shows when the operational parameters of an electrical circuit or system are being exceeded, not how loud or soft something *sounds*. The problem with the VU meter is that it doesn't show very *exact* information about the *electrical* levels, either!

The Peak Reading Meter

Instead of measuring a short-term average of audio levels as the VU meter does, the peak reading meter reads the absolute maximum, instantaneous, peak levels of audio.

The peak meter does not really do the job as far as perceived loudness is concerned, either, but it does display with greater accuracy the *audio* levels it measures. Because high-frequency transients and wide-bandwidth signals are desirable and feasible elements of today's audio—and because fairly exact distortion tolerances must be observed—a peak meter would seem to be the obvious choice over a VU meter.

Why, then, the proliferation and longevity of the VU meter? One answer is that the VU meter has been standardized throughout the international audio world; the peak meter has not (at least not in the United States). The confusing variety of peak meter types can be disconcerting to anyone used to the good old VU.

The "PPM"

In Britain and parts of Europe, one type of peak meter has been established as the standard, and it is used by the BBC and others. It is called the Peak Programme Meter, or "PPM," and works very nicely as a peak reading meter, with some limitations. Visually, its pointer rises somewhat faster than the VU meter, and falls much more slowly, so it does take some getting used to for someone familiar with the response of VU meters to audio signals. The PPM is a much more accurate absolute audio measurement device, designed to convey maximum audio levels to the human *eye*; it does not attempt to relate them to the ear at all.

The PPM is beginning to be accepted in the United States, and it is probably the only meter other than the VU found here to any great extent, but there are still far fewer PPM than VU meters. However, the fact that the PPM is a *standard* meter is helping dissolve one reason the VU is preferred. As the PPM becomes more accepted in the United States, perhaps it will push aside the VU and provide a more accurate standard meter.

One further note on the PPM standard: Although the meter's operation is standardized, its calibration and meter face notations are not. The meter shown in figure C.1 is the EBU-A scale meter, which is perhaps the easiest to get used to for those familiar with VU meters. If you set it up according to manufacturer's

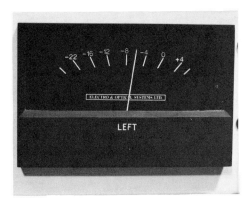

Figure C.1. The Peak Programme
Meter (PPM), with EBU-A scale.

instructions, you can observe levels much as you would with a VU meter, so that the pointer does not go above "0." Once you adjust to the timing response of the meter, it's smooth sailing.

Non-Mechanical Meters

Advances in fluorescent and liquid-crystal displays and their associated circuitry have made possible meters with no moving parts, which can respond instantly to audio signals and don't suffer from mechanical inertia. But because people are used to working with mechanical-needle meters that *do* have lag time, many of the new displays are designed to offer either "VU" or "peak reading" characteristics. Some of them also offer separate "overload" indicators or peak memories with numerical readouts that retain the highest peak values.

One manufacturer, Dorrough, markets an add-on meter that displays both peak and average levels (see Figure C.2). An arc of LEDs is arranged like the curve of a VU meter face; audio signals cause the LEDs to light up starting at the left and moving to the right for louder signals. A single LED indicates the peak audio levels, while at the same time a solid band of LED shows the average levels weighted to adjust for perceived loudness. The relatively high cost of this metering system has limited its penetration of the general meter market.

Metering for Digital Equipment

VU and peak-reading meters for analog equipment both set the "0" reference to leave a little "headroom" above "0"—that is, the needle can go a little bit above "0" before reaching the point of distortion. In part, this is because different pieces of gear offer varying amounts of headroom, and because the relationship

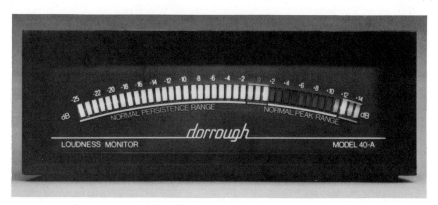

Figure C.2. The Dorrough Meter.

between actual electrical levels and meter movement varies with meter mechanics and the type of program material being metered.

Digital recording offers a much more black-and-white decision process for metering: "0" on a digital meter is the *highest* signal a digital recorder can record. Any signal stronger than digital "0" will be distorted significantly; the digital process cannot "describe" that signal because it has run out of 1's and 0's. (See Chapter 15, "Emerging Technologies and Techniques," for more information on digital audio.)

The trick with digital recording, then, is to keep the highest audio peaks as close to "0" as possible *without* going past "0." In practice, most manufacturers recommend that a test tone showing at "0" on a VU meter be adjusted to show -15 to -20 dB on a digital recorder's meter. This leaves 15 to 20 dB of headroom above the program operating level.

Appendix D
Tips on Recording from the Telephone

For news and information programming, audio from the telephone is a staple. Even in these days of satellite transmission, fiber optics, and digital technology, the telephone remains the most common conduit for on-location sound (actuality) that must hit the air quickly. And despite the fact that improvements in audio technology have made telephone audio even more of an "earsore," a phone feed often is the only way to get something newsworthy from a remote location on the air in a timely manner. And it's likely to remain so for some time to come.

Programmatic Concerns

Your first approach should be to keep the use of "phoners" to a bare minimum. Don't use a phone feed for anything other than a breaking story, and keep it as *short* as possible. Feature pieces or other non-dated productions should never use phone-quality audio. (Below are some ways to avoid the use of phoners entirely for distant interviews.)

Interfacing

When you record phone audio, be sure to use the proper equipment. Recording *from* the phone in the studio is more difficult than feeding *into* the phone from the field.

One simple device for recording from the studio phone is the **voice coupler**. This small box is permanently wired into a phone or line and provides a quarter-inch phone jack *output* for feeding a line-level signal to a console or recorder input. When using a coupler, it is most convenient to have the telephone instrument on-line equipped with a push-to-talk switch on its receiver. This is because the telephone receiver has to be "off the hook" while the feed is coming in, and the push-to-talk switch turns off the receiver's mouthpiece microphone when it is not depressed, thus ensuring that studio noise and conversation will not be included in the recording. (The coupler also allows feeding a line-level signal *into* the phone line as well, in lieu of "clipping on" to the receiver.)

For professional-quality phone feeds, *two-way* phone recordings, phone interviews, or broadcasts, you need a much more complex arrangement that usually involves a variation on the "speaker phone" or "telephone hybrid." This is beyond the scope of this book.

Improving Phone Audio Quality

Once the phone has been properly interfaced with a line-level input on a console or similar device, some amount of audio processing is usually in order. This can be done as the phone feed is being recorded, or the feed can be recorded "flat" (without processing) and then processed during subsequent production or dubbing. The audio processing that is useful for phoners can be divided into three steps: **filtering, equalization,** and **compression.**

Filtering. The first step, filtering, should use a device with a very steep "shelving"-type high frequency roll-off (a "low-pass filter"). This should be set to roll off at three to four kHz (but adjusted by *ear* to each phone feed). There is little or no audio above this frequency on a standard phone line, but there is *noise*. The longer the distance of the call, the more noise there will be on the line, generally. The filter's roll-off point should be adjusted relative to the amount of noise on the line. The trade-off to removing much of the noise is loss of high-frequency audio (i.e., intelligibility), so not all the noise can be filtered out. Your ear will determine the exact adjustment for the filter on that particular line, balancing the amount of noise removed to the amount of intelligibility lost. It is better to err on the side of intelligibility here, meaning that a little noise left in is preferable to a quiet but "dull" phone voice, which is more difficult to understand.

On some phone calls, or with some phone interfacing devices, low-frequency noise ("hum") is a problem. This can generally be removed without further audio quality degradation by the use of a "shelving"-type low-frequency roll-off ("high-pass filter"), set to around 150 Hz. So called "notch-filters" can also be used to remove this hum or any other discrete tones found on phone lines. A good device of this kind is the UREI 565 filter set.

Equalization. The next step is equalizing the phone line to increase intelligibility. Using an equalizer (see Appendix E) to reshape the frequency response of the phone line within its audio bandwidth can result in marked improvements in intelligibility. The equalizer should be patched into the audio chain *following* the filter(s). (Many processing devices offer high-pass and low-pass filters *plus* equalization together in a single, multi-stage unit.)

Although equalizer settings will be different for every phone line, the following basic curve is usually helpful, with the sections of the curve listed in decreasing order of importance.

1. 6 dB CUT at 400 Hz, wide bandwidth
2. 3 dB BOOST at 2.5 kHz, narrow bandwidth
3. 3 dB BOOST at 200 Hz, narrow bandwidth
4. 2 dB CUT at 800 Hz, moderate bandwidth

Basically, what this equalization curve does is decrease the energy in the middle of the phone line's bandwidth and increase the energy on both ends, in an attempt to flatten out the frequency response. The typical phone line's excess of energy in the 400 Hz region has a particularly negative effect on intelligibility. Reducing 400 Hz region energy alone will improve almost any phone line's sound.

Compression. Because of the reduction in energy caused by equalization, the phone line's intelligibility is improved, but its overall *volume* or loudness is reduced. For this reason, a moderate amount of *compression* after equalization is recommended. This will restore or even enhance the loudness of the phone line, which further improves its listenability, beyond the intelligibility increase from equalization. Compression can also serve as a protection device by helping to catch any excessive audio peaks that the phone line signal may have. (These peaks may even have been exaggerated by the equalization.)

More importantly, when the phone audio is going to be mixed with other full-fidelity audio (i.e., a phone interview, where the interviewer is in the studio and the guest is on the phone), compression of just the *phone* audio can help increase its apparent loudness relative to the studio voice. Without such compression, proper loudness-matching of the elements to the ear will result in widely divergent VU meter readings between the studio and phone audio. (Typically, an uncompressed phoner hitting 0 VU will match the loudness of a close-miked studio voice reading around -10 VU.) This can result in difficulties when matching *that* studio-voice recording to other studio-voice-only recordings in the same program, in which the studio voice is generally recorded at a much higher VU level. It is also an inefficient use of the dynamic range available on the tape, resulting in an *overall* noisier ("hissier") recording.

One drawback to compression is that while the phone audio's apparent loudness is increased, so too is any background noise on the phone line. In many cases, this noise level is rather high to begin with, and compression just makes it worse. Therefore, as with any audio processing tool, use it with moderation.

Dynamic Noise Filtering

Another effective processing device for phone improvement is the Dynamic Noise Filter or "DNF," manufactured by dbx, Symetrix, Audio and Design Recording, and others. This device serves to filter out noise between the words of the voice on the phone, and can often clean up a noisy line without much negative effect on the desired audio. Some DNF units are easy to operate, and other, more flexible designs are quite complex. Some are designed specifically for telephone audio. Beware of using a DNF on digitally processed phone lines (such as the ITT/ROLM system and others), or other extremely noisy, satellite-fed long distance lines. In these cases, the "gating" (opening and closing around the words) effect of the DNF may make the noise more distracting by its "coming and going" with the words than if it were just there at a constant level all the time. In many standard phoner situations, however, a good, simple DNF can be a useful and expedient tool for improving phone audio.

Additional Enhancement

Some people have experimented with phoners played back through so-called **aural exciters**, with some favorable results. These devices are patented processors intended to enhance the realism or richness of high-fidelity recordings, but seem to have some ability to improve the intelligibility and listenability of phoners, without a trade-off in excessive noise increase. These devices are manufactured by Aphex, EXR, and others, and are expensive. They must be used with moderation, but often they can help to put the "edge" back in otherwise dull-sounding phone audio.

The Tape-Sync

A technique that can eliminate the phone sound entirely from an interview done by phone is one called the **tape-sync** or **phone-sync** (also called a "double-ender" or a "simul-rec"). It requires more production time, and is therefore generally inappropriate for breaking news stories, but can be helpful in feature-type stories or other highly produced pieces, where putting phone-quality audio on the air is especially inappropriate.

The process requires a stereo console and two-track machine at the studio end, and any good recording equipment at the remote end. At the studio, assign the studio voice *only* to the *left* channel console output and record it only on the left track of the tape. Assign the phoner output *only* to the *right* channel console output and record it only on the right track of the tape. (It is helpful if the interviewer in the studio can hear a mono sum of both tracks in the headphones.)

Meanwhile, on the remote end, the guest merely conducts a normal phone conversation with the interviewer, speaking into and listening from the telephone receiver. However, someone at that location simultaneously makes a high-fidelity recording of the guest's end of the conversation by placing a microphone near the guest's mouth and rolling tape. This requires no interface with the telephone. In fact, it is important that no phone audio "leak" into the microphone from the telephone receiver earpiece, so the technician should be sure to place the mike on the opposite side of the guest's mouth from the telephone receiver and instruct the guest to hold the phone tightly to the ear and not to move around a lot.

Once the interview is completed, the recording made at the remote location is sent to the studio. There, put the recording on one tape machine and cue it to the beginning of the interview. Cue the studio (two-track) recording to the same point, which you find by listening to the right (phoner) track. Then start both machines at the same time, mix their outputs, and make a new, combined recording on a third recorder. Use only the *left* (studio mike) track of the studio recording in this mix.

Use the right track purely as a reference, since it is the only common element (or "sync-track") between the two tapes. Monitor this track occasionally in "cue," to see how far apart in timing the two tapes are drifting (which they always do). Once the two tapes have drifted sufficiently far apart to affect the dynamics of the conversation, stop all recorders, leave fader levels untouched, rewind the two playback machines a few seconds, re-sync them, and re-start the recording.You can make a pick-up edit in the new mix recording later. Any audible leakage on either end will make sync-drift instantly apparent, whereas without leakage, a full half-second or so of drift is often tolerable before re-synching is required.

If you're careful, and there is not a lot of background noise on either tape, you can re-sync "on-the-fly," by stopping the machine that is getting ahead for a second or two, and then restarting it (while the person on the lagging machine is speaking, of course). Quick fades down and up around the stop usually help. By the way, varispeed (varying the tape speed) during the synching process is not recommended, because it usually creates more error than it fixes, except when a gross speed error exists on either the studio or (more likely) the remote-end recording.

You can add audio processing to either side of the conversation independently, in an attempt to match acoustics, or whatever. Differences in microphones can be readily apparent to the listener in such a situation, so make every effort to put the remote guest in a quiet, "dead" environment, and use identical or similar sounding mikes on both ends.

Should the remote tape be lost in transit, or not arrive in time, you can mix-down or "sum" the studio two-track recording with optional audio processing on just the phone track. Regular phone-interview recording is the result; nothing lost, except time.

Other Tips

Remember that in most cases, you need not be satisfied with the quality of a phone line on the first attempt. Redial the call if the first connection is noisy, distorted, or low-level. If the call is long distance, call the operator and say, "This is station KXYZ, and we have been unable to get a broadcast quality line to (phone number). Can you please help us get one?" Occasionally the words "Press Urgent" have some effect, especially when dealing with overseas operators. Of course, if IDDD (International Direct Distance Dialing) is not available to the desired location and a call must be ordered for later delivery, you take what you get.

When someone is speaking into a regular telephone receiver on a phone feed or interview (especially from an outdoor pay phone) and the sound is muddy or distorted, ask the person to rap the receiver mouthpiece sharply against a hard surface a few times. This serves to break up any coagulations of carbon granules in the microphone that humidity may have caused (much like a saltshaker in the summertime). Often this will improve the sound.

Appendix E
An Introduction to Audio Processors

Audio processing is defined as the artificial manipulation of audio. It can be divided into three areas: manipulation of *frequency response, dynamic range,* and *time*. In the first case, the processors are called **equalizers** or **filters;** in the second, **compressors, limiters, expanders,** and **gates;** and in the third, **reverberation** and **delay units** of various types. There are occasional hybrids between categories.

Equalizers and Filters

These devices are designed to change the frequency response of an audio signal, so the resulting sound has a different tonal balance after being filtered or equalized. A "dull"-sounding recording can be "brightened" by having its proportion of high frequencies increased or "boosted" by an equalizer. A "tinny"-sounding recording can be "mellowed" by having its high frequencies reduced or attenuated (or "cut") by a filter. An equalizer can usually boost or cut, and generally a filter can *only* cut frequencies.

The actual design and layout of an equalizer or filter varies from unit to unit, but equalizers are generally denoted as being of the **graphic** or **parametric** type, with the hybrid "paragraphic" showing up now and then (see Figures E.1 and E.2). Filters are generally referred to as **low-pass** (filters out *highs*), **high-pass** (filters out *lows*), or **band-pass/band-reject** (*filters around/filters out* a certain middle band of frequencies). An extreme version of the latter is the **notch filter,** which can severely attenuate a very narrow band of frequencies, and leave all other frequencies basically untouched (see Figure E.2).

Compressors, Limiters, Expanders, and Gates

Compressors, limiters, expanders, and gates are all devices that change the dynamic range of an audio signal. For example, if a voice recording has VU meter readings that vary from -10 VU to 0 VU, a **compressor** can make that same voice read from -10 VU to -5 VU, or from -5 VU to 0 VU, or whatever. In other words, it *reduces* the dynamic range of a sound, or makes the difference between its loudest and quietest extremes smaller. A **limiter** does the same thing, but in a somewhat more brutal fashion. It acts as a sort of brick wall that does not allow any audio level to exceed a certain point, generally for protection purposes to avoid overmodulation, distortion, or tape saturation. Compressors can be used in a more creative fashion to increase the perceived loudness of a sound without increasing its maximum audio level. In other words, the meter never goes into the red, but stays at a higher level *more often* due to compression, which to our ears sounds *louder*. The *average* level over a period of time can be increased without the absolute maximum level being made any higher (see Figure E.3).

Expanders and **gates** are much less useful devices that basically do the opposite of compressors and limiters, respectively. They *increase* rather than reduce dynamic range, and are rarely used in broadcast productions.

Reverberation and Delay

These devices are used almost exclusively for special effects or in music and drama recordings. They can simulate a different (larger) acoustic space than the one in which the sound was really recorded. They can also be used to create surreal or "spacey" kinds of sounds, and can be quite entertaining and convincing.

A tape recorder can also be used to create a similar (though less versatile) effect by feeding its output back into its input. While the tape machine is recording something from a mixing console, put its monitor switch in the *PB* or *TAPE* mode, and carefully bring the recorder's output up into the mix on the console, so that now the recorder is recording the original sound *plus* a bit of its own recording of it, with the latter delayed in time by the amount of time it takes for a point on the tape to travel from the record head to the playback head (see Figure 14.4). You can experiment with tape speed as well; 15 ips produces a faster tape echo than does 7–1/2 ips.

The Dynamic Sibilance Controller

This device, usually referred to as a **de-esser**, combines some functions of an equalizer and a compressor/limiter, in an attempt to reduce some of the excessive "S" sounds that some close-miked voices exhibit. They cut high frequencies in this sibilant region (roughly 5 to 8 kHz), but *only* when sibilance is present. In this way, non-sibilant audio in this same frequency area is not lost, but when a quick burst of it comes along, the "de-esser" drops the level of this frequency band very quickly, and equally quickly restores things to normal once the sibilance has passed. Excessive use of this device can make a person seem to have a severe speech impediment, so exercise care in its use (see Figure E.2).

Summary

These devices are handy tools to help solve problems, but they are *never* a primary solution. There is almost always a better way to fix the problem, but when worse comes to worst, audio processing *may* help. Moderation is the key here; overuse of any of the devices is a common trap, so beware. When using any one of these devices, experiment to become intimately familiar with its operation and its effect on various sounds before you use it on serious production. This will improve your eventual results as well as save you much time in the heat of the production battle.

Figure E.1. A Parametric Equalizer (Ward-Beck Systems). This model is built into a mixing console.

Figure E.2. A Rack of Audio Processing Equipment. From top to bottom: a ``de-esser'' or dynamic sibilance controller, a telephone interfacing device, a paragraphic equalizer, a notch filter, another paragraphic, and another notch filter. This system could be used to separate phone lines simultaneously, or one stereo tape.

Figure E.3. A pair of simple compressors.

Appendix F
Analog Tape Track Configurations

CASSETTE FORMAT

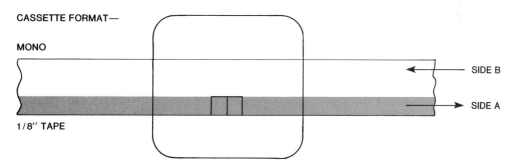

Figure F.1. **Cassette format—Mono.** Almost all mono cassette recorders use this bidirectional format, operating at 1–7/8 inches-per-second (ips). Cassette tape's width is 0.150 inches, or slightly more than 1/8 of an inch.

CASSETTE FORMAT

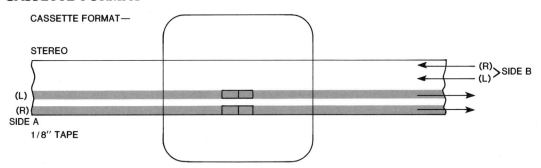

Figure F.2. Cassette format—Stereo. Stereo cassette recorders use two adjacent tracks in this bidirectional format. Playback of a stereo cassette on a mono cassette machine provides a compatible mono sum of the two stereo tracks at the playback head.

REEL-TO-REEL FORMAT

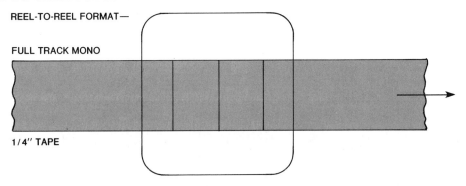

Figure F.3. Reel-to-Reel format (1/4 inch)—Full-Track Mono. This monaural format uses the entire width of the tape in one direction only. Standard tape speeds for all reel-to-reel formats can run anywhere from 15/16 ips to 30 ips, but professional broadcast (non-multitrack) recorders use 1/4 inch tape at 7½ ips and 15 ips.

REEL-TO-REEL FORMAT

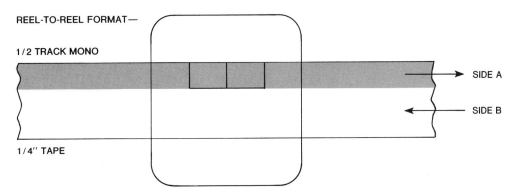

Figure F.4. Reel-to-Reel format—Half-Track Mono. This monaural format uses half of the width of the tape in a bidirectional format.

REEL-TO-REEL FORMAT

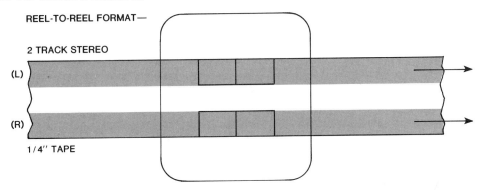

Figure F.5. Reel-to-Reel format—Two-Track Stereo. This is currently the most commonly found professional broadcasting format. This format splits the tape into two tracks with a rather wide ``guard band'' in between, for stereo recording, only in one direction. (Format shown is the U.S. two-track; European formats use wider tracks and a narrower guard band.) Also known as ``half-track stereo.'' When this format is used for monaural recording, it is occasionally referred to as ``twin-track mono.'' The upper track corresponds to the left channel input/output and the lower track corresponds to the right channel. (Half-track mono plays back compatibly on this format, but provides a left-channel-only output).

REEL-TO-REEL FORMAT

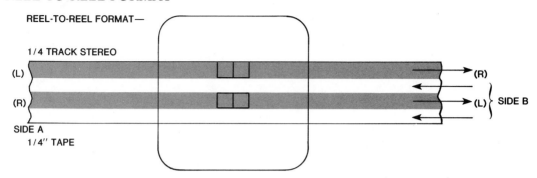

Figure F.6. Reel-to-Reel format—Quarter-Track Stereo. This format splits the tape into four bands with guard bands in between, for use as two pairs of stereo tracks in a bidirectional format. Unlike the cassette format, the two tracks of each stereo pair are not adjacent but alternate, such that the top track is the left channel, and the third track (from the top) is the right channel of the side playing forward. Tracks #2 and #4 are the right and left channel respectively of the "other side." Mono summing can only be done electrically after stereo playback.

CART FORMAT

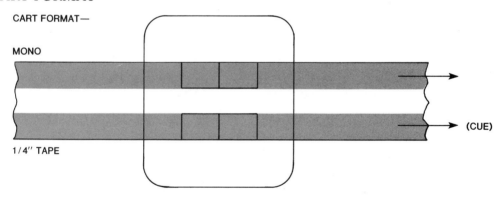

Figure F.7. Cart format—Mono. This two-track, one-direction format is used on all mono broadcast (continuous loop) cartridge machines at 7½ ips. The upper track is for audio, the lower track is for cue tones.

CART FORMAT

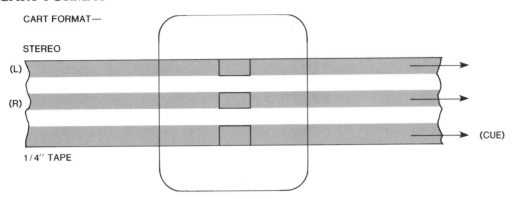

CART FORMAT—

STEREO

(L)

(R)

(CUE)

1/4″ TAPE

Figure F.8. Cart format—Stereo. This three-track, one-direction format is used on all stereo broadcast cartridge machines, usually 7½ ips. (Some cartridge machines have a 15 ips option.) The upper track is usually for left channel audio, the middle track for right channel audio, the bottom track for cue tones.

Sample Production Plan

Sample Technical Plan for Music Program

Technical Notes	Program Material	
Bring up music (guitar), hold for :35, then bring under for *Insert A* (Music peaks at +3 dB).	*Doc & Merle Watson* Cannonball Rag	2:00
Add applause cart (:10 secs) at end of music. Crossfade to ambience cart and roll Cut #2, *MC Wallace*. . .	*Insert A (Announcer)* in: ''That's some pickin'. . . out:''. . . our MC onstage.''	1:15
0 level—should be -6 dB on MC.	*MC Wallace* in: 11Welcome to the . . . out: ''. . . Peg Leg Sam.''	1:45
Backtime the applause for *Peg Leg Sam* :06 secs from the end of MC Wallace, and mix into master tape ''A''	*Peg Leg Sam* (set begins w/applause)	:11
Level 0 dB, then jumps to +3 dB at 1:00 into *Talk*. Level normal at start of song ''Greasy Greens.''	*Talk and jokes* *Greasy Greens*	1:24 3:24
Equalization needed on ''Greens''. . . roll off bass, boost high end slightly	*Hard luck story*	4:00
Check ambience change at splice— occurs at 3:15 into *Hard luck* story	out: 16 secs applause; and ''thank-you's''	
Fade applause after second ''thank-you'' (occurs :10 secs into applause) and roll *Insert B*	*Insert B (Announcer)* in: ''At this 3rd annual. . .'' out: ''. . . Malvina Reynolds''	1:24

NPR Newsmagazine Clocks

Morning Edition

MORNING EDITION [R]
FORMAT CLOCK

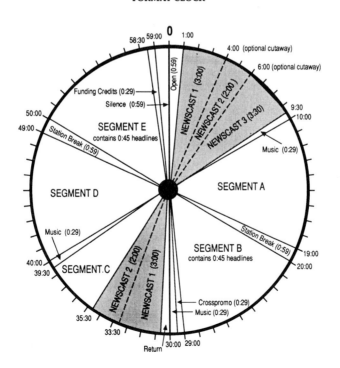

All Things Considered

FORMAT CLOCK
December 1991

FORMAT CLOCK
December 1991

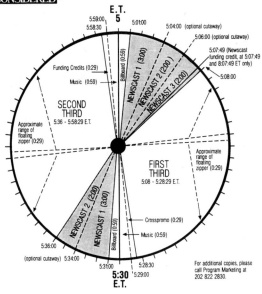

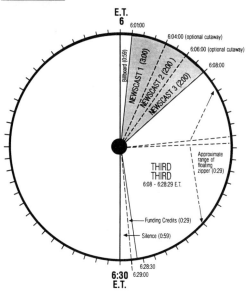

NATIONAL PUBLIC RADIO®   NATIONAL PUBLIC RADIO®

Weekend Edition

FORMAT CLOCK
November 1991

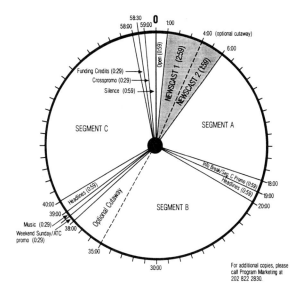

N A T I O N A L   P U B L I C   R A D I O®

Weekend All Things Considered

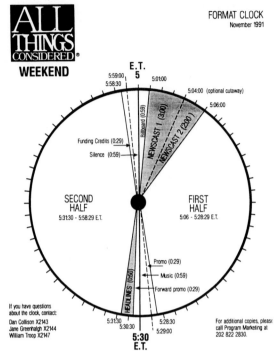

ALL
THINGS
CONSIDERED®
WEEKEND

FORMAT CLOCK
November 1991

E.T.
5

5:59:00
5:58:30
5:01:00
5:04:00 (optional cutaway)
5:06:00

Billboard (0:59)

Funding Credits (0:29)

Silence (0:59)

NEWSCAST 1 (3:00)
NEWSCAST 2 (2:00)

SECOND
HALF
5:31:30 - 5:58:29 E.T.

FIRST
HALF
5:06 - 5:28:29 E.T.

HEADLINES (0:60)

Promo (0:29)

Music (0:59)

Forward promo (0:29)

If you have questions
about the clock, contact:
Dan Collison X2143
Jane Greenhalgh X2144
William Troop X2147

5:31:30
5:30:30
5:28:30
5:29:00

For additional copies, please
call Program Marketing at
202 822 2830.

5:30
E.T.

N A T I O N A L   P U B L I C   R A D I O®

Talk of the Nation

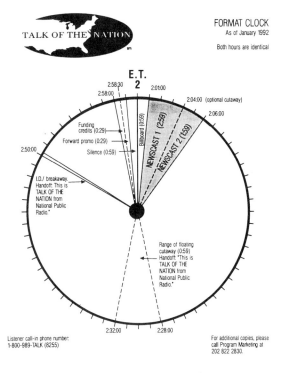

TALK OF THE NATION ℠

FORMAT CLOCK
As of January 1992

Both hours are identical

E.T.
2

2:58:30
2:58:00
2:01:00
2:04:00 (optional cutaway)
2:06:00

Funding
credits (0:29)
Forward promo (0:29)
Silence (0:59)

Billboard (0:59)
NEWSCAST 1 (2:59)
NEWSCAST 2 (1:59)

2:50:00

I.D./ breakaway.
Handoff: This is
TALK OF THE
NATION from
National Public
Radio."

Range of floating
cutaway (0:59)
Handoff: "This is
TALK OF THE
NATION from
National Public
Radio."

2:32:00
2:28:00

Listener call-in phone number:
1-800-989-TALK (8255)

For additional copies, please
call Program Marketing at
202 822 2830.

N A T I O N A L   P U B L I C   R A D I O®

Library Research

by Robert Robinson

Taking a look at what other people have written about your topic can be helpful. The **Reader's Guide to Periodical Literature (RG)** is the basic low-tech index to magazine articles in the popular press (*Time, Newsweek, People, McCalls, Aviation Week, Science*, etc.). *Reader's Guide* is those thick green volumes available in just about every school and public library in the United States and Canada. But now in many libraries, *Reader's Guide* is available on a compact disc (CD) that you access with a personal computer (PC). You just type in what you are looking for (a name, a subject, etc.), and it tells you where to find stories related to that subject. Similar to *Reader's Guide*, and also available on CD, is **Magazine Index**, which indexes about 400 magazines back to the early 1960s. Another standard resource is **National Newspaper Index** which covers the *New York Times, Washington Post, Los Angeles Times, Christian Science Monitor*, and *Wall Street Journal* back to the late 1970s.

If your library has a PC and CD drive, it probably has several other indexes or full-text products on CD that will be helpful to you. Many major newspapers and magazines are available on CD now, as they have been available for years on microfilm. Many encyclopedias and other large, expensive reference works are also available on CD and often sell for less than the printed versions. One advantage of the CD versions is that by typing in a few search terms, you can instantly find and display the full text of stories and print them on the printer attached to the PC. This '90s speed and ease makes library research far less painful and more productive than it used to be.

If you need to find information more specialized than that in the popular press, one of the **on-line databases** may have what you need. **Dialog** is a collection of 350 different databases, each with specialized medical, business, environmental, news, or scientific information. The advantage of on-line databases is the cost, as little as $2 (1992 pricing) for instant acquisition of data. This depends on the amount of time needed on line to access the information. On-line rates are similar to telephone charges and are reduced during non-business hours. Many Dialog databases are available in **Knowledge Index,** a cheaper "after dark" service that is also available through Compuserve. Other on-line databases worth exploring are **NewsNet** (mostly newsletters and news wires), **VU/Text** and **DataTimes** (each has at least 50 full-text newspapers), **Nexis** (full text of hundreds of magazines, newspapers, news wires, and broadcasts, including NPR broadcasts), and **Burrelle's** (full text of television news and NPR broadcasts).

Libraries have many books that reporters find to be gold mines of information, but the following directories are particularly useful: The *Directory of Associations* can quickly tell you what groups have an interest in your topic and how to get in touch with them. The *Washington Information Directory* lists, by interest area, the federal government agencies, congressional committees and subcommittees, and interest groups in the Washington, D.C., area. People can be located and their biographical data verified with *Who's Who in America*, or *Current Biography*, or *Contemporary Authors*, or *Contemporary Musicians*, or *Contemporary Newsmakers. Thomas' Register* tells you which companies manufacture a certain product; *Standard and Poors* or *The National Directory* tells you where a company is located.

Robert Robinson has been library director in National Public Radio's news library since 1975. He began working at NPR in 1974 as the assistant program librarian in the tape library. Robinson has also worked as an editor on NPR's national desk and produced news stories for ALL THINGS CONSIDERED *and* MORNING EDITION. *He received a B.A. in Psycholinguistics from Allegheny College in 1972, and an M.L.S. from the University of Maryland in 1973.*

Glossary

A-wire—The main wire service news wire for newspapers.

A/B reels—Odd-numbered cuts are assembled onto the A reel, and even-numbered cuts on the B reel. When played back from two tape decks through a mixing console, the cuts alternate between reels for the proper sequencing, with short mixes possible between them.

acoustical distance—The perceived distance a sound source is from a microphone.

actuality—An interview or on-location voice recording in a news story. Also known as "cut," "act," or "sound bite."

adapter cable—Cable with different input and output plugs used to connect one audio source to another.

advisories—Notices on the news wire to alert subscribers about upcoming stories.

alligator clips—Spring-loaded clip connectors used to make temporary electrical connections.

ambience—In acoustical terms, the surrounding or pervading acoustic atmosphere, the sound environment.

ambience beds or ambience tracks—Sounds, recorded on location, that can be mixed under narration and actualities.

analog audio—An electrical sound system that responds to the continuous stream of pressure ridges in the air by producing a continuous electrical signal that varies in the same way the sound waves did. The result is an electrical "analogy" of the sound.

anchor—The primary on-mike or on-camera speaking talent during a news program. NPR uses the term "host" instead.

and so—The conclusion of a report. In broadcast journalism, it often is the element that the listener most remembers.

angle—The element that gets the listener to pay attention; a new approach to a topic. It is not an opinion or a point of view.

assembly editing—Dubbing audio elements from one or more sources onto a tape in sequence.

assignment editor—A person who assigns stories to reporters and manages the traffic flow of news stories.

aural exciter—A patented processor intended to enhance the realism or richness of high-fidelity recordings. It can also improve the intelligibility and listenability on phoners, without a trade-off of excessive noise increase.

automatic level control (ALC)—A gain system that monitors what's coming in from the microphone or other sound source and automatically adjusts itself up and down to ensure a safe average recording level. Also known as **automatic gain control (AGC)**.

auxiliary (AUX)—An additional line-level input usually found on home stereo equipment.

axis—A vertical line on a graph marking the center of a microphone's pickup pattern.

backgrounders—Stories that explain the events leading up to the main story.

backing—The side of plastic magnetic tape that provides structure for the tape. Edit marks are placed on the backing.

backtiming—The process of deciding where two sounds must occur together, and then measuring back in time to determine when each element must be started to arrive at that point simultaneously.

balanced connection—A three-wire audio connection in which two wires carry mirror images of an audio signal and one wire acts as a shield. This reduces noise in the line.

band-pass/band-reject filters—Filters that cut around or cut out a certain middle band of frequencies.

beat—The location or subject matter covered by a reporter.

bed—See **ambience bed.**

bias tone—A high frequency, inaudible tone added during recording to make the magnetic patterns flow more smoothly on the tape. This current must be adjusted for different types of tape.

bidirectional or **figure-eight**—Microphones that are sensitive to sound from the front and the back but not from the sides.

binary—A system of numbers using only 1's and 0's. (The traditional, decimal number system uses numbers from 0 through 9.)

boundary microphones—See **pressure zone microphones.**

breaking news—A hard news story that has just happened or is changing rapidly.

broadcast wire—A news wire written for radio and television broadcast copy.

bulk eraser—An electromagnet that erases tape without unspooling or removing the tape from its housing. Also known as a **degausser.**

Burrelle's—An on-line database that provides full text of television news and NPR broadcasts.

cadence—The rhythm and rate of speech. It must be preserved when editing.

calibration (CAL)—Adjusting console, tape recorders and any other equipment to a specified standard, so their measurements are equal.

Cannon connector—See **XLR.**

capstan—The rotating drive-shaft of a tape recorder.

carbon microphone—The low-quality microphone used in most telephones. Sound waves going into a carbon microphone cause the particles of carbon to jostle around and strike each other, modulating an electric current passing through them.

cardioid—A popular type of unidirectional microphone pickup pattern that takes its name from the Greek word for heart.

cart or **cartridge**—A continuous loop of quarter-inch tape contained in a plastic cartridge.

cart deck or **cartridge machine**—A tape deck that records and plays carts. The tape cycles in a continuous loop inside the cartridge. An inaudible cue tone is recorded on the tape during each recording, which allows the tape to cue itself.

cassette—A plastic housing containing two spools, a length of recording tape, and various rollers and guides that permit smooth motion of the tape during recording and playback.

CBC style—The Canadian Broadcasting Corporation system that structures a radio piece in three-element sections—sound, script, interview actuality.

chromium dioxide—A recording tape oxide often referred to as chrome type, because most tapes in this category are made with chromium dioxide (CrO_2) particles. Requires high bias and 70-microsecond equalization.

clipping—Extreme and sudden distortion of the audio signal.

close-up—A closely miked sound that, in audio terms, is analogous to a tightly framed picture in film or television.

cold reading—Reading copy aloud without rehearsal.

color story—A soft feature story that usually contains personality information about a prominent person.

combo—A studio where the producer or talent does the speaking and mixing.

compact disc (CD)—A plastic disc holding a digitally encoded recording that is read by a laser beam.

compressor—A device that reduces the dynamic range of a sound, or minimizes the difference between its loudest and quietest extremes.

condenser microphone—A microphone in which two metallic membranes (one of which is electrically charged) are suspended very close to each other. Sound waves striking one membrane cause it to move closer to or farther away from the second membrane. This movement creates a variation in electrical charge of the other membrane. This tiny electrical signal is then amplified in the microphone. Condenser mikes require a power source.

copy editor—An editor who deals mostly with a report after it has been written, to check for consistency, grammar, etc.

crossfade—Reducing the volume of one audio source while simultaneously increasing the volume of another.

crossfade editing—A computer editing function that provides a choice of transitions ranging from an abrupt cut to a variety of styles and lengths of crossfades.

crystal—A microphone that uses a piece of piezoelectric crystal, such as quartz, to transform sound waves into an audio signal.

cue—(n.) A feature that allows one source to be monitored while playing another. Or a setting on a tape machine that allows a tape to be monitored in fast forward to facilitate rapid location of a particular section of the tape.

cuts—Same as **actualities**.

DataTimes—An on-line database that provides full-text access to stories from at least 50 newspapers.

daybook—A listing of important governmental meetings and public events provided for journalists by the wire services.

de-esser—See **dynamic sibilance controller**.

deadpot—Same as **deadroll**.

deadroll—Starting a sound source at a specific time without hearing it in the mix, in order to have the sound end at a specific time.

decibel (dB)—A unit of measurement that describes the ratio of two sound or audio quantities. It can also be used to compare an electrical power level with a standard level of one milliwatt (dBm), to compare a voltage with a standard of one volt (dBv), or to compare the sound pressure level of a measured sound with a standard silence level (dBspl).

degausser—See **bulk eraser**.

delay—The interval of time between a sound and the repetition of that sound.

delay unit—An electronic device that accepts and stores an audio signal, then sends it out again after a controllable amount of time has passed. Older analog units use a tape loop to create the delay, but modern delay units use digital technology.

denatured alcohol—A type of ethyl alcohol used to clean the heads of tape machines. It does not contain water.

desk editors—Radio editors who are comparable to section editors at newspapers. They are responsible for the news in a given geographical or topical area.

desktop editing—Using a computer workstation to assemble digital audio elements.

Dialog—An on-line collection of 350 different databases, each with specialized medical, business, environmental, or scientific information or news.

digital audio—A recording system that represents sound waves by sampling them and storing the sampled values in binary code.

digital audio broadcasting (DAB)—A transmission system that uses digital binary code to broadcast and receive radio signals.

digital audio tape (DAT)—A tape format using a rotary-head recording system, similar to that found in video recorders, to record CD-quality stereo sound on a DAT cassette.

digital compact cassette (DCC)—A stationary-head digital recorder that

uses psychoacoustic coding to reduce a digital recording's data to fit 90 minutes of sound on a tape. It is able to play analog cassettes as well.

digital signal processing (DSP)—An electronic system that manipulates audio to change volume or tone, add spatial elements, alter pitch or running time, or make other changes.

diphthongs—Combinations of two vowels sounded in one syllable.

dropouts—Lost instants of recorded sound sometimes caused by an improper splice.

dub—To record a copy of an audio tape onto another tape.

dynamic automation—Computerized mixing that mimics the functions of a mixing board by allowing the operator to continuously vary adjustments of the volume of one or more elements in a mix while the computer memorizes the adjustments.

dynamic microphone—A microphone consisting of a metal diaphragm moving in the field of a magnet. The small movements caused by sound waves striking the diaphragm induce an electrical signal.

dynamic noise filter (DNF)—A device to filter out background noise on the phone. The amount of filtering increases as the volume of the sound decreases.

dynamic range—The distance between the quietest sound and loudest sound in a recording.

dynamic range chart—A conceptual diagram of the limitations in volume extremes inherent in an audio system. Too high a level causes distortion, too low a level causes the audio to be masked by system noise.

dynamic sibilance controller—A device for reducing some of the excessive

"S" sounds of some close-miked voices. It cuts high frequencies in this sibilant region (roughly 5–8 kHz), but only when sibilance is present. More commonly known as **a de-esser.**

earphones—See **headphones.**

edit—1. To review a story with an editor before recording it. 2. To physically or electronically cut tape elements.

edit block—A piece of machined metal with a specially designed channel for holding tape and angled slots to permit cutting the tape on a specific angle.

edit covering—Using ambient sound mixed under a voice montage to mask noticeable edits or ambience changes in the voice recordings.

edit mode—A tape machine function that disengages the take-up reel motor. Tape can be played and spilled onto the floor.

editor—A journalist, usually a supervisor, who makes assignments, briefs hosts, consults with reporters during the course of their reporting, or checks reports after they have been written for content, style, and accuracy—or all of the above.

electret condenser—Condenser mikes that have one permanently charged membrane.

entrance covering—To fade in an ambient sound bed before a voice to make the transition less abrupt.

EQ—See **equalizer.**

equalizer—A device designed to change, or **equalize,** the frequency response of an audio signal. The resulting sound has a different tonal balance. A "dull-sounding" recording can be "brightened" by having the proportion of high frequencies increased or "boosted" by an equalizer. Equali-

zation can be used to boost or cut a range of frequencies.

erase head—The head on the left side of the tape recorder that scrambles the magnetic orientation of oxide particles on tape, allowing them to be reorganized by the record head.

exit covering—Concealing the end of a sound effect by fading it out under a group of closely spaced words.

expander—A device that widens the dynamic range of a sound.

expert interview—An interview with someone who is knowledgeable about the issue at hand.

explanatory tape—Recorded tape in which a person tells the premise of the story, gives background information, or tells what the situation means.

eyewitness interview—An interview with someone who was present when an event occurred.

fade—To reduce gradually a sound source's volume.

fader—A volume pot that controls the level of voltage in a circuit by moving a control up and down.

feature—A soft news story or sidebar that gives background information, description, personality profile, or takes an unusual approach to telling a story about an individual or topic.

feed hub—The hub on the left side of a reel-to-reel tape recorder where blank tape is placed for recording. Also known as **supply hub.**

feed spool—The spool on the left side of a cassette.

feedback—An output signal being channeled back into its input. Usually it creates a loud, piercing sound. When this is done at low amplitude on a three-head tape recorder, it can create an "echo" effect.

ferric oxide—Most commonly used oxide on recording tape.

fiber optic cable—Hair-thin strands of pure glass cable that carry modulated light with more than 600 times the information-carrying capacity of electrical signals through copper cable.

field recording—Recording audio material using portable equipment outside the studio.

figure-eight—See **bidirectional**.

file—(v.) To submit a news or feature story for broadcast.

filter—A device designed to change the frequency response of an audio signal, so that the resulting sound has a different tonal balance. A "tinny-sounding" recording can be "mellowed" by having its high frequencies reduced or attenuated ("cut") by a filter. A filter can generally only cut frequencies.

flange—One of the sides of a metal tape reel.

"Foley-work" equipment—A sound-effects system set up in the form of a multiple-sectioned sandbox, on the studio floor, with each section containing a different walking surface (flagstone, dried leaves, grass, twigs and branches, gravel, sand, water, etc.) to add sound effects for films, television, and radio drama.

foreign desk—The assignment desk that covers international news.

frequency—The number of vibrations a sound wave or electrical current makes in a second, measured in cycles per second, or Hertz (Hz), or thousands of Hertz (kHz).

frequency masking—See **masking**.

frequency response—How well an audio system can reproduce all frequencies of the sound it is processing without amplifying or attenuating any of those frequencies more than the others.

full-up or **foreground**—Closely miked recorded sounds that are like close-ups in film. They convey single images that the listener must be able to recognize without seeing them and without narration describing them. They can be used to make transitions or to begin or end scenes.

fundamental frequency—The lowest frequency component of a sound. The fundamental frequency determines the pitch of the sound.

funnel—An interview structure that opens with a general question and then moves on to particulars.

futures file—An organizing tool for editors to keep track of upcoming events.

gate—An audio device that senses when volume level drops below a selected threshold and mutes the audio when that happens.

gooseneck—A flexible metal tube, generally six to 18 inches long, that can be used to extend the reach of a microphone stand or clamp.

graphic equalizer—An equalizer with linear faders that adjust the tone quality of a sound. Also see **parametric equalizer**.

grease pencil—A china marker or soft waxy pencil used to mark tape for editing and to note console reference marks.

grip point—A point that is a set distance from the playback head at which one grasps the tape from the tape recorder and places it in the cutting block. This allows the cut to be made at the proper place.

habitual pitch—The pitch normally used for speaking.

hard disk—A data storage system used by computers.

hard news—Generally refers to breaking, daily stories, concentrating more on the who, what, where, and when than the why. Contrasts with **features.**

hard wired—Pieces of equipment interconnected by wire.

harmonics—Vibrations that are multiples of the fundamental frequency of a sound, which affect the timbre or tone color of a sound.

head—The part of a tape recorder that actually records sound on tape, or reads the sound from the tape. The head is a specially designed magnet whose poles are bent around in the shape of a letter C, so they almost touch each other across a narrow gap. For recording, an electrical current is applied to the head. This creates a fluctuating magnetic field, which will rearrange the magnetic particles on a tape as it is pulled past the head. In playback, the magnetic patterns on the tape interact with the magnetic poles of the head and create an electrical current.

headphones—Small speakers that are worn over the ears and used for monitoring during recording and private listening. Also called **earphones.**

headroom—Additional power level above 0 VU that a sound can reach before it becomes distorted.

heads out—Audio tape wound on a reel so the beginning of the tape is on the outside of the reel ready to be played.

hertz (Hz)—Cycles per second. This is a unit of measurement for the frequency of a sound wave.

high impedance (HI-Z)—Mikes that have impedance values from 10,000 to 50,000 ohms.

high-pass filter—A filter that cuts out low frequencies and passes high frequencies.

host—The primary narrator and interviewer during a newsmagazine.

host introduction—Same as **lead-in.**

hot tape—Recorded interview material that is emotional, or a strong statement spoken with energy and feeling that captures the listener's interest and provokes an emotional response.

hub—The plastic or metal center of a tape reel on which the tape is wound.

hypercardioid—Microphones that are even more sensitive than cardioids to sounds coming from directly in front of them. Useful for miking from a longer distance.

idler arm—A spring-loaded tape guide on an open-reel tape recorder, used to help maintain consistent tape tension. When the tape runs out, the spring tension swings the idler arm down, stopping the tape transport functions. Also called a "tension arm."

idler wheel—A roller on an open-reel tape recorder, which the tape threads around. Driven by the friction of contact with the tape, the idler wheel spins, and the inertia of the spinning wheel smooths out small variations in the speed of the tape.

impedance—Resistance to the flow of alternating current (AC) electrical signals. Measured in ohms (Greek letter omega or "Z"). Generally, the output impedance of a microphone or amplifier should match the input of the next piece of equipment in the audio chain. A low-impedance output connected to a high-impedance input will result in a substantial drop in power, while a high-Z output fed to a low-Z input can result in distortion.

in the mud—Recording levels too low to make the sound audible over the noise floor.

in the red—Recording levels that exceed 0 VU. The recording is too loud and may be distorted.

inches per second (ips)—The speed reel-to-reel tape moves across the tape heads.

inflection—The changes in pitch and stress that occur within spoken words. It clarifies the meaning of the words.

input—The point where signals are fed into a tape recorder, console, or sound system.

insert editing—Allowing new audio to be rerecorded over an existing section of audio (sometimes called a punch-in). The existing audio is erased as the new material is inserted.

interpersonal speaking distance—Territorial space distance for conversations based on the familiarity of the speakers. This distance varies from culture to culture.

jack—A connector leading to the input or output of an audio source or patch bay.

keeper reel—Reel containing edited tape to be used in final production.

kHz (kilohertz)—One thousand hertz, or cycles, per second.

Knowledge Index—An on-line database containing many of Dialog's databases. It can be accessed only in the evening.

lavalier microphones—Small mikes that hang by a strap around the speaker's neck, or are clipped on at chest level. They can be either dynamic or condenser microphones. Also known as "lavs."

laying up—Taking many audio elements and transferring them onto open tracks on multitrack tape or a computer workstation. Each is placed in the appropriately timed location relative to the other elements.

lead—The opening sentence in a news story.

lead-in—The host's or newscaster's live introduction to a report, two-way, commentary, etc. Also called **host introduction**.

leader tape—Non-oxide plastic or paper tape used to visually identify sections of a reel of tape, such as the head, tail, or internal sections.

level—Volume or intensity of a sound or a signal.

level-dropping or **"attenuating" cable**—Allows a line-level source to be plugged into the mike input jack of a tape recorder.

level matching—Subjectively listening to the elements of a production to ensure that the apparent loudness of each element is similar.

libel—To knowingly, publicly write false statements about another person.

light phoner—An interview on a humorous or quirky topic that often is used to bring levity to a newsmagazine.

limiter—A device that does not allow an audio signal to exceed a certain level. Generally protects against overmodulation, distortion, or tape saturation.

line—(1) A short description of a report, two-way, commentary, etc. It is used by producers, editors, hosts—anyone who needs to get a quick understanding of what the story is about. Writing it helps reporters focus their report. (2) Another name for a **shotgun** microphone. (3) See **line level**.

line in—An input jack of a tape recorder that receives a line level signal for recording.

line input—An input designed to receive line level signals.

line level—An audio power level greater than microphone level but less than speaker level. It is the standard for interconnecting most electronic audio equipment.

line out—The output jack of a tape recorder that feeds a signal at line, not mike, level.

line up—To adjust all of a studio's tape machines' meters so that a "0 VU" reading shows up on them whenever that same reading appears on the console meter.

live—In radio, a report is live when it is broadcast at the same time it is delivered by the reporter or program host.

log—(v.) To use a stopwatch or tape counter to keep running times or location references for taped material, making detailed notes on the content and quality of each segment of tape.

long shot—Placing the sound source beyond the normal pickup range of the microphone. The sound will seem "boomy" and fainter than close-miked sound.

loop—See **tape loop**.

loudness—The level of amplitude or intensity of a sound as subjectively perceived by the ear.

low impedance (LO-Z)—Mikes with resistance values in a range from 50 to 500 ohms.

low-pass filter—A filter that cuts out high frequencies and passes low frequencies.

Magazine Index—A publication that indexes about 400 magazines back to the early 1960s.

manual level control—Allows the operator to set the recording level manually while monitoring a built-in meter.

masking—When one sound is obscured by a simultaneous, louder sound close to the same pitch (frequency masking), or by a louder sound happening shortly before or after the first sound (temporal masking).

medium shot—Placing the sound source just out of the optimum pickup pattern of the microphone.

metal—Recording tape that requires a different bias and EQ from normal or chrome tapes, and higher-than-normal recording power. Uses particles of pure metal instead of oxides. Used in Type IV analog cassettes, DATs, and Hi-8 and S-VHS video cassettes.

microphone level—The lowest power level of all audio components. Mike level must be boosted by a preamp before it can be mixed with other elements.

MIDI (musical instrument digital interface)—Originally a protocol for controlling synthesizers and other digital musical instruments, its use has expanded to include control of audio recorders, mixers, and other digital devices.

mil—One thousandth of an inch.

mini disc—An optical disc-recording system that uses psychoacoustic coding to help fit up to 74 minutes of stereo digital audio on a 2½-inch disc.

mix-minus—Special output from a console designed to provide an audio feed to someone at a remote location. It contains everything in the mix except the speaker's voice, to avoid feedback or echo.

mixer—A portable console that can control the levels of several sound sources or microphones and combine the output into one signal that can be connected to the *AUX* or *LINE* input of a tape machine or cassette recorder.

mixing—Blending the relative volumes of two or more sound sources through a console or mixer.

monaural (mono)—A recording system with only one master channel, similar to listening with one ear.

monitor—A loudspeaker used for listening to the recording or playback of a sound.

montage—Layering a variety of short elements to create a single sound image.

mult box—A large box, with many output jacks, that receives the feed from a microphone. Each reporter can connect a tape recorder to one of the jacks on the box, and receive a signal from the microphone. (Sometimes called a splitter box or press box.)

multipath interference—Temporary loss of an FM radio signal caused when the radio picks up the signal from the radio station and also the reflection of the signal off of nearby buildings or hills.

multitrack—A tape recorder that is able to record more than two tracks at the same time. It enables the playback of several tracks while recording new tracks in a synchronized manner.

National Newspaper Index—An index that covers the *New York Times, Washington Post, Los Angeles Times,* *Christian Science Monitor,* and *Wall Street Journal* back to the late 1970s.

news analysis—An explanation of events or issues that focuses on why they happened or what is at stake.

newscast—A short series of news stories read by one person (newscaster), highlighting the most important information of the hour.

news conference—An organized meeting with someone in the news where journalists can ask questions. Also called a "press conference."

news judgment—The journalistic process by which a determination is made about what is important and what is not—which stories will be covered, how they will be covered, and how they will be presented.

newsmagazine—A 30–120 minute news program usually featuring longer, prerecorded news stories introduced by a host.

newsmaker or **participant interview**—An interview with a participant in an event or an advocate of an issue.

NewsNet—An on-line database that provides full text of newsletters and news wires.

news peg—An event to which you can tie a news story.

news spot—A brief (usually no longer than 45-second) report that is part of a newscast.

Nexis—An on-line database that provides full text of hundreds of magazines, newspapers, news wires, and broadcasts, including NPR broadcasts.

noise reduction—A sound processing system such as Dolby or dbx, that reduces the hiss in audio recordings.

notch filter—A filter that can severely attenuate a very narrow band of frequencies and leave all other frequencies basically untouched.

off-mike—Recording a voice or sound too far away from—or off—the normal pick-up pattern of a microphone. The voice will sound distant and indistinct.

off-tape monitoring—A setting on a tape recorder that allows the operator to listen to the sound being recorded a fraction of a second after it is on tape.

off the record—Information revealed by a source that either cannot be used for a news story or cannot be attributed.

ohm—A measurement of resistance in direct-current (DC) circuits, or of impedance in audio or other alternating-current (AC) circuits. Often abbreviated as the Greek letter omega or as "Z."

omnidirectional microphone—A microphone sensitive to sound from all directions.

on-line databases—Reference indexes available through a computer and a telephone modem.

on-mike—Placing the sound source within the pickup pattern of the microphone.

on the record—Information that can be quoted and attributed in a news story.

on the satellite—A short hand term meaning that satellite transmission is involved. Another slang term for satellite is "the bird."

open-reel audio tape recorder—A tape recorder that openly moves the audio tape from a feed reel to a take-up reel. The tape is not enclosed in a cassette or cartridge.

optimum pitch—The best pitch for the normal speaking voice. It is usually about one-third of the way up from the lowest note to the highest note a person can sing.

oscillator—An electronic device that generates a pure tone at any frequency. The oscillator produces the electrical signal at a steady frequency and at a constant level. It is often used for calibrating audio inputs and outputs.

oscillograph—An electronic visual representation of a sound wave.

outcue—The last few words or sounds of an audio element or program.

output—1. The point on a console or component from which a signal is sent. 2. The outgoing signal being sent from one device to another.

outtakes—Sections of recorded tape not used in the final production.

overlapping—Mixing a longer piece in sections so that each new section begins with the same material that ended the previous section. The sections can then be spliced together, eliminating the repeated material.

oxide—The side of audio tape that faces the playback head. It is made of particles of magnetic metallic oxide.

PA—See **public address**.

pack journalism—A number of news reporters from different news organizations simultaneously covering the same story or beat. The term usually is a derogatory one because it implies that the reporters do not think or act as individuals.

pancakes—Reel-to-reel tapes wound onto hubs without flanges attached to the sides.

parametric equalizer—An equalizer that permits adjustment of several different parameters of the audio. For each frequency band of the equalizer there are adjustable controls for center frequency, bandwidth, and amount of boost or cut. Constrast with a **graphic equalizer**, which typically has controls only for boost or cut for each frequency band.

patch bay—A bank of jacks hard-wired to the inputs and outputs of audio equipment in a studio.

pause—A button or switch for momentary interruption of the tape motion during *RECORD* or *PLAY*.

peak programme meter (PPM)—An audio measurement device that indicates loudness peaks in the program material. It is designed to relate maximum audio levels to the human eye so they can be viewed.

peak reading meter—A meter that reads the absolute maximum instantaneous peak levels of audio.

perceived loudness—How loud a sound seems to the human ear.

phase—The time relationship between two or more sound waves or electrical currents. If they are exactly synchronous, they are said to be "in phase."

phase cancellation—When the time relationship between two or more sound waves or electrical currents is not synchronous, the amplitudes of the signals interfere with one another, lowering the volume of some frequencies and boosting others.

phone-sync—See **tape-sync.**

phoner—An interview conducted over the phone. It can be live or taped.

pickup edit—A place in a mix or track that allows the recording to be stopped and re-recorded with a small overlap. The two elements are then cut together to eliminate the overlap.

pickup pattern—The direction(s) in which a microphone is most sensitive to sound.

pinch roller—Rubber roller that pushes the tape against the capstan to drive

the tape from the feed reel to the take-up reel.

pitch—The highness or lowness of a sound determined by its fundamental frequency of vibration. Sounds in the bass region are low in pitch, while those in the treble region are high-pitched.

play—To mechanically advance the tape recorder to listen to a recording.

playback head—The device on a tape recorder that senses the fluctuating magnetic patterns stored on a tape.

playlist editing—A computer audio editing system that places electronic markers at the beginning and end of audio sections, and then creates a list of which sections to play and in what order.

plosives, also known as **P-pops**—Bursts of air produced by consonants such as P, B, and T that cause distortion when the microphone is straight in front of the mouth.

pot—A rotary console volume control, short for potentiometer, a variable resistor. See **fader.**

potentiometer—A resistance device that controls the voltage in a circuit.

PPM—See **peak programme meter.**

press packet—Written background information about a person, issue, or group that is distributed by the person or organization.

pressure zone microphones—Microphones that typically are used on a flat surface such as a table, wall, or floor, and have a hemispherical pickup pattern with a very coherent sound for distant recordings. Also known as **boundary microphones** or **PZMs.**

primary source—Someone who has direct knowledge of an event, a decision, an issue, etc.

production editor—An editor who deals with the production, as opposed to the assignment, end of the reporting process.

production script—A script that has all the elements, outcues, and timing for a radio production.

program editors—Editors responsible for the overall content of a given program. They help decide what stories will be covered, how they will be covered, and what aspects of the stories should be included.

psychoacoustic coding—Digital audio processing that applies knowledge of the characteristics of human hearing to determine what sounds in an audio signal will be audible, then removes the inaudible ones. The resulting signal has much less data, so it takes only a small fraction of the storage space or broadcast spectrum that the original unprocessed signal would require.

public address (PA)—A sound amplification system usually consisting of a microphone, amplifier, and loudspeaker designed to reinforce a voice or other sounds for a large gathering.

punch-in—See **insert editing**.

PZM—See **pressure zone microphone**.

quantize—To quantify each value of a wave form as a discrete number. The values are compared to a stepladder of discrete positions, and then rounded to the nearest step.

quarter-inch phone connector—Plugs and jacks used to connect audio equipment. They come in mono and stereo versions and are commonly used for headphone jacks and line-level audio connections.

radio mike—See **wireless mike**.

radio time—Compressed time. Translating real time to radio time necessar-

ily compresses information through editing.

random-access memory (RAM)—A type of computer memory chip that can have data recorded into it and then read out in any order. Used in samplers and other digital audio recorders.

raw tape—The complete tape gathered for a story, before any editing or selection process.

RCA phono connector—A type of plug or jack most often used in home stereo equipment. It is only a mono connector, often used in color-coded pairs for stereo connections.

Reader's Guide to Periodical Literature (RG)—The basic index of magazine articles in the popular press (*Time, Newsweek, People, McCalls, Aviation Week, Science*, etc.).

record—To mechanically advance the tape recorder to store electronic impulses as magnetic patterns on the oxide of the audio tape. Most recorders require that both *PLAY* and *RECORD* buttons be depressed simultaneously to engage this function.

record head—The second head of a tape recorder. It creates a fluctuating magnetic pattern in the oxide on audio tape to represent the audio information being recorded.

record safety—A switch that ensures that the record function on a machine cannot be accidentally engaged, causing erasure of the signals on the tape.

recording ratio—The relationship between the raw tape recorded and the length of the final story.

reel-to-reel—See **open reel**.

regular condenser—Mikes that require external power to charge the membrane and run the amplifier in the mike.

reporter two-way—An interview with a reporter who has covered an event or an issue.

resolution—The number of encoding steps on the stepladder of values in digital recording.

reverberation—A gradually diminishing series of sound reflections.

reverse threading—Threading the tape through the capstan and pinch roller so that when the PLAY button is depressed, the tape will play backward. Used for **backtiming**.

review—A setting on a tape machine that allows a tape to be heard while rewinding to facilitate rapid location of a particular section of the tape. Similar to *CUE*.

ribbon microphone—A sensitive microphone that has a ribbon diaphragm within a magnetic field.

safe—See **record safety**.

sample—To record a sound using digital equipment. Short-duration samples can be stored in a device called a "sampler," which may use random-access memory (RAM) storage rather than a tape or a disc.

sampling rate—The number of times each second that the analog-to-digital converter takes a measurement.

shotgun—A type of supercardioid microphone that picks up sound from a long distance.

show editor—The person with overall responsibility for the content of a news program.

sibilance—Excessively sharp whistling sounds produced while pronouncing "S," "SH," "CH," "Z," and other sibilant sounds.

sidebars—Reports that spin off from the main story and help explain it.

slander—To knowingly say false information about another that injures his or her reputation.

snapshot automation—Audio elements are placed in a computer, arranged sequentially, and assigned a series of points in time. For each point in time, a volume control setting can be specified for each audio element in the mix. The computer then "electronically mixes" the elements, gradually changing volume settings from one snapshot to the next or making immediate changes at each snapshot.

social distance—The distance from another person at which one feels comfortable conversing. It varies from culture to culture.

soft pieces—Reports that add color or human interest to the news.

sound bed—Recording of ambience or music played under a foreground sound.

sound bite—A very short actuality, often just a phrase.

sound portraits—A sidebar that gathers sound from a series of small events and weaves them with interviews, creating a sound impression of people, places, or things.

sound tape—The recorded ambience bed.

source—See **input**.

sources—People who provide information for reporters.

spectral density—The relative power of a sound's fundamental pitch and its harmonics (the amount of harmonic energy the sound contains). The higher the spectral density (i.e., the more powerful the harmonics contained in the sound), the louder the sound will seem to the ear.

spectrum—The range of audible frequencies.

splicing tape—Sticky one-sided tape used to hold two edited pieces of recording tape together. It is slightly narrower than its corresponding-width magnetic tape.

splitter box—See **mult box.**

stand up—A report that contains no actualities.

stereo—Audio recording and playback using two or more microphones, two tracks, and two speakers to give a natural image of sound from left to right.

stereo cut—A 63-degree angle on the edit block used to minimize the difference in time between the left and right channels of a splice in a stereo recording.

studio—A soundproofed room where voices are recorded. Sometimes the complex of production rooms with recording equipment and performance room is called a studio.

subtractive editing—Computer audio editing system similar to razor-blade style removal of unwanted audio material.

supply hub—See **feed hub.**

tails out—Audio tape wound on a reel so the end of the recorded material is on the outside of the reel. The tape must be rewound before it can be played back.

take-up reel—An empty reel placed on the right-hand hub of a tape machine to collect the tape as it moves past the playback head.

take-up spool—The spool on the right side of a cassette. See **feed spool.**

talk to time To deliver copy in the appropriate allotted time.

taped or **tape-delayed**—A report recorded onto tape and broadcast at a later time. Many live programs also include taped segments.

tape editing—A physical or electronic task (cutting the tape and joining it together again). A technique for manipulating audio information, like written words on a page, by "cutting and pasting" to rearrange it in a more concise form.

tape editor—A person who physically or electronically manipulates tape to condense, refine, and organize it for production.

tape loop—Recorded sound effects, music, or voice edited into a loop played continuously to extend running time or create repetition.

tape-sync—A telephone interview during which each person is simultaneously tape recorded in different locations, and then both tapes are later combined on a third tape. This is done to avoid having phone-quality recording for one voice. Also called "phone-sync," "double-ender," or "simul-rec."

tempo and **rate**—The speed at which one talks.

temporal masking—See **masking.**

tension arm—Same as **idler arm.**

three-to-one ratio—A rule of thumb for placing two speakers and two mikes: The distance from your mouth to the interviewee's mike should be *at least three times* the distance from your mouth to your mike, and vice versa.

tie-tack—A small mike that can be clamped onto the tie or other clothing. Also called **lavalier,** or "lav."

timbre—The tone quality of a sound determined by the number of harmonics that occur, and their relative intensities.

timing—The pacing, movement, tempo, or length of a radio program.

tracking—Recording vocal narrative.

tracks—The vocal narrative in a report.

transducer—A device that changes mechanical vibrations (sound) into electrical signals or vice-versa, such as loudspeakers and microphones.

transition—Transporting the listener from place to place or idea to idea with changes in sound.

two track—A tape recorder that records information on two tracks (left and right).

two-way—An interview in the studio or over the phone with a reporter and one guest. Also **2-way**.

unbalanced connection—An audio connection using only two wires. One wire carries the signal; the second is called the ground wire. Unbalanced connections are more susceptible to electrical hum.

unidirectional—Mikes with this characteristic are most sensitive to sounds coming from the front and least sensitive to sounds from the rear.

unity gain—Aligning the console and tape machines so they are lined up to an absolute zero point. Nothing is added or subtracted from the level of the signal as it travels from one tape machine to another, through the console.

upcut—Cutting off a portion of the sound or word in the editing process.

uplink—A satellite ground terminal capable of sending a signal to a satellite.

variable playback speed (varispeed)—A device that adjusts the speed at which a tape is played back. It can be used to correct the slowdown that comes when recording with weak batteries or to vary the pitch or speed of a recording. When speed is increased, pitch and tempo also go up; when speed decreases, the pitch and tempo drop.

voice coupler—A small box permanently wired into a phone or phone line that provides a quarter-inch phone jack output for feeding a line-level signal to a console or recorder input.

voice quality—The basic nature of one's voice.

voicer—A short news story that has only the reporter's voice and no actuality.

volume—Loudness.

volume unit (VU)—A standardized, international unit measuring the short-term average of audio levels.

vox pop—The comments of ordinary people, collected unscientifically, usually in public places. The term comes from the Latin "vox populi" (voice of the people).

VU meter—An audio meter that measures the average volume of a signal.

VU/Text—An on-line database that provides full-text stories from at least 50 newspapers.

windscreen—An open-cell foam rubber screen placed on microphones to reduce the effect of plosives and wind.

wire service—National and international news-gathering agencies (e.g., the Associated Press, Reuters, United Press International, Agence France Presse) that provide daily news to print and broadcast customers.

wireless mike—A mike attached to a small, battery-operated radio transmitter that sends the mike's signal to a special radio receiver connected to a console or the input of a recorder. Also known as a **radio mike**.

wires—Collectively, the **wire services**.

wrap-around—A news story in which the reporter, newscaster, or host introduces an actuality and then adds at least one sentence after it.

XLR connector—This jack has three pins arranged in a triangular pattern and surrounded by a round collar of metal. The corresponding plug on the cable, which "mates" with this jack, has three holes in the same triangular pattern. Used for most professional microphone connectors.

Y-adapter—A cable that can connect two microphones to one input jack.

zero VU or **0 VU**—Aligning a sound to 0 Volume Units, also shown on many VU meters as 100 percent modulation.

Index